CIRCUS AND STAGE

CIRCUS AND STAGE

THE THEATRICAL ADVENTURES OF ROSE EDOUIN AND GBW LEWIS

MIMI COLLIGAN

© Copyright 2013 Mimi Colligan
All rights reserved. Apart from any uses permitted by Australia's Copyright Act 1968, no part of this book may be reproduced by any process without prior written permission from the copyright owners. Inquiries should be directed to the publisher.

Published by Monash University Publishing
Building 4, Monash University
Clayton Victoria 3800 Australia
www.publishing.monash.edu

Published in association with the State Library of Victoria
328 Swanston Street
Melbourne Victoria 3000 Australia
slv.vic.gov.au

Monash University Publishing brings to the world publications which advance the best traditions of humane and enlightened thought. Monash University Publishing titles pass through a rigorous process of independent peer review.

www.publishing.monash.edu/books/cs-9781922235022.html

Series: Biography

Design: Les Thomas

Front cover image: Mongo Mongo, an Aboriginal rider with Ashton's Circus in New South Wales, in *Illustrated Sydney News*, 23 June 1855. Reproduced courtesy of the State Library of Victoria.

Back cover images: (Left) Rose Edouin as a young actress, c.1864. Reproduced courtesy of the State Library of Victoria. (Right) George Lewis, in the *Melbourne Tatler*, 21 May 1898, p. 18. Reproduced courtesy of the State Library of Victoria.

National Library of Australia Cataloguing-in-Publication entry:

Author:	Colligan, Mimi, author.
Title:	Circus and Stage: The Theatrical Adventures of Rose Eouin and GBW Lewis / Mimi Colligan.
ISBN:	9781922235022 (paperback)
Notes:	Includes bibliographical references and index.
Subjects:	Eouin, Rose, 1844-1925.
	Lewis, George Benjamin William, 1818–1906.
	Entertainers--Australia--Biography. Entertainers--Europe--Biography. Entertainers--Asia--Biography. Entertainers--Australia--History. Entertainers--Europe--History. Entertainers--Asia--History. Performing arts--Australia--History. Performing arts--Europe--History. Performing arts--Asia--History. Theater--Australia--History. Theater--Europe--History. Theater--Asia--History.
Dewey Number:	791.092

Printed in Australia by Griffin Press an Accredited ISO AS/NZS 14001:2004 Environmental Management System printer.

The paper this book is printed on is certified against the Forest Stewardship Council ® Standards. Griffin Press holds FSC chain of custody certification SGS-COC-005088. FSC promotes environmentally responsible, socially beneficial and economically viable management of the world's forests.

In memory of my parents,
for fostering historical inquiry in their unschooled child.

CONTENTS

Acknowledgements ix
About the author xi
Note on sources xiii
Introduction xv

Chapter 1.   Mr George Lewis, gymnast, ring master and equestrian . . 1
Chapter 2.   The Edouins in England 17
Chapter 3.   On tour in Australia 26
Chapter 4.   George in Asia 41
Chapter 5.   The Edouins return to Melbourne 50
Chapter 6.   Lewis moves from circus to stage 60
Chapter 7.   Lewis's grand dramatic burlesque and ballet company
             in India. 82
Chapter 8.   Melbourne and India 95
Chapter 9.   India and China 102
Chapter 10. Employing the Williamsons, 1875–1876 114
Chapter 11. The Victorian Academy of Music, 1876–1879 128
Chapter 12. The Lewises at the Bijou Theatre, 1880–1885. 165
Chapter 13. Retirement and back to England, 1885–1893 181
Chapter 14. Return to Australia and 'poverty', 1894–1907 194
Chapter 15. Rose home in England 210

Bibliography 221
Index 227

ACKNOWLEDGEMENTS

As a researcher and historian of nineteenth-century entertainments I kept 'tripping over' Mr and Mrs G. B. W. Lewis in theatre advertisements and reviews in newspapers ranging from the London *Era* to Melbourne *Punch*. My friend and fellow theatre historian, Elisabeth Kumm of Melbourne, discovered that Mrs Lewis was also known as London child star Rose Edouin. For the next few years the Lewises were among the many theatricals we researched. Elisabeth's interests soon diverged to another theatre couple, the Broughs, and she generously gave me much of her research to that point on the Lewises. I became quite obsessed with George and Rose, especially when I found that they had taken theatre to Asia. Then there was George's earlier circus career and so on. Soon I was travelling to London to read microfilms of Indian newspapers from the British Raj period at the British Library. Here a generous friend, Diana Renard of Kilburn, allowed me to stay with her while I spent days at the British Library just a short train trip from her home. The late Keith Davis inspired me with his family album containing photographs of the Lewis company in India and I thank his daughter Gil Bosaid for permission to use some of these *cartes-de-visite* in this book.

Another mentor was the late Bridget Everett, with whom I had shared an interest in Cremorne Gardens, Richmond. Bridget did not live to write her book on Cremorne but through her posthumous papers, mainly photocopies, now at the State Library of Victoria, she contributed many references in this book. Two colleagues from Kolcata offered help on the Indian section of this book: Sudipto Chatterjee now of Loughborough University, UK and Parichay Patra now a Ph.D. candidate at Monash University.

Thanks are also due to Frank Van Straten of Melbourne, Elizabeth Morrison of Canberra and the afore mentioned Elisabeth Kumm who took time off from their own writing to read my early drafts painstakingly. Mark St Leon, doyen of Australian circus history, generously checked my circus chapters and helped with some 'last minute' queries. Veronica Kelly and Richard Fotheringham of the University of Queensland encouraged me to go on with the book. I also thank research colleagues: Allister Hardiman, of Tullamarine, illustrator and researcher for his wide knowledge of forgotten musicians and actors and for finding a lovely *carte-de-visite* of Rose Edouin; Richard Morton, former editor of the *Victorian Historical Journal* who alerted me to the origin of an S. T. Gill circus engraving; Peter Johnson, architect and friend, who gave helpful advice on how to find information on properties connected with the Lewises and found a drainage plan of one of the Lewises' houses, Shanghai Villa, and Amy Hawley, who proofread an early draft and improved my style. Special thanks to actor Gemma Reeves of Dublin who gave me Rose Edouin's scrapbook, which had been bought in a London antique shop and given to her mother, actor Anita Reeves. Gemma decided that the scrapbook, having been 'on tour in Europe' since 1909, should return to Australia.

The two libraries whose collections are the most important to this work are the British Library, London, and the State Library of Victoria. I acknowledge the help given by the staff over the years: at the State Library of Victoria, including Anne Glover, Kerri Hall, Fiona Jeffery, Joan Maslen and Margot Jones, Publishing Project Manager for her support towards the preparation of this book. Also the always helpful attendants who found unfindable books and focussed microfilm readers for me. At the British Library in the Asian and African room, Hedley Sutton and his staff kindly helped a jet-lagged antipodean with the intricacies of the BL catalogue. Thanks are also due to staff at the Mitchell Library, State Library of New South Wales; Hong Kong University Library; New York Public Library for the Performing Arts; the Harvard Theatre Collection, Harvard University, Boston and the city libraries at San Francisco and Los Angeles. The staff of the Victorian Performing Arts Collection made available objects belonging to Rose Edouin Lewis and theatrical *cartes-de-visite* and I thank Patricia Convery, former research officer for her help. The staff of the Public Record Office Victoria were generous with my requests for files ranging from Letter Books, and Health Records to Wills and Inquests. Graeme Haig of Sydney found genealogical records on the mysterious Lewis and Bryer families. Finally I thank my friends Bill and Jenny Raper and Teresa Pagliaro for putting up with my endless gossip about the Lewises and for reading some of the book's drafts.

Thanks finally to Monash University Publishing for publishing this work, and to staff members Joanne Mullins and Les Thomas.

ABOUT THE AUTHOR

Dr Mimi Colligan writes on 19th century popular culture. *Canvas Documentaries*, her history of panoramic entertainment in Australia and New Zealand (including theatre panoramas), was published in 2002 by Melbourne University Publishing.

A primary school 'drop-out' through ill health, she later graduated from university with an honours degree; she worked as a research assistant in Monash University's English and History Departments, and was awarded a Ph.D. from Monash University in 1987.

An interest in images as historical documents has led to her writing and contributing to Performing Arts Museum and Ballarat Art Gallery exhibitions. She has also curated exhibitions, including 'Cremorne Gardens, Richmond' for a property developer, and 'Melbourne Theatres in Transition 1840s–1940s' for the Royal Historical Society of Victoria. She also researched and wrote the Heritage Council's report *Her Majesty's Theatre 1886–1986*.

Mimi has published numerous articles in scholarly journals on subjects ranging from biographical articles on often obscure entertainers for the *Australian Dictionary of Biography* to the State Library of Victoria's Shakespeare window. She also researched images and wrote many *Stamp Heritage Books* for Australia Post while Senior Research Officer from 1987 to 1993.

Mimi is a Fellow of the Royal Historical Society of Victoria; an Adjunct Research Fellow with the National Centre for Australian and Indigenous Studies at Monash University; a committee member of Theatre Heritage Australia Inc.; a Board Member of the International Panorama Council; and a member of the Victorian Working Party of the *Australian Dictionary of Biography*, as well as a contributor.

Mimi has attended and given papers on panoramas/cycloramas at many IPC conferences in China, the USA and Europe. Travel for conferences (largely self-funded) over the last ten years enabled her to research this book at libraries in Hong Kong, Kolkata, London and New York.

NOTE ON SOURCES

Few personal records of the Lewises survive. For an insight into the Lewises' lives we must rely largely on civil registrations, public records, newspaper advertisements, articles and theatre reviews and occasionally a silk playbill from their Asian tours. Recently a small scrapbook made by Rose Edouin (or her son) surfaced in Dublin. This book details her appearances in England in the 1890s together with some clippings from her earlier and later career. Although some press interviews with George Lewis have been found, there are few reminiscences of him, though we sometimes 'hear' his voice when he gives evidence at various civil court cases in which he was involved. With Lewis's wife Rose there are more clues. There are newspaper reports of her various farewell speeches from stages as far apart as Melbourne and Calcutta as well as reports of interviews and lectures. Here the biographer and reader must retain a healthy scepticism to evaluate the truth or otherwise of the claims of advertising and the opinions of journalists and critics. There was often a nexus between editorial and advertising text. Theatre managers might expect, but not always get, favourable opinions of their productions in relation to the advertising fees they were charged.

INTRODUCTION

Why write a biography of the now largely forgotten theatrical couple Mr and Mrs G. B. W. Lewis (George Lewis and Rose Edouin)? First, George and Rose were significant show business people in the early days of entertainment during the gold rush in Victoria, she as a juvenile performer and popular young actress, he as an ambitious equestrian circus proprietor associated with the building of the first Princess Theatre in Spring Street and later a stage entrepreneur. Second, they were agents of empire in the post gold-rush period of the 1860s and 1870s. The Lewis Dramatic Company was the first to take Western theatre to post-Mutiny India. There Rose was star and 'directress', while manager George built several theatres including the Theatre Royal, Calcutta. Their enterprise accorded with the Imperial ideal of the time of bringing British culture to the far flung Empire. After nine years in India and touring to Shanghai and Hong Kong they returned to Melbourne where they opened the Bourke Street Bijou Theatre. They invested in property in the early development of St Kilda Road but suffered in the 1890s bank crash. But that was not the end – Rose went on to become a valued character actress in Australia, New Zealand and UK. This narrative of their long careers can be seen as a kind of case study of show business and its changes over time and will, I hope, give an insight into popular theatre in three continents from the mid-nineteenth to early twentieth centuries.

Why have the Lewises been forgotten? Whereas Melba, J. C. Williamson, George Selth Coppin and Harry Rickards still to some extent remain in the public memory, the Lewises were on a 'lower' level of popular culture and were not as consistently 'successful'. Melba was perhaps Australia's greatest opera singer. Williamson was a clever actor and an enormously successful entrepreneur and his name 'J.C. Williamson', remained in the 'firm' he founded until 1974. Coppin was a good comedian, adventurous entrepreneur and, importantly, a parliamentarian; he was good at marketing himself. Rickards was a singer-comedian and founder of Australia's Tivoli vaudeville circuit that survived into the 1970s.

From the 1850s, Australian entertainment was crowded by other talented theatre people. Yet, individuals such as Gustavus Vaughan Brooke, Bland Holt, Nellie Stewart, Fanny Cathcart, Mary Frances Scott-Siddons, Mary Gladstane, and Robert and Florence Brough are all but forgotten. The careers of Williamson's sometime partners, Arthur Garner and George Musgrove, are seldom mentioned. Fame is ephemeral. There seems to be an indefinable factor that perpetuates the memory of some theatrical personalities over others. This factor is not necessarily lasting success nor is it always genius.

Entrepreneur and circus performer George Benjamin William Lewis and his actress wife Rose Edouin (née Bryer) rarely receive much attention in histories of Australian theatre. Lewis, whose career as a circus gymnast, theatre lessee and manager in Australia, China and India spanned half a century, was a near contemporary and would-be rival of George Coppin. Rose (Edouin) Lewis, a versatile and popular actress during her long career, is only occasionally noted in theatre histories and reminiscences. This dual biography takes the form of a chronological narrative divided by accounts of the separate careers of Lewis and Edouin until their marriage in 1864. From this time the emphasis is mainly on the performing career of Rose Edouin Lewis as George takes on a less publicised role as manager and entrepreneur. The show business lives of the Lewises and their important contribution to the spread of British theatre culture in the Australasian and Asian regions are detailed but the reader will find many unanswered questions about the couple and their families. These must remain mysteries until any so-far unknown sources are found.

Australian entertainment during the nineteenth century was lively, and with standards often comparable with the best of British provincial theatre, with Melbourne perhaps being ranked next after Manchester on the provincial theatre scene. The Lewises, above all, provided *popular* theatre. This was at a time when anything from Shakespeare and melodrama to farce, pantomime and burlesque could be termed 'popular'.

G. B. W. Lewis, known as George Lewis at the time, was the first lessee of the Astley's Amphitheatre, Spring Street, Melbourne. This building later became the first Princess's Theatre. In 1876, after seventeen years touring in Asia with his circus and drama companies, Lewis became the first lessee of the Bourke Street Academy of Music, later known as the Bijou Theatre, with Rose as 'Directress'. For a time in the late 1870s, they had also managed the Prince of Wales Opera House in Bourke Street. Rose was still absorbed in running a children's theatre school at their home, but by the late 1880s they had virtually retired from the theatre. Their son, George Encyl Lewis, although a keen musician, would soon gain his articles as an architect with offices in Collins Street.

Both Rose and George had been entertainers from an early age. George claimed to have walked from London to Liverpool in the early 1830s at the age of 14 to join a circus. Rose and her siblings had been child performers in

INTRODUCTION

London theatres from 1850, and Rose had starred as Puck in Shakespeare's *A Midsummer Night's Dream* at Sadler's Wells Theatre under the direction of actor-manager Samuel Phelps in 1855 when she was only 11 years old. Just before he arrived in Victoria in late 1853, George Lewis claimed to have toured successfully in Europe as a circus gymnast and ringmaster. Rose and her brothers and sisters were taken to Australia by their parents in 1857. It is easy to see what brought them to the colony of Victoria within only four years of each other: the Australian gold rush.

Chapter one

MR GEORGE LEWIS, GYMNAST, RING MASTER AND EQUESTRIAN

George and Rose Lewis celebrated their silver wedding anniversary on 19 November 1889. A Melbourne society weekly saw it as a splendid affair. The couple had invited 120 guests to a ball at their Melbourne home, 1 George's Terrace, near the corner of Commercial and St Kilda Roads.[1] George Benjamin William Lewis, retired theatre and circus entrepreneur, owned all four houses in the terrace.[2] Lewis's much younger actress wife, also retired from the stage, wore 'a trained gown of white and the palest shade of green brocade, the design, outlined in gold and blue, with side panels of amber satin; clusters of ostrich plumes … were effectively used for trimming'. Diamond and ruby ornaments and a bridal bouquet completed her outfit.[3] They made an impressive pair: Rose, aged 44, in her opulent gown; and George, six-foot-three, (190.50cm) 'straight and tall'[4] despite his age – it was also his 71st birthday. It had been a long journey from their humble beginnings in Regency London and early Victorian Brighton to the St Kilda Road address of a man of property in booming Melbourne.

George Lewis was born on 19 November 1818, the son of William Lewis, a labourer, and his wife Susan. He was christened George Benjamin William at St Clement Danes church, London, on 22 December 1818.[5] The family lived in humble circumstances in the tenements of Wild Court between Lincoln's Inn Fields and the theatre district of Drury Lane.[6] Most of Lewis's claims about his early circus career were made late in life and are difficult to check. For example, he talked of 'running away to the circus' at

---
1 *Table Talk*, 22 November 1889, p. 16.
2 City of Melbourne Rate Books 1870–1895.
3 *Table Talk*, 22 November 1889, p. 16.
4 *Age*, 'Melodious Memories', 2 July 1938.
5 Church of Jesus Christ of Latter Day Saints International Genealogical Index for the British Isles.
6 London Metropolitan Archives; see also British History online: http://www.british-history.ac.uk/report.aspx?compid=74284#n2.

the age of 14 and walking all the way to the north of England where his first job was as the hind-quarters of an animal.[7] This would have been about 1832. He named Hengler's, a circus popular in the mid to late nineteenth century, as the company he toured with to Europe just before he arrived in Australia in 1853. The late English circus historian John Martin Turner has shown, however, that Hengler's did not 'take off' as a company until the 1840s.[8] Furthermore, in his close study of Hengler's, Turner could produce no evidence that they ever toured to the continent of Europe.[9] Lewis recounted how, during his time of European travel, possibly in 1851, he was held up by bandits when performing in the circus at Bologna in Italy.[10] In another reminiscence he claimed to a journalist that he had been in the popular Pablo Fanque's circus in northern England.[11] Pablo Fanque was the *nom d'arena* of William Darby, born in Norwich in 1756 of African descent.[12] So far the only likely reference to George Lewis being in Fanque's company is found in the *Manchester Times*, 15 April 1843, where a Mr Lewis is listed as 'Conductor of the Circle' when the Pablo Fanque troupe was at Ashton-Under-Lyne near Manchester. Such a position involved a kind of 'choreography' of equestrian processions, tournaments and battles – a good grounding for his later career as an equestrian circus proprietor. Again, Lewis is hard to pin down between 1843, when he seems to have been with Pablo Fanque in Manchester, and 1850 when he was definitely performing gymnastics with the child 'Lilliputian Tom' in a show at Gravesend, Kent, near London. In any event, George[13] Lewis claimed to have arrived in Australia with £30 000, which he said were the profits from a tour of Russia. It is so far impossible to check whether his claims about Russia and Austria were mainly self-promotion.

Although one of the precursors of the modern circus, equestrianised dramatic spectacles (hippodramas) and equestrian circus were quite different from those of the late nineteenth century, when wild animals and trapeze

---

7   *The Theatre*, 1 August 1906, p. 5.
8   J.M. Turner, *Victorian Arena: A Dictionary of British Circus Biography*, Vol. 1, Lingdales Press, Formby, UK 1995, p. 64.
9   John M Turner, *Historical Hengler's Circus*, Part One, Lingdales Press, Formby, UK 1989.
10 *Australasian*, 10 June 1905, p. 1346. See also *Imperial Review*, Vol. 42, 1907, pp. 66–7.
11 'A stage veteran' by Autolycus (probably Henry Gyles Turner who was Lewis's friend and pall-barer at his funeral), *Argus*, 31 May 1905.
12 See John (Martin) Turner, 'Pablo Fanque, Black Circus proprietor', in Gretchen Holbrook Gerzina, ed., *Black Victorians Black Victoriana*, Rutgers University Press, New Brunswick, 2003.
13 George Lewis does not seem to have used the initials, 'G. B. W.' professionally until about 1867.

CHAPTER ONE

An early equestrian circus. Pablo Fanque at London's Astley's, in *Illustrated London News*, 20 March 1847, p. 189.
Private Collection

artists had begun to replace the traditional equestrian flavour, or more recent style entertainments such as those featured by Circus Oz, Cirque de Soleil and Flying Fruit Fly Circus where the only performers are those of the human species. From the late eighteenth century the original 'circus' entertainments were usually performed in purpose-built structures called amphitheatres and included trick riding, clowns and acrobats. By the early nineteenth century equestrian spectacles, known as hippodramas, were presented in London amphitheatres and included adaptations of Shakespeare's *Richard III* or specially devised plays such as *Turpin's Ride to York*, *The Battle of Alma* and *Mazeppa*, the latter loosely based on Byron's poem. As well as waltzing to music, the horses were called upon to rear at a signal from their riders, simulate kicking and biting, and act dead, as in the case of Richard III's horse White Surrey and Turpin's Black Bess. The hippodramatic shows featured spectacular scenery and costumes, richly caparisoned horses and

CIRCUS AND STAGE

A scene from Astley's (London) version of Richard III, in *Illustrated London News*, 6 September 1856 p. 251.
Private Collection

trick riding. The most famous venue for these entertainments was Astley's Amphitheatre in London on the south side of the Thames. It contained a stage with a ring circle in front and tiers of boxes for the audience on three sides. By the 1850s Astley's was at the height of its fame. With the added attractions of rope dancers (now called tight-rope performers), bare-backed riders, gymnasts and jugglers, the shows relied heavily on the dramatic and athletic talents of man, woman and horse. Historian Arthur H. Saxon has observed that 'Even Shakespeare's plays were reduced to mere vehicles for displaying the talents of the leading costumiers, designers and machinists of the day'.[14]

By the 1850s George Lewis had acquired management skills as well as those of riding and gymnastics. No doubt attracted by the gold rush in Victoria with its promise of good audiences, Lewis left the port of Deal, Kent, on 7 September 1853 on the ship *Woodbridge*, and arrived at the port of Geelong, 90 kilometres from Melbourne, on 31 December 1853. He was

---

14   Arthur H. Saxon, *Enter Foot and Horse*, Yale University Press, New Haven, 1968, p. 54.

CHAPTER ONE

listed as married and 40 years old. Shipping lists, however, are not always correct; he was 35 and his only companion on the voyage was a boy called Tom (no surname) listed as 14 years old.[15] Although records of his first marriage have not been found, the certificate for his second marriage in 1864 indicates that he was a widower at the time.

Lewis and Tom seem to have teamed up in September 1850, when they were advertised in England's leading theatrical newspaper the weekly *Era* as 'Lewis and Lilliputian Tom', performing in an equestrian circus at the Royal Terrace Gardens at Gravesend, Kent.[16] The previous April, Lilliputian Tom attracted attention at the City of London Theatre when it was reported that he was:

> a diminutive posture master, surnamed Lilliputian Tom ... whose graceful *posés* elicited loud and well-merited applause. The child is remarkably clever executing the most difficult feats without that apparent effort which usually renders this class of entertainments so painful to the spectator.[17]

The identity of Lilliputian Tom has remained impenetrably obscure. He was probably adopted, an orphan or waif, as were many children who were 'apprenticed' as circus performers. It is possible that Tom was a dwarf or midget.[18] It is also possible that Lewis had more than one partner, or 'pupil' who was given the name Lilliputian Tom.[19]

Soon after arriving in Melbourne, Lewis worked under canvas as a gymnast with his 'pupil' Tom in Joseph Rowe's American Circus in Lonsdale Street. Rowe billed them as 'the Incomparable Artistes MR GEORGE LEWIS And LILLIPUTIAN TOM, Whose Miraculous Feats bring down nightly applause'. A Melbourne *Herald* review described Tom as a 'fine strapping little fellow, between 9 and 10 years of age' who 'performed a variety of posture feats never performed in Melbourne ... we understand that his present instructor commenced breaking him in at the early age

---

15   PROV, VPRS 947, Passenger List, *Woodbridge* 1853.
16   *Era*, 8 September 1850, p. 1; *Era*, 17 August 1851, p. 1.
17   *Era*, 22 April 1849.
18   A person calling himself Lilliputian Tom continued to perform well into the 1860s. He was appearing in 'The Great Australian Circus' in Sydney in January 1868, see *Sydney Morning Herald*, 13 January 1868; and in Verletti's Troupe at Maitland in 1869, see *Maitland Mercury and Hunter River General Advertiser*, 3 June 1869. This performer is not to be confused with the clown Tom Lewis whose real name was Bingham Tomlinson, died Hobart 1876. See *Mercury*, 27 September 1876.
19   Apart from the quotation from the *Herald*, 7 January 1854, I have so far been unable to find a description or reminiscence about this performer.

of three and a half years'.[20] The brutal language of this report reflects the nineteenth century indifference to childhood,[21] when children were often treated as young adults before their time: in this case almost as animals to be trained to entertain.

The review, in the Melbourne *Argus* of 7 January 1854, details the various feats performed by the pair:

> In one scene Lewis raises Lilliputian Tom from the ground by his feet; tosses him into the air; catches him as the boy descends with his head towards the earth in the palm of his right hand and then plays with him as with an orange or a ball, by tossing him from one hand to the other some seven or eight times, the boy's feet being all the time uppermost. Another feat is, to so bend the boy's body as to nearly make his hands and heels join, and then revolve him over his wrist some twenty circles at a time as fast almost as top would spin.

Today this type of performance might be labelled as a form of child abuse, but in the nineteenth century it was very popular. This act most likely had ancient origins in contortionism, tumbling and acrobatics, but by this era had become known as a 'Risley act' after the exhibitions given by one of Lewis's American near contemporaries 'Professor' Richard Carlisle Risley (aka Richard Risley Carlisle).[22] It was also very dangerous. There was a story that one of Risley's 'sons' was dropped and killed during one these foot juggling performances.[23] In true 'variety' style Lewis and Tom, dressed in yellow costumes sprinkled with stars,[24] shared the bill with several different acts: equestrienne Madame Yeamans, 'The Sylph of the Circle; 'The Grand Equestrianism' of Mr J. L. Smith; the American clown Mr E. Yeamans; and the contralto Madame Sara Flower singing a 'favorite composition'.[25]

Rowe's Circus, a wooden building with a canvas roof, situated on the corner of Lonsdale and Stephen (later renamed Exhibition) Streets had opened in May 1852. So popular was the venue – one of the few in Melbourne at the time – that performances were given nearly every day during 1854, from

---

20 *Melbourne Morning Herald*, 7 January 1854.
21 Anne Varty, *Children and the Theatre in Victorian Britain: 'All Work, No Play*, Palgrave Macmillan, UK, 2008, chapter one.
22 Frederik, L. Schodt, *Professor Risley and the Imperial Japanese Troupe: How an American Acrobat Introduced Circus to Japan and Japan to the West*, Stone Bridge Press, Berkeley, California, 2012, p. 36.
23 J. M. Turner, *Victorian Arena: A Dictionary of British Circus Biography*, Vol. 1, Lingdales Press, Formby, UK 1995, p. 111. Risley's dates: 1814–1874.
24 Howard Vernon, 'Howard Vernon's Life', *Advertiser*, 1923.
25 *Argus*, 16 January 1854.

CHAPTER ONE

Rowe's Circus in Lonsdale Street, Melbourne. Drawing by S. T. Gill, in *Arm-Chair*, 25 February 1854. Dixson Library, State Library of New South Wales

early January to 20 October when it closed for the last time.[26] According to the London theatre weekly *Era* of 30 April 1854, 'Professor Lewis and his pupil are engaged at £50 per week'. While this is a startling sum, the same article reports that 'profits have been more than five hundred pounds per week'. Melbourne's population was small and there was little competition compared to London or the British provinces, but the gold rush was at its height and prices – such as Boxes 8s, Pit 5s, and 2s.6d – were much higher than their British equivalents. George Lewis and Tom were still performing with Rowe's Circus only two weeks before the first night of Lewis's new venture, an antipodean version of the famed Astley's Amphitheatre.[27] The advent of this new equestrian circus around the corner in Spring Street meant the end of Rowe's business but he returned to San Francisco with reputedly $100,000 in cash and treasure.[28]

---

26   John Spring, 'Computerised Listing of Melbourne Public Performances, 1850–1869', Monash University, 1981.
27   *Argus*, 28 August 1854.
28   Albert Dressler ed., *California's Pioneer Circus Founder, Joseph Andrew Rowe*, H. S. Crocker Inc., San Francisco, 1926, p. 19. Rowe returned (with less success) to Australia in the late 1850s.

CIRCUS AND STAGE

Lewis had set about building an equestrian theatre modelled on London's Astley's Amphitheatre with an American hotel keeper Thomas Mooney. The *Argus* of 28 August 1854 ran a detailed description of the new Astley's Amphitheatre in a report of an inspection by Melbourne worthies including the Mayor and the Colonial Architect. As well as a stage, the theatre had an arena where normally the pit and stalls would have been. The dimensions were: length 110 feet (33.5 metres), width 80 feet (24.38 metres) and height 40 feet (12 metres). There was seating for an audience of up to 2000, plus standing room. The theatre was:

> Finished at the south end with a semicircular gallery, running back from the floor at an angle of 45 degrees, furnished with seat above seat to the very ceiling. This is called the half-crown gallery; on the opposite sides of the house there are rows of pit seats and dress-circle boxes.

In contemporary articles and advertisements, Thomas Mooney was named as the builder and proprietor who was leasing the theatre to George Lewis. Doubts have been raised about who was the principal in this enterprise. Lewis's obituary in the *Leader* 23 July 1906, states that he had earned £100 per night with Hengler's Circus in Russia and elsewhere and had spent most of the £30 000 he arrived with on building the Spring Street theatre. On the other hand, journalist J. M. Forde, writing 50 years later as 'Hayseed' and 'Old Chum' in the *Truth* and *Sydney Sportsman* respectively, discounts this story, saying that he found no record of Lewis being a star of Hengler's and suggests that it is more likely that Lewis asked Mooney to back the project.[29] Thomas Mooney had done well on the Californian and Victorian goldfields and is said to have later returned to the United States.[30]

Some time during 1854, Lewis employed actor and equestrian Henry Birch as an agent or 'talent scout' to engage equestrians, rope dancers and other circus performers from the venues of London and the Continent. Birch attended shows at London's Vauxhall Gardens looking for such talent.[31] Pending the promised arrival of London circus people, Lewis opened Astley's Amphitheatre on 11 September 1854 with a series of 'GRAND MUSICAL AND COMIC ENTERTAINMENTS'. Advertisements boasted that Lewis and Lilliputian Tom were 'The two greatest Gymnasts in the World' – who performed their feats as seen 'before Her

---

29 *Truth*, 11 August 1906; and as 'Old Chum', *Truth*, 10 February 1912.
30 Melbourne *Truth*, 10 February 1912.
31 See below, evidence of Birch at the trial Berg v Lewis, *Argus*, 12 May 1855.

CHAPTER ONE

Majesty Queen Victoria, their Majesties the Emperors of Russia and Austria … &c &c'.[32] It is possible that such performances had netted Lewis the £30 000 about which he had bragged on arrival, but I have yet to find any evidence of their appearances before European royalty.

The 'grand' musical entertainments seem to have been rather tame with such gems as 'Why Do I Weep for Thee?' and 'I'm Thinking Now of Thee Jamie' sung by Miss Octavia Hamilton, contralto. Mr Barlow and his 'Negro Entertainments' enlivened the proceedings with 'Songs, Dances, Jokes, Wit, Animals, Birds and Insects'.[33] Robert Barlow was famous for his rendering of the popular minstrel song 'The Blue Tailed Fly'. As 'Sole Lessee' Lewis trumpeted in his advertisements that he had dispatched to Sydney to secure the services of the great Irish soprano Catherine Hayes, known as 'The Swan of Erin' then touring the colonies.[34]

The equestrians from London were late in arriving so Lewis engaged Henry Burton's Circus Troupe from Monday 2 October.[35] It was during this season that the Amphitheatre's first equestrian drama was given: *Turpin's Ride to York*. Burton, who had been travelling the colonies since 1851 with his own circus troupe, played Dick Turpin, and George Lewis made one of his rare appearances in drama as Dick's 'brother of the road' Tom King.[36]

Lewis's troubles were compounded when, to his intense embarrassment, Catherine Hayes, a soprano 'second only to Jenny Lind', decided, despite various financial inducements, not to sing at Astley's, preferring instead the old Queen's Theatre in Queen's Street.[37] Lewis was constrained to publish an 'Explanation' defending the acoustics of the building in his advertisements for 28 October, referring to Mr Barlow's 'inimitable imitation of the "Blue Tail Fly" … when 2000 spectators … have heard the humming of Barlow's fly as distinctly as if the fly hummed in their own bed-chamber'.

The first of three ships carrying horses and performers engaged by Birch finally arrived. By 30 October 1854, Lewis could advertise a 'Grand Company of Equestrians, and beautiful Stud of Horses', and that Mr Chas Devere the 'celebrated American clown from California' would perform together with Mr E. Yeamans (the Clown from Rowe's circus). The first

---

32 *Argus*, 22 September 1854.
33 ibid. In the English speaking world the 1840s and 1850s were the highpoints of 'nigger' minstrel entertainments. The majority of the entertainers were white singers and actors with 'blacked-up faces'.
34 *Argus*, 16 October 1854.
35 *Argus*, 28 September 1854.
36 *Argus*, 27 October 1854.
37 *Argus*, 25 October 1854.

CIRCUS AND STAGE

'Street Acrobats Performing', from Henry Mayhew's *London and the London Poor*, London 1861, Vol. III. Republished by Dover Publications, New York, 1968, p. 82

performance of the 'famous riders' Mr and Mrs Melville was announced for 1 November.[38] The *Calabar*, which arrived on 3 November 1854, brought the top clown from London Astley's, Tom Barry, equestrians James Melville, Tom and Emma Lee, a rider and rope dancer respectively, and their 'petite family' of child performers.[39]

Lewis took large advertising space in the Melbourne newspapers, linking somewhat erroneously his efforts at the equestrian circus with the massive shows of ancient Rome. At the same time, he assured the public that Tom Barry really was the one and only clown from London and that Mrs Lee was 'the daughter and pupil of Cooke' (the Scottish circus proprietor) and a great rope dancer. Among other things, Barry was famous in London for his 1844 journey down the Thames in a bath-tub apparently pulled by geese.[40] According to 'Old Chum's' reminiscences in Melbourne *Truth* of 10 February 1912, Barry repeated this act on the Yarra before leaving Melbourne in May 1855!

It is likely that Emma Lee,[41] billed as the 'first rope dancer in the world', was indeed a member of the famous Cooke circus family. She was probably the daughter of Thomas Taplin Cooke, the legendary Scottish circus proprietor who during the early part of the century had fathered nineteen children, most of whom grew up to be circus performers. According to an obituary of her husband in the *Era* of 6 October 1878, Emma Lee was the sister of circus proprietor James Cooke. The *Argus* reviewer applauded Emma's husband 'Mr Lee' as a skilled rider and gave detailed and admiring descriptions of Emma's extraordinary act on the tight-rope, where she sat on a chair at a table, both precariously balanced on the rope, and poured herself liquid refreshment:

> Mrs. Lee's tight-rope performance is amazing. The lady is as much at home in her aerial setting as if she were on *terra firma*. She balances on the narrow footing of the rope a chair, in which she sits and a table on which are candles, decanters glasses, &c., and seems quite at her ease'.

---

38 *Argus*, 31 October 1854. The Melvilles were from Sydney.
39 None of these performers was among the cabin passengers. Apart from the cabin passengers listed in the newspapers, the passenger lists for this ship have not survived.
40 *Illustrated London News*, 28 September 1844.
41 There are many circus performers called Lee, a difficult name to trace in entertainment history. For example, there was a family of Lees performing in Sydney at Malcom's Circus in 1853. Tom Lee was performing at Astley's London in June 1854.

The performance also introduced the Lee children – 'La Petite Emily', 'Miss Lee' and the 'Infant Edward Lee' – in a playlet, *The Duchess of Puddledock*.[42] As illustrated by the Crummles family in Dickens's novel *Nicholas Nickleby*, juveniles were prized as stage performers in Victorian England, with their managers often understating their ages to retain their status as 'Infant Prodigies'.

The Bergs (or Burghs), another family of equestrians and dancers, arrived by the *Stebonheath* on 23 December 1854. The family included Adolphe, 43, his wife Marie (or Minna), 24, his 13-year-old sister Antoinette and 9-year-old brother Robert.[43] In advertisements on 1 January 1855, Lewis apologised for the non-appearance of these and other 'stars', mentioning that the 'long voyage had relaxed the muscular vigor of some of the artistes' but went on to describe the new talent: Mons Klaer 'In his peculiar Act as the Juggler of Venice'; Antoinette Burgh, 'The Taglioni of the Cirque' (referring to the famous ballet star of the 1830s and 1840s); Mr H. Walker 'of Astley's Amphitheatre London will go through his extraordinary evolutions on the slack Rope'; Mr Adams 'Will appear on the swiftest steed of the circle'. Pablo Fanque (a 'man of colour' whose real name was Bill Barham and who was a nephew of William Darby, the black British acrobat and circus proprietor, the original 'Pablo Fanque') was another member of the new troupe.[44] Fanque's specialty, 'La Perche', astonished the *Argus* reviewer:

> The performer climbs a pole ... which is balanced ... by assistants ... Mr. Fanque ascends the pole with the agility of a monkey. Arrived at the summit, he performs a variety of antics ... the whole of his performance being accomplished with graceful action and gesture.

'Mr. Lewis [as Ring-Master] ... contributes to the amusement of the crowd by the resignation with which he endures the clown's jokes, verbal and practical'. The review compares Melbourne's Astley's favourably with 'any provincial [i.e. not London] establishment in Great Britain.'[45]

By February 1855, Lewis's offerings at the Amphitheatre seemed to have settled into the 'equestrian' and 'hippodramatic' entertainments typical of a London amphitheatre. As well as the usual circus feats, the equestrianised drama, *Timour the Tartar*, was produced on 5 and 6 February.[46] The H. M.

---

42   *Argus*, 28 November 1854.
43   PROV, VPRS 947, Inward Passenger List *Stebonheath*, 23 December 1854.
44   *Age*, 1 January 1855. See John Turner, *Victorian Arena: A Dictionary of British Circus Performers*, Vol. 1, Lingdales Press, Formby, UK, 1995, p. 99.
45   *Argus*, 1 January 1855.
46   *Age*, 6 February 1955.

CHAPTER ONE

Milner equestrian adaptation of Lord Byron's poem *Mazeppa* thrilled audiences later in the month.[47] There are no illustrations of how this colonial production might have looked, but the famous ride by the semi-naked Mazeppa strapped to his horse most likely was, as in London, performed by the horse and rider climbing higher on ramps and higher still to the back of the stage, finally in the distance being replaced by 'dummies' and cut-outs of horses.[48]

The engagement of the Bergs proved disastrous for Lewis, and sealed the demise of his amphitheatrical enterprise. Soon after her arrival, Mlle. Antoinette Berg injured her knee while riding an ill-prepared horse and was unable to perform for about three weeks. In another incident Robert Berg fractured his arm. Adolphe Berg sued Lewis for breaking their contract and forcing Antoinette and Robert to rehearse too soon after their 109 day voyage, thus causing their injuries. Adolphe Berg was to receive £50 per week for the 'trick acts' to be performed by Antoinette and Robert Berg. Lewis counter-claimed that the Bergs were not 'equal to the first riders of England, France and Germany' and therefore he had to terminate their contract.[49]

The case came to the Supreme Court on 11 May 1855 with the eminent Judge (later Sir) Redmond Barry presiding. Lewis was defended by prominent Melbourne lawyers Richard Ireland and George Higginbotham, but a jury of four found in favour of the Bergs who were awarded £500.[50]

The newspaper reports of the case are valuable in the way they define such things as 'trick horses' and 'trick acts'. William Barlow, a rider, gave the following explanation:

> Doing a "trick act" means, first standing on a horse galloping round, then striking graceful attitudes, then jumping over garters, then leaping over broad canvas sheets, finishing with a jumping through balloons and the like. A "trick horse" means a horse that can dance a minuet or polka by himself after training.

Under the management of George Lewis, Melbourne's Astley's proved much less successful than its London namesake. It was probably too large

---

47 *Argus*, 26 February 1855.
48 See 1851 illustration by Tenniel, Alan Wykes, *Circus!*, Jupiter Books, London, 1977, p. 92. The role of Mazeppa, originally written for a male actor/rider was made 'infamous' in London during the 1860s when the scantily-clad female, Adah Isaacs Mencken, performed it for E.T. Smith's Astley's. Melbourne theatre-goers enjoyed a similar spectacle when English actress/equestrienne Fannie Brown took the role at the Theatre Royal in 1866, see *Argus*, 8 June 1866.
49 *Argus*, 14 May 1855.
50 *Argus*, 12 May 1855.

an enterprise even for a gold-soaked Melbourne to have supported at the time. On 17 June 1855 Lewis declared himself insolvent. Under the heading, 'CLOSING OF ASTLEYS', the *Argus* stated:

> We are now sorry to record ... that Mr. Lewis, after a most arduous managerial career of nearly 12 months, has been compelled to succumb to the pressure of the times. The heavy damages in which he was cast as the defendant in the cause of Berg vs. Lewis ... [incurred] ruinous expenses but still Mr. Lewis struggled on ... The bad weather of the past month proved the grand climax of his misfortunes, and on Friday Mr. Nunn [Lewis's manager] announced that the amphitheatre would be closed after that evening ...[51]

The paper went on to bemoan that the 'unfortunate state of theatricals at present is remarkable for the great number thrown out of employment'. An examination of Supreme Court Civil Briefs shows that Lewis was severely in debt during 1854–1855. By July 1855 he owed his agent Henry Birch £3000.[52] Thomas Mooney suffered even greater losses than Lewis. The *Melbourne Morning Herald*, 4 December 1855, reported that Mooney was 'hopelessly mortgaged'. He had incurred debts of £11 981 in building the National Hotel, Astley's Amphitheatre, and the Mazeppa Hotel and that the ground landlord Mr Benjamin, would 'reap the benefit and advantage of the whole buildings'. Benjamin had lent Mooney £1000 at 20 per cent, and other mortgages had been entered into with D'Arcy Murray and Mr Kennedy. All this suggests that Lewis's claim to have paid for the construction of the building was untrue.

Not yet defeated however, Lewis reopened the Amphitheatre the next day in the vain hope of recouping his losses and 'trading out' of trouble. But this was unrealistic. From late June to mid-July 'benefits' were held for the various stars lured to Melbourne by Birch on Lewis's behalf, but the last benefit, for Lewis himself, clashed with the opening night of the new Theatre Royal in Bourke Street so few people came.[53] Astley's closed 'for want of support' on 20 July.[54] The *Argus* of 7 September reported that Lewis's 'splendid stud of horses' would be auctioned.

---

51   *Argus*, 18 June 1855.
52   PROV, VPRS 267/P1, Unit 71, File 2483.
53   *Melbourne Morning Herald*, 16 July 1855. A 'benefit' was a mainly nineteenth century entertainment phenomenon where a percentage of the takings was given to the various stars and performers, usually towards the end of a season, see Phyllis Hartnoll, ed., *Oxford Companion to Theatre*, Oxford University Press, Oxford, 1983, p. 74.
54   *Argus*, 21 July 1855.

CHAPTER ONE

Lewis was reduced to teaching riding at Astley's and briefly held the licence for the Mazeppa Hotel to which it was attached.[55] He soon left the Amphitheatre altogether, taking the remnants of his stud of horses and performers on tours of the goldfields.[56] From this time they performed in a tent. He returned to Melbourne in 1856 and his troupe performed at Coppin's Cremorne Gardens in the nearby suburb of Richmond and at the Theatre Royal.[57] Recognising the popularity of juvenile performers and the need to 'start young', Lewis placed advertisements in the 'Wanted' columns of the Melbourne press later in 1856 seeking 'Little Girls and Boys as Apprentices to the Equestrian Profession'.[58] Some of the children who were to appear in his later tours may have been enrolled at this time, such as Jessie and Marie Wild aged nine and six, who had arrived in Victoria with their parents in 1852.[59]

The 'white elephant' status of the Melbourne edition of Astley's Amphitheatre could not be thrown off. Henry Burton's circus troupe opened there on 10 September 1855, but lasted only two weeks. Such was the competition from the infamous performer Lola Montes at the Theatre Royal and the renowned tragedian, Gustavus Vaughan Brooke at Coppin's Olympic Theatre.[60] The amphitheatre was empty for months at a time. Remodelled in February 1856, it was renamed the Royal Amphitheatre by the ubiquitous theatrical entrepreneur George Coppin as leaseholder. In April 1857 the building was again transformed by Coppin into the first Princess's Theatre.[61] By the 1860s, circus entertainments given under canvas 'big tops' had proved superior to the amphitheatre or theatre-based circus spectacle. For the remainder of the nineteenth century, Melbourne was served by touring circus companies such as Burton's, Bird and Taylor's, St Leon's, Wirth's, and FitzGerald's.

---

55 *Argus*, 20 July 1855.
56 See advertisements in *Geelong Advertiser*, 5 June 1857; *Mount Ararat Advertiser*, 9 October 1857; *Ballarat Star*, 2 October 1857; *Mount Alexander Mail*, 8 September 1858; *Bendigo Advertiser*, 11 September 1858.
57 Richmond rate books show that Lewis occupied large stables on Balmain Street, Richmond, on the boundary of Cremorne Gardens.
58 *Argus*, 2 July, 15 December 1856.
59 PROV, VPRS 947, Inward Passenger List for Bengal Merchant. Wild was a surname prominent in circus and travelling shows in England. See *The original, complete, and only authentic story of "Old Wild's"...: Being the reminiscences of its chief and last proprietor, "Sam" Wild*, ed., "Trim" [ie W. B Megson], London, 1888, reprinted Society for Theatre Research, London, 1989.
60 *Argus*, 18 September 1855.
61 *Argus*, 14 April 1856.

CIRCUS AND STAGE

From a perspective of some 155 years later, it is clear that Lewis and Mooney had imagined the prosperity of the Victorian gold rush would support their shows and over-extended themselves financially. As Bagot observed, in his biography of George Coppin, by late 1855 there were too many amusement venues in Melbourne.[62] Nevertheless, equestrian dramas, or 'hippodramas' as they were sometimes called, continued to be performed in Melbourne theatres, including the Princess's, well into the 1860s. As late as May 1866, the visiting American combination the Great World Circus of Wilson, Cooke and Zoyara performed at the Haymarket Theatre in Bourke Street.

Although something of a failure, Lewis's venture into circus and equestrian entertainment encouraged a rich influx of circus performers to Melbourne and inaugurated the Spring Street site as a continuing one for theatre. It is now occupied by the 127 year-old Princess Theatre, a treasured part of Melbourne's theatre life.

For the next eighteen months Lewis travelled provincial Victoria with a modest equestrian troupe. During June–July 1857 he was engaged at Melbourne's Theatre Royal and it was there that he probably met the Edouin (real name Bryer) family of juvenile ballet and pantomime performers. Recently arrived from England, the Edouin Family was engaged at the Theatre Royal from 13 July for six performances of their vaudeville entertainments, *Frolics in France* and *Hole in the Well*. Lewis's equestrian productions of *Mazeppa*, *El Hyder* and *Dick Turpin* followed their programmes at the theatre in late July.[63] Among the Edouin family was 13-year-old Rose, later to become Lewis's wife.

During the next few years both the Lewis and the Edouin troupes were touring the countryside to the goldfield towns, one often following the other. One might imagine that George was impressed by the talented young Rose and her siblings.

---

62   Alec Bagot, *Coppin the Great*, Melbourne University Press, Melbourne, 1965, p. 201.
63   *Argus*, 5 June 1857; *Argus*, 13–18 July 1857; *Argus*, 20–31 July 1857.

Chapter two

THE EDOUINS IN ENGLAND

Around the time when 26-year-old George Lewis was trying to make his way in provincial equestrian circus in the north of England, Rose Bryer was born in Brighton, Sussex on 29 January 1844. Her parents were John Edwin Bryer, 'professor of dancing', and his wife Sarah Elizabeth. Sarah was a young widow when she married John in May 1832. Born Sarah May in Brighton, Sussex c.1809, she had married William Lind in April 1829 but was soon widowed.[64] Given her later history as a teacher of stagecraft Sarah might have been a ballet dancer. In a Dickens-like story included in the 1902 Souvenir Programme dedicated to Rose's stage golden jubilee, her mother was described as being once the 'belle of the pretty watering place' who had married 'one of the handsomest men, well-to-do … and a clever fellow'.[65] John Edwin Bryer, (son of an excise officer) was a year younger than Sarah and is listed as an ivory turner (a long-lost craft where ivory was used for items such as handles and combs) on his first child's baptism certificate in 1833. By the 1840s he appears in the Brighton directories as a 'professor of dancing'.[66] As a 'pretty watering place' in its post-Regency and post-George IV period, Brighton would still have been a good place for such an occupation.

Meanwhile Sarah had given birth to six children: Edwin Charles (later known as Charles) born 1833, John William born 1840, Eliza born 1842, Rose born 1844, William Frederick born 1846, and Julia born 1849. There is something of a mystery in this family with seven years between the first two children. The mother might have suffered miscarriages or had still births. On the other hand the father might have committed some crime which entailed his disappearance for seven years. Somewhere along the way he became a dancing master, and while Rose claims that she had made her

---

64 Information from the East Sussex Record Office, Lewes, UK.
65 *Souvenir of Mrs. G. B. W. Lewis' Professional Jubilee Testimonial Benefit, Theatre Royal October 3rd 1902.* Miller Printing Company, Melbourne, 1902, p. 7.
66 *Pigots Directory of Sussex 1839–1840.*

mother teach her dancing, John Edwin Bryer must also have taught the children many of their stage skills. Then, in 1850, something happened that caused the couple to separate. To quote her daughter's Souvenir Programme, 'she lost her husband'. In later speeches Rose talked of the family being 'fatherless and penniless'.[67] It seems that Mrs Bryer left Brighton, possessing only two shillings and took her children to London to avoid the shame of being seen as a deserted wife in her home town.[68] In the British Census held on 30 March 1851 the Bryer family, consisting of Sarah 42 'teacher of dancing', Edwin 17 'teacher of dancing and singing', and Eliza 9, Rose 7, and William 5, are listed as living at 409 The Strand. This was a few doors from the Adelphi Theatre, probably a place of work for some of the family. One wonders where John aged 11, and the youngest child Julia, aged about 15 months, were on census night. There is no mention of John Edwin Bryer, the father of the family.

The eldest child, Charles Edwin, was known to the younger children as 'Teddy' or 'little father'.[69] He seems to have taken the responsibility of giving school lessons to his siblings and earning money for the family by playing in theatre orchestras. When their Brighton medical practitioner, Dr Sanders, found them in reduced circumstances in London, he organised a benefit for them to perform in their native town. This earned them £100.[70] Soon the other children became theatrical performers. With the stage name of Edouin, given to them by their French dancing teacher in London,[71] they started performing in London theatres and other places of entertainment.

As can be seen in *Nicholas Nickleby*, juvenile performers like Dickens's 'infant phenomenon' Ninetta Crummles were popular in British theatre, sometimes to a ridiculous degree. Not all were constantly drugged with gin and kept a child beyond their years like Dickens's Ninetta. For instance, Jean Davenport and her actor-manager father T. D. Davenport, on whom Dickens is supposed to have modelled Crummles and his 'infant phenomenon', matured to become a successful actress in America as Jean Davenport Lander.[72]

---

67   *Englishman*, 15 January 1874.
68   *Souvenir of Mrs. G. B. W. Lewis' Professional Jubilee Testimonial Benefit* ... op. cit., p. 7.
69   ibid., pp. 8–9.
70   ibid., p. 7.
71   Melbourne *Punch*, 10 October 1889, p. 228. The French dancing teacher found the name Bryer not theatrical enough, asked them their father's given names and formed 'Edouin' out of 'Edwin'.
72   See various articles by Malcolm Morley in *The Dickensian* including, 'More About Crummles', Vol. 59, 1963, pp. 51–56 and 'Dickens goes to the Theatre', Vol. 59, pp. 156–171. For Jean Davenport Lander, see *American National Biography Online*.

CHAPTER TWO

Also in America, child stars Kate and Isabel Bateman grew up to be serious actresses.[73] As well as amusing other children, child actors attracted adults for many reasons: there was piquancy in tiny tots acting as ladies and gentlemen, let alone the appeal to any psychosexual proclivities among the adult audience.[74] As with most British theatrical traditions, it was exported to America, Australia and New Zealand. Troupes such as the Lees, the Marsh Troupe, the Wisemans, the Edouins, the Nelsons and later the Pollards, were attracted by Australian's prosperity. The juvenile stage was to be a constant theme in Rose Edouin's career, from her own performances and, from the 1870s, by teaching acting and dancing to young people.

After attending boarding school for a short time Rose, aged six, played one of her first stage roles as the Child in the eighteenth-century play *The Stranger* by German writer August von Kotzebue, with the tragedian G. V. Brooke at the Marylebone Theatre in May 1850.[75] In an autobiographical speech from the stage many years later Rose remembered how she was:

> brought away from school on the Sunday and danced with my elder sister on the Monday our afterwards celebrated Dutch Dance. That was my *début*. In 1851 I left the boarding-school for the stage and have never been back since. We danced in nearly all the London theatres … We danced at the old Covent Garden … the night the theatre was destroyed by fire. In our family were the first living Marionettes in Leicester Square, when I played all the leading low comedy business … At the Strand Theatre … I was the Infant Grimaldi. I dare say many may think it strange that a little girl should play clown … There was nothing in the profession that I was not taught. I could dance, tumble … I have been the only female clown.[76]

During the summer, Eliza, John, Rose and Willie were engaged to perform at the open-air pleasure park known as Cremorne Gardens, Chelsea. They were billed as 'Les Petits Edouins' performing 'Characteristic Oriental Military Dances'.[77] Later in the year Rose toured with the family troupe.

---

73   T. Allston Brown, *History of the American Stage*, Dick & Fitzgerald, New York, 1870, p. 25.
74   See Anne Varty, *Children and the Theatre in Victorian Britain: 'All Work, No Play*, Palgrave Macmillan, UK, 2008, chapter one.
75   *Englishman*, 15 January 1874. In one of her farewell speeches Rose is vague about dates: she played with Brooke in 1850, see playbills; and W. J. Lawrence, *The Life of Gustavus Vaughan Brooke*, W.&G. Baird, Belfast, 1892.
76   *Englishman*, 15 January 1874.
77   *The Times*, 26 July 1850.

By 1852 Rose was playing 'all the low comedy business' at the Living Marionette Theatre in Leicester Square and on tour in the English provinces.[78] Marionette shows were enjoying something of a vogue in London in 1852. A Royal Marionette Theatre with wooden marionettes was opened in Adelaide Street near the Strand in January 1852.[79] The Living Marionette Theatre soon cashed in on the craze by forming a company of juveniles who acted like marionettes, lip-syncing to dialogue and songs performed off stage and presenting them in Leicester Square. The *Era*, of 2 May 1852, carried a piece reporting that 'Henry Lee of Covent-garden theatre has put forth a … programme of musical and other entertainments …' at the Theatre of Varieties, Linwood Gallery, Leicester Square. Also promised was an entertainment of a 'mysterious nature, combining some new features of attraction'. This turned out to be the 'Living Marionettes'. (Also advertised as Peter Parley's Royal Living Marionette Theatre).[80] The *Morning Chronicle* described the show: 'The children are treated on the Marionette principle – that is, they act and move their lips, while the speakers remain hidden in the *coulisse*.'[81]

An undated article from the *Era* compared the two marionette genres:

> Delighted and amused as we were with the ligneous representatives of the histrionic art at the Marionette Theatre, we must confess to a more exalted surprise and gratification when witnessing the performances of a corps of Living Marionettes … Hitherto the difficulty has been to curb the juvenile tongue … Here we have a troupe of some barely above the nursery years, and none … in the "teens", pourtraying [sic], with the most minute fidelity of action, the characters in a drama.[82]

The Royal Living Marionette Company, including Rose and her siblings, went on a provincial tour after a successful season in London. The tour encompassed Nottingham, Sheffield and Derby, where the newspapers gave glowing reviews which the management, together with London reviews, included in one of its undated handbills entitled 'Opinions of the Press':

---

78 *Englishman*, 15 January 1874.
79 George Speaight, *A History of the English Puppet Theatre*, Robert Hale, London, 1990, p. 242; *Illustrated London News*, 17 January 1852.
80 V&A Theatre and Performance Archives, 'Royal Living Marionettes' folder (1852–1853). Playbills including 'Opinions of the Press' [n.d.]. The name 'Peter Parley' was used by authors of children's literature; notably by the American Samuel Griswold Goodrich (1700–1860) but no connection is apparent. Henry Lee might have used it as a pseudonym.
81 ibid.
82 ibid.

CHAPTER TWO

> An extraordinary humour is exhibited in these performances by a little girl apparently about eight years old, Miss Rose Edouin, who with her sister, Miss Eliza Edouin, and a little boy, Willie, aged five are perhaps the most able of the corps.[83]

Plays and vaudevilles performed by the children included versions of *Jack Sheppard* (where Rose played the title role), *Robert Macaire*, *The Forest of Bondy*, *Macbeth*, and *Box and Cox*.[84]

Years later, retired theatrical John Ennis claimed to have been the manager of the 'Living Marionettes'. He remembered the young Julia Mathews, who was later to have success in Australia and who developed into a star in London and the USA, and Lydia Thompson, who founded the famous 'Blondes' vaudeville troupe, successful in London and America, as being in the company.[85] Yet playbills of the time show that Rose, her elder sister Eliza, and her talented younger brother Willie (later to star in comedy on Broadway and in the West End) often seem to have similar billing with Julia Mathews and others.[86] Mathews, born 1842, and her parents went to Australia in 1854.[87] Lydia Thompson's name does not appear in the existing playbills of the Living Marionettes – born 1836 she might have been too 'old' for juvenile performances at this time and was already dancing at the Haymarket.[88]

The children also had parts in the Strand Theatre Christmas pantomime *Harlequin and Gulliver*, where Rose played Clown in the Harlequinade.[89] Rose also played Grimalkin in *Harlequin Puss in Boots* in the Sadler's Wells Christmas pantomime.[90] Interestingly, the company visited the Edouin home town of Brighton playing at the Theatre Royal.[91] It is not known if the family was recognised as the former Bryers. By August 1853, 'the Edouin Family' was performing in Lewes (a little to the east of Brighton) at the Corn Exchange Star Hotel where a temporary stage had been erected. Rose was mentioned

---

83   V&A Theatre and Performance Archives, 'Royal Living Marionettes' folder.
84   ibid.
85   *Era*, 21 May 1882, p. 9. Mathews' dates: 1842–1876, Thompson's dates: 1836–1908.
86   V&A Theatre and Performance Archives, 'Royal Living Marionettes' folder, playbill dated 18 April 1853.
87   Jean Gittins, 'Julia Mat(t)hews', *Australian Dictionary of Biography*, Vol. 5, Melbourne, 1974, p. 227.
88   Kurt Gänzl, *Lydia Thompson Queen of Burlesque*, Routledge, New York, 2002, p. 15.
89   Sadler's Wells Theatre, November 1852, playbill reproduced in *Souvenir of Mrs. G. B. W. Lewis' Professional Jubilee Testimonial*, op. cit.
90   Playbill dated 1852.
91   *Era*, 19 June 1853.

as a clever Clown.[92] She appeared with Willie later in the year in *Ernestine and Georgette*.[93] Rose is next noticed in December 1853 as a Clown in *Taffy was a Welshman* at the Strand. A highlight of the Edouins' 1854 repertoire was a dramatisation of Dickens's just completed novel *Hard Times*, where Eliza and Rose played Sissy Jupe and Luisa Gradgrind as children.[94]

In November 1855, the actor-manager Samuel Phelps of the Sadler's Wells Theatre engaged Rose to play Puck in his production of *A Midsummer Night's Dream*. Phelps had, with two others, taken a lease on Sadler's Wells theatre in what was then semi-rural Islington in 1843, and for the next eighteen years produced and starred in most of Shakespeare's and other English classical plays.[95]

Rose was awestruck on first meeting Phelps, who did much to popularise Shakespeare in the mid-nineteenth century. Her brother Charles escorted her to the theatre but, as she remembered many years later, her brother:

> didn't know the road, and as we had no money, we had to tramp it. The consequence was that we lost our way, and wandered about for hours … we were shown into the presence of the great man. He looked like a king, and I regarded him with awe … The end of it was I was engaged to play Puck. Next day I was kept in bed all day to study the part in greater comfort. When I attempted to get up, the family exclaimed, "Come, Rose, do a flip-flap".[96]

Rose's performance at the age of not-quite-12 seems to have been more than that of just another 'infant phenomenon'. *The Times* review singled her out among the cast as being particularly effective in the part:

> the managers of Sadler's Wells are most fortunate in the possession of a clever little girl, named Rose Edouin, who plays the character of Puck. In former times this truly national sprite was represented on the stage as a mere abstract fairy, like the rest, but now he wears a big head, and in depicting his love of mischief Miss Edouin introduces a series of gestures worthy of being drawn on the margin of the most elaborated book of elfin legends. Not one of her gestures is human, but she remains throughout the type of one of those fanciful existences that, hatched

---

92 *Era*, 14 August 1853.
93 *Who Was Who in the Theatre*, compiled from *Who's Who in the Theatre*, volumes 1–15 (1912–1972), Gale Research Co, Detroit, c.1978.
94 *Era*, 20 August 1854.
95 Shirley S. Allen, *Samuel Phelps and Sadler's Wells*, Wesleyan University Press, Middletown, Connecticut, 1971, p. 81. Phelps's dates: 1804–1878.
96 *Table Talk*, 12 June 1896, p. 6.

in the first instance by popular belief, has been rendered so definite by poet and painter as almost to become realities.[97]

The 'big head' would have been inspired by the large papier mâché heads worn in pantomime at that time. Phelps became Rose's mentor, instilling a love and study of Shakespeare in the young girl. He taught her stage skills until the family departed for Australia.[98]

In March 1856, Rose was in *The Sister of Mercy* at the Garrick Theatre.[99] The Edouin children were certainly kept occupied with performances in 1856 – even five-year-old Julia appeared at the Strand Theatre with her ten-year-old brother Willie in the panto *Holly Tree Inn*.[100] They seem to have been in demand to act children's parts in adult drama. Miss Edouin (Eliza), 'with the permission of Messrs Greenwood and Phelps' (of Sadler's Wells), played the child in the melodrama *Kate Wynsley; or, A Woman's Love* at the Strand Theatre.[101]

Dancing at John Henry Anderson's *Bal Masque* at Covent Garden Opera House was another type of engagement. 'Professor' Anderson, 'Wizard of the North' was a magician who at the time had the lease of the Opera House. Eighteen years later, speaking in a Calcutta theatre, Rose recalled dancing until 2 am, before a disastrous fire destroyed the building.[102] Another role taken by Rose was that of Belphegor's son with tragedian Charles Dillon in *Belphegor* at Sadler's Wells (her performance as Puck was mentioned in the review).[103] The siblings must have been amused with Willie getting the role of Belphegor's son in a burlesque of the tragic play.[104] More Sadler's Wells Shakespearean roles were assumed by Rose during 1856: Fleance in *Macbeth*,[105] and Cupid in *Timon of Athens*. It is probable that their eldest brother Charles Edwin was managing the children's busy careers. In early 1857, for example, eight-year-old Julia was given the role of the child in *A Wicked Wife*, a melodrama at the Haymarket Theatre where she was also playing in the pantomime *Babes in the Wood*.[106]

---

97 *The Times*, 27 November 1855, p. 10.
98 *Souvenir of Mrs. G. B. W. Lewis' Professional Jubilee Testimonial Benefit* ... op. cit., p. 9.
99 *Who Was Who in the Theatre*, compiled from *Who's Who in the Theatre*, volumes 1–15 (1912–1972), Gale Research Co, Detroit, c. 1978.
100 *Era*, 13 January 1856.
101 *Era*, 3 February 1856.
102 *Englishman*, 15 January 1874; *Athenaeum*, 15 March 1874 p. 337.
103 *The Times*, 27 April; *Era*, 27 April 1856.
104 *Era*, 5 October 1856.
105 *Morning Chronicle*, 7 September 1856.
106 *Era*, 22 February 1857.

Some time in 1856 the father of the family returned. According to an article about Willie Edouin, his father John Edwin Bryer had gone to Australia in the early 1850s and had returned in 1856 when he persuaded the family to emigrate.[107] Perhaps he hoped that the still prosperous gold towns of Victoria would prove profitable. He could also point out that, three years earlier, their former colleague in the Living Marionettes, 11-year-old Julia Mathews had been taken by her parents to Australia. There she was playing starring roles on the goldfields and in the theatres of Sydney and Melbourne.[108]

Years later in a speech to a theatre audience Rose expressed some regret at having to leave London and lays some blame on her father: 'I remained [in London theatre] until 1857 when *my mother was induced* [my italics] to take us to Australia. We had some pretty little pieces written for us, took a farewell benefit, and away we went.'[109]

On 12 March 1857 the 'clever family' gave their last performance at the Strand,[110] after which the children and their parents travelled to Liverpool to embark on the clipper ship *Algiers* for Australia. John Edwin Bryer was, for some unknown reason, calling himself John Edwin Jones, 47, mechanic.[111] It would have cost the family of three adults and five children more than £100 to travel steerage on the *Algiers*.[112] Bryer's wife Sarah, and the children, were registered under the name of Edouin on the *Algiers*' passenger list. It is interesting that they did not all use the name Bryer. It could be that John Edwin Bryer was wanted by the law, or that John Edwin Jones was merely a pseudonym for a new life in a new country. Edouin was to remain the family's stage name. Apart from the Souvenir Programme and shipping lists, I have found a few references to Rose's parents, mainly in their death and probate papers. Sarah Elizabeth Bryer died intestate in Calcutta on 29 June 1873, leaving property of £105 which was distributed to her daughters Rose and Julia and her surviving son Willie.[113] John Edwin Jones Bryer, musician,

---

107   Clipping on Willie Edouin at New York Public Library. A comprehensive search of Australian passenger lists and other records has so far found no mention of John Edwin Bryer going to Australia before 1857.
108   Jean Gittins, 'Julia Mat(t)hews', *Australian Dictionary of Biography*, Vol. 5, p. 227.
109   *Englishman*, 15 January 1874.
110   *Era*, 15 March 1857.
111   PROV, VPRS, Unassisted Passenger Lists to Victoria 1852–1923 for *Algiers*, March 1857.
112   *The Times*, 16 March 1857, advertisement for White Star Line *Algiers*: £14 per adult no food or bedding provided.
113   PROV, VPRS 28/P, Unit 226, File 99/637.

CHAPTER TWO

died on 23 November 1888 and the six children whose names are listed on his death certificate tally with those of Rose and her brothers and sisters.[114]

There was deep family sadness about the behaviour of the father, so that when Rose was interviewed for her 1902 Testimonial she talked of her mother as having 'lost her husband' in 1850. Another reason for this attitude to their father was that by 1866 he had started a de facto relationship with Isabella Jane Wing, who was to be the mother of three more of his children.[115] By this time, John Edwin Bryer had taken on a new occupation; that of livery stable proprietor in the Melbourne suburb of Fitzroy using the name J. E. Jones.[116]

Among other reasons for the emigration was, of course, the lure of the gold rush in the colony of Victoria, with Melbourne as the prosperous city where lucky diggers spent their gold on entertainment. The population of Victoria jumped from 76 162 in 1850 to 538 546 in 1860.[117] Another inducement might have been the promise of a warmer climate for a family which, like many others of the time, was infected with tuberculosis.[118]

The family is detailed on the Passenger List as: John E. Jones 47, mechanic; Sarah Edouin 48, wife; Edward Charles Edouin 23; John Edouin 16; Eliza Edouin 13; Rose Edouin 11; Willie Edouin 9; and Julia Edouin 7. Typical of juvenile performers, most of the children were in fact about two years older than the given ages. The *Algiers* (1001 tons), carrying 307 passengers in intermediate and steerage, arrived at the port of Melbourne on Thursday 25 June 1857.[119] The Melbourne theatres were contacted and the family found that one of their London employers, Gustavus Vaughan Brooke was the lessee of the Theatre Royal in Bourke Street. Here was someone who knew their talent first-hand. Soon, they were to make their Australian debut.

---

114 Edwin Jones Bryer, Death Certificate, November 1888.
115 Marriage and Death Certificates of Blanche Cameron née Bryer, 1890 and 1964; Death Certificate of Charles Edwin Bryer b.1867 and Birth and Death Certificates of Herbert Ernest Jones Bryer b.1871.
116 Sands and McDougall, *Directories of Melbourne, 1857–1874*.
117 *Victorian Year Book 1973*, Commonwealth Bureau of Census and Statistics, Victorian Office, No. 87, p. 32.
118 At least three of the siblings were to die of lung-related illnesses.
119 *Argus*, 26 June 1857; PROV, VPRS 947, Unassisted Inward Passenger List, *Algiers*, 1857.

Chapter three

ON TOUR IN AUSTRALIA

Melbourne was still part of New South Wales when the first theatre opened in February 1842 only fifteen years before the arrival of the Edouins. The first theatre was a ramshackle timber structure, part of the Eagle Tavern, a Bourke Street public house. At first named the Royal Victoria Theatre, but later known as the Pavilion, the Theatre Royal and the Victoria Saloon, its inaugural programme consisted of a series of 'amateur' performances led by professional actor George Buckingham. Early performances included such plays as *Rob Roy* and *The Widow's Victim*. In the days before separation in 1850, Melbourne theatrical promoters had to apply to the Colonial Secretary in Sydney for a theatrical licence.

In 1845, a more substantial theatre of brick and stone, known as the Queen's Theatre Royal or simply the Queen's, was built in Queen Street by Melbourne city councillor John Thomas Smith. Actor-managers associated with the Queen's included Conrad Knowles, Francis Nesbitt and the man who was to dominate the profession during the gold-rush years and after, George Selth Coppin. As well as the standard English repertory of Shakespeare plays and melodrama, Melbourne's first 'home grown' pantomime *Goblins of the Gold Coast or Melbournites in California* was given its premiere at the Queen's in May 1850.

The gold discoveries of the 1850s, and the accompanying increase in population, led to an expanded demand for entertainments. Over the following 30 years seven large theatres were built in Melbourne, some designed to hold up to 3000 people, as well as several smaller music halls, not to mention Astley's Amphitheatre previously mentioned. The focus of the city's entertainments shifted from the western end to a block bounded by Bourke Street East, Spring Street, Lonsdale and Stephen Streets. Theatrical stars such as the actor G. V. Brooke, the singers Catherine Hayes and Anna Bishop, and the scandalous performer Lola Montes (or Montez) drew large houses at the Theatre Royal Bourke Street and Coppin's Olympic Theatre in Lonsdale Street. Both these venues opened in 1855.

CHAPTER THREE

The quality of popular drama in colonial Australia probably reflected the standard found in the provincial theatres of contemporary England. There was a repertoire of Shakespeare, often bowdlerised and adapted to current taste, and melodrama, pantomime and burlesque, comedy and farce popular in London and provincial cities such as Manchester or Sheffield since the late eighteenth century. For instance, many of the plays performed in Melbourne and in the goldfield towns were written no later than the 1840s.[120] Sometimes the London plays were localised – as seen in Stirling Coyne's farce *Did You Ever Send Your Wife to Mordialloc?* This was first produced in London in 1846 as *Did You Ever Send Your Wife to Camberwell?* – Camberwell was then on the outskirts of London and Mordialloc lay on the outskirts of Melbourne. The play was adaptable to many locations, with Brighton, St Kilda and, in America, Brooklyn, being substituted in the title. At the other end of the theatrical spectrum there was Kotzebue's serious comedy-drama *The Stranger*, first performed in English in 1798. Other plays such as *The Lady of Lyons* (1838), *Louis XI* (1854), and *A New Way to Pay Old Debts* (1833) were immensely popular in mid-century Melbourne.[121]

Within a month of arriving in Melbourne, the Edouins were dancing and playing in vaudevilles at the Theatre Royal. The city's population by then numbered 51 000. At that time, a vaudeville was a 'light and amusing' entertainment quite different from the later Americanised term 'vaudeville' which had separate acts and, in Australia, evolved into the sub-genres 'variety' and 'revue'. The Edouins' 'vaudevilles' were performed as light relief as, for instance, an afterpiece to the drama *The Lady of the Lake*, starring Melbourne's favourite tragedian G. V. Brooke (who was also then the lessee of the Royal). As noted, Brooke gave Rose one of her first stage parts at London's Marylebone Theatre.[122] The reviews of the Edouin's were generally favourable, although the Sheffield-born medico and theatre critic, Dr James Edward Neild, sounded a general note of warning about the perils to child performers of their parents' 'lust for gold'.[123]

> No one can deny the talents of the Edouin Family, or the wonderful skill with which they must have been trained – But we never look upon such exhibitions without a feeling of regret that the bloom, if not the

---

120 John Spring, 'Computerised Listing of Melbourne Public Performances, 1850–1869', Monash University, 1981.
121 ibid.
122 See chapter two.
123 *Examiner*, 18 July 1857, p. 13. Neild's dates: 1824–1906.

innocence, of childhood and youth should be sacrificed to the acquired taste for precocity on the part of the public – if such taste really exists – or; to the lust for gold on the part of the parents.

On the other hand, the Edouins did not offend the *Herald*'s critic who saw their 17 July performance, timed to end at 11 pm for 'the younger branches of City families':

> The Edouin family played in the first two pieces, *Frolics in France* and a petite ballet entitled *Hob in the Well* ... the ballet exhibits these clever children to still greater advantage. The antics of Willie, as a sort of Pierrot, convulsing with laughter, not only the juvenile portion of the spectators, but the 'children of larger growth.' The young ladies are graceful dancers, and, intelligent pantomimists, and at various intervals gained significant marks of approval from their patrons. The little Julia – a perfect *bijou* of a ballerina – was encored in a sort of diamond edition of a horn-pipe ... The 'family', including Mr. Charles Edouin, who had rendered good service to the ballet as the 'old man', was summoned to receive the usual compliment.'

Before leaving London, one calling himself Edouin Bryer (probably Edwin Charles the Bryers' eldest son) had commissioned the London playwright Frederick Fox Cooper to write an 'interlude' *Frolics in France*, for Rose, Eliza, Willie and Julia to perform in Australia.[124]

This short play was a vehicle for the four youngest Edouins to display their versatile talents. It was in the style of the 'protean' dramas of the early nineteenth century where an actor or actress played multiple roles. By mid-century, plays such as *The Spoiled Child*, *The Actor of All Work* and *The Actress of All Work* were popular among juvenile performers.[125] As Lady Clarinda, engaged to Sir Willoughby Dalton (played by Eliza), Rose exhibited no fewer than five different characters: a languid English aristocrat, Lord Lavender Lollington; a tempestuous ballet dancer, Mlle Taglioni Vestris Twerlington; an un-named peddler; a fiery French officer, Hercule Achille; and an old woman, Miss Totterly. Rose brought forth each of these different identities as the plot unfolded with Lady Clarinda tricking her fiancé on his clandestine trip to Paris. Willie was Tiger Tim, Sir Willoughby's servant, a part which

---

124 Applications to the Lord Chamberlain for Theatre Licences. (British Library, LCP ADD. MS. 52, 962 Z). Such applications were required until 1968.
125 See Anne Varty, *Children and the Theatre in Victorian Britain: 'All Work, No Play*, Palgrave Macmillan, UK, 2008, p. 118.

allowed him to quote *Macbeth* to his master's annoyance and clown behind his back. Seven-year-old Julia played Lady Clarinda's diminutive servant Tiny Tippet. Rose must have had a deep regard for the play as, more than 50 years later, she was still acting in and producing variants of the text.[126]

In contrast to Dr Neild, the performances of the children also delighted the critic of the weekly journal *My Note Book*.[127] He wrote, 'They act in fact with the same freedom from effort, and with the same apparent absence of constraint, as do children in the playground ... They exhibit, in fact, an example ... of the tendency seen in nearly all children to something histrionic.' He went on to describe the performances:

> Master Willie is one of the most comical little fellows I have for a long time seen, he took a kind of Figaro part ... and the briskness and vivacity of his acting, and the genuine drollery of his physiognomic expression were as complete as anything I have seen in adult actors. Miss Rose Edouin takes half-a-dozen *transition* characters – a fine lady of the Johnsonian epoch with powdered head apparatus and judicious beauty spots; a fop exquisite of the same period; a French danseuse; a fire-eating captain; a voluble cheap John, and an ancient spectacled maiden lady. These characters are as a matter of course interwoven with the action of the piece, and require a rapid change of dress ... nor is the ready assumption of a different manner one whit less remarkable than the change of costume; – the languishing air of the beauty, the yawning simper of the petit maître, the French-English of the tripping ballet queen, the swagger of the irascible militaire, the rattle of the impudent peddler, and the cracked voice of the old maid succeed each other with a like readiness. Miss Eliza Edouin who does the 'walking gentleman' displays no less striking ability in her knowledge of emphasis, gesture, and stage action, and the little mite, Julia, is the most mercurial of microscopic actresses.

While not resiling from his general disapproval of child performers, even Dr Neild had to concede, after their last performance, that he was not 'insensible to the really extraordinary merit of these clever children.'[128]

After their first season in Melbourne at the Theatre Royal, in *Frolics in France* and *Hob in the Well* and *The Bachelor's Daughter*, the Edouins departed for appearances at the theatres of Geelong and Daylesford accompanied by

---
126 See chapters fourteen and fifteen.
127 *My Note Book*, 18 July 1857, p. 238.
128 *Examiner*, 25 July 1857, p. 13.

their mother and eldest brother Charles.[129] At Geelong, a seaport some 90 kilometres south-west of Melbourne, they appeared at the Theatre Royal in the town's Market Square.

In the meantime, George Lewis's Astley's Amphitheatre equestrian company took their place at Melbourne's Theatre Royal, presenting the galloping horse dramas of *Mazeppa*, *St George and the Dragon* and *Timour the Tartar*. Lewis had just completed a six weeks' season at the Geelong Royal where one of Lewis's riders, Henry Harwood (real name Biggs) had claimed attention for his ability to act as well as ride. He played Mazeppa without using a 'double' or 'dummy' as he rode on the 'Wild Horse of Tartary'.[130] Actor Richard Younge took the role in Melbourne. Despite 'brilliant armour and costumes of the knights' and the 'magnificent trappings' of the horses, the Melbourne production of *Mazeppa* lacked the excitement of performances in London or at the Spring Street Amphitheatre, or in a big tent, as recalled by reviewers in the *Herald* and in the weekly *My Note Book*. Although the stage was 're-boarded to suit the horses hoofs', the animals did not have a suitable arena around which to gallop and the *Herald* critic found Mazeppa's 'fiery steed' to be 'rather a lazy beast'.[131] This was humorously illustrated by Melbourne *Punch* at the end of July.

In Geelong (population 23 000), the Edouins shared the bill with a group from the Melbourne Royal led by Mr and Mrs Heir (better known by their stage names of Robert Heir and Fanny Cathcart) who came to Melbourne with Brooke in 1855. Also in the company were J. C. Lambert, Henry Edwards, and Mr and Mrs McGowan. Opening on 20 July, the Royal company brought to Geelong a repertoire of comedy and drama such as *A Roland for an Oliver*, *The Lady of the Lake* and *Adrienne Lecouvreur*, as well as the ballets and vaudevilles of the Edouin Family.

After the long season of horse dramas by Lewis's company, an 'old playgoer' writing the review of the first night in the *Geelong Advertiser* seemed glad to see the old drama back in its rightful place with the Heirs and the Edouins, but this sensitive critic expressed shock at the use of 'strong' language and oaths by the Edouin children:

> The petite vaudeville "Frolics in France" introduced the Edouin family to a Geelong audience. The acting of these juveniles is amusing enough.

---

129 They might have travelled to Geelong by steamer or by the recently opened railway.
130 *Lorgnette*, 5 October 1885, p. 2. Harwood later became an actor-manager on the Australian stage, his dates are 1830–1898. For a detailed description of *Mazeppa or, the wild Horse of Tartary*, see Saxon op. cit., chapter 7.
131 *Herald*, 21 July 1857.

CHAPTER THREE

An engraving from London's *Punch*, 1855, showing how Mazeppa was staged.
Newspaper Collection, State Library of Victoria

A cartoonist's view of Lewis's production of Mazeppa at Melbourne's Theatre Royal. Melbourne *Punch*, 30 July 1857.
Newspaper Collection, State Library of Victoria

> The plot of the piece is of the most flimsy description, but gives scope for some excellent mimicry and jest. One drawback to thoroughly enjoying the performance is the stupid oaths interlarded with one portion of the dialogue. Whatever disguise is assumed, the audience does not forget that three out of the four Edouins are little girls, and to hear from such lips such expressions as "I wish to the Lord" is simply disgusting. The children are quite talented enough to be able to dispense with the supposed additional "fun" which we presume the author thought he was giving the dialogue ...[132]

Perhaps because of this criticism the Edouins seem to have dropped *Frolics in France* from their Geelong repertoire. For example, after the drama *Adrienne Lecouvreur*, the children appeared in a vaudeville called *The Bachelor's Daughter* with John, Eliza, Rose, Willie and little Julia ending the performance with their suite of dances.[133] The season lasted more than three weeks.

In late July, having bought a van or wagon and painted the sign 'The Celebrated Edouins' on its sides, they started a tour of the interior, moving from one goldfield settlement to another. It must have been stressful for the little family driving around the Victorian goldfields with a horse and cart in the depth of winter along crude and muddy roads. Mrs Sarah Edouin Bryer was later described as 'a courteous little lady'.[134] She chaperoned her growing children through very rough social conditions. During the years of their travels, Sarah was aware of the importance of respectability in the life of an actress since the occupations of 'actress' and 'prostitute' were, in the eyes of many, not disconnected. Since Eliza and Rose would soon reach puberty, Sarah would have impressed upon them that off the stage they must behave modestly and avoid any attachment to the opposite sex.

Although Geelong had possessed a good theatre in Market Square built prior to the gold-rush period, theatre on the diggings often meant little more than a tent or a large room attached to a public house with a couple of tables serving as a stage.[135] Centres of entertainment were still merely large rooms attached to rough public houses dotted along Main Road near the diggings.

The Edouins travelled to Ballarat, the premier gold town, population 17 000. There they played at the Montezuma, a theatre attached to a pub of the same name. Ballarat then was a far cry from the prosperous inland city it later became. Only three years earlier it had been the site of Australia's

---

132 *Geelong Advertiser*, 21 July 1857.
133 *Geelong Advertiser*, 25 July 1857.
134 *Truth*, 11 August 1906, p. 2.
135 ibid.

CHAPTER THREE

first (and only) armed rebellion, the Eureka Stockade, after diggers refused to pay the exorbitant mining licence fees demanded by the government. Not until 1859 was the imposing brick and stone Theatre Royal built on Sturt Street.

Now removed from provincial Geelong and its straight-laced theatre critic, the Edouins restored *Frolics in France* to its place on the playbills for the 3 August opening. The rough but more cosmopolitan audience of Ballarat's Montezuma Theatre found no fault with the 'Extravaganza, written expressly for the Edouin Family by Fox Cooper Esq.'[136] Sharing the programme with a local stock company led by Charles Walsh, the 'little family' stayed at the Montezuma until 29 August. A brief review reported that: 'The Edouin Family continue to be as attractive as ever ...'[137] Males would have predominated in their audiences on the goldfields but women and children would also have attended.

Other family companies were to be found travelling around the goldfields and to larger towns. The Misses Wiseman, a local Ballarat family, opened at the Charlie Napier Theatre in Main Road while the Edouins were playing down the road at the Montezuma. Tight rope dancer Madame Lee and her 'petite family' featured in George Lewis's first Australian circus venture in 1854; they also performed in Adelaide and Dunolly during the late 1850s, while Marie Carandini and her adolescent daughters gave vocal concerts around Victoria and Tasmania.[138] Anna Maria Quinn, a six year old Irish-American tot, had starred in *The Actress of All Work* and spouted soliloquies from *Hamlet* to enthusiastic audiences from 1855 in the Australian colonies.[139]

The Edouin family is mentioned in Fanny Wiseman's reminiscences 'Pleasant Memories', published in 1906. As a child, Wiseman belonged to a similar juvenile troupe and her experiences mirrored those of the Edouins while touring the goldfields:

> At the same theatre, my sister and I played with the talented Edouin Family – Charlie, Eliza, Johnnie, Rose, Willie and Julia – now alas, all gone with the exception of Rose (Mrs G. B. W. Lewis) and Willie.
>
> At the conclusion of their engagement they started travelling through all the mining and agricultural towns. It was during their stay at one

---

136 *Ballarat Star*, 4 August 1857.
137 *Ballarat Star*, 22 August 1857.
138 Marie Carandini (1826–1894), London-born soprano, arrived in Tasmania in 1833.
139 *Argus*, 18 July 1855.

of the town-ships – I cannot recollect the name – that Eliza, the eldest daughter died.

We too went out on the same route, billed as the Wiseman Family, and did remarkably well and although we were stuck at times, it was not for lack of funds, but from a plethora of mud. Mud! It was more like glue! Our repertoire consisted of a 'musical comedietta, entitled Village Coquette, also April Fool; Love in Humble Life; The Wild Irish Girl; Betsy Baker; Little Back Parlour and The Bloomer.

Going from Smythesdale to Carisbrook our horses 'jibbed' and refused to go an inch further – it was lovely. The wheels were sinking deeper and deeper in the mire, when, fortunately for us, my father saw a man coming along with a wagon and a team of bullocks and as the wagon happened to be empty its owner offered for a trifling consideration to transfer us and our belongings to it and take us the rest of the way. When we arrived at our destination about 7 o'clock at night, we were cold, wet and hungry – for we had not time to have a proper meal – but our hearts were made happy by seeing a large crowd around the – shall I say Hall? – no, I won't, for it was merely a long dining room; the Stage consisted of two large tables put together. There were no dressing rooms, of course, so we had to dress in the hotel, and horror! We were forced to walk through the audience in order to get to the "stage"! My brother Dick didn't mind in the least – in fact, he rather enjoyed it – but Emily and I were simply disgusted – to think we could not make our entrance in the orthodox manner, but had to step on the tables – oh! it was terrible! – to us.[140]

By September 1857 the Edouins were playing with some success at the smaller diggings of Forest Creek (now Castlemaine), where the population had reached about 15 000, and the small town of Daylesford. But great sadness arrived when on 2 October Eliza Edouin died aged only 15. While her siblings performed for the miners in a makeshift theatre on the Daylesford diggings, the girl died alone at the Mount Alexander Hotel from inflammation of the lungs.[141] The local newspaper the *Mount Alexander Mail*

---

140   Fanny Wiseman, 'Pleasant Memories', *Illustrated Sporting and Dramatic News*, 1 November 1906, p. 16. I am indebted to Ballarat historian Peter Freund for this reference.
141   Death Certificate; *Argus*, 6 October 1857. Several of the Edouins were to die of tuberculosis-related illnesses.

CHAPTER THREE

of 9 October reported their 'severe bereavement', mentioning 'Miss Eliza, a young lady of great accomplishments … this sad event has necessitated a suspension of their excellent performances'. Yet only three weeks after Eliza's death, the Edouins were on the road again.

They travelled to another gold town Sandhurst (later known as Bendigo), with a population of 15,000, opening at the Haymarket Theatre in their 'Vaudevilles Farces and Ballets'.[142] The 'Lilliputian Edouin Family' was reported to have had 'good houses' and the *Bendigo Advertiser* of 30 October published a favourable review noting that: 'Though juvenile performers, they require no allowance made for their youth, but at once, as regards their excellence, are fair rivals for histrionic superiority with actors of maturer years'. Heartbreakingly without Eliza, Rose was still playing Lady Clarinda and her disguises, but the part of Sir Willoughby had to be played by her seventeen-year-old brother John.[143]

By 11 December the family had reached the new goldfield of Ararat where they opened at the Duchess of Kent Theatre, another place of amusement attached to a hotel. A long review in the *Mount Ararat Advertiser* of 15 December 1857 singled out John Edouin for his dance piece *I and My Double*, where in a two-sided costume he portrayed a soldier and sailor. Around this time, the Edouin Troupe turned from the goldfields to travel the towns along the south-west coast of Victoria. They probably were advised that there would be good paying audiences among the wealthy squatters of the western district who often took vacations at Portland, Warrnambool and Port Fairy. From Portland, it was a short trip by steamer to Adelaide where more audiences could be found.

The journey to Portland was long, arduous and uncomfortable. Roads down the hills of Ararat to the plains beside the Grampians Mountains were badly marked, dusty and potholed in the summer. It took the best part of a month to reach the coast. They found Portland, Victoria's oldest seaport, a small prosperous town with many pubs, including the large bluestone Mac's Hotel containing a suitable room where they could perform. The family opened on there18 January 1858. The *Portland Guardian* of 20 January 1858 carried a large advertisement detailing their programme, including the ubiquitous *Frolics in France* together with a Stirling Coyne farce *An Unprotected Female*, with Willie, Rose and John in the main parts, followed by various ballets

---

142   *Bendigo Advertiser*, 24 October 1857. Sandhurst was officially renamed Bendigo in 1891.
143   *Bendigo Advertiser*, 7 November 1857.

danced by Rose, Julia and John. A Mr B. Ricards played Sir Willoughby to Rose's Lady Clarinda. Her eldest brother Charles was manager. The family performed twice on Saturday to 'accommodate the Schools and Families residing at a distance'.[144] There was a hiatus in their Portland season when they found that their theatrical license had expired. Obtaining a theatrical license was a legal requirement for all performances in the colonies. Their absent father intervened acting as their agent in Melbourne on 27 January and, calling himself John E. Jones, he applied to the Colonial Secretary to renew the license for 'a mother and her 5 children' stranded at Portland.[145]

A renewal of the licence was obtained and for the next month the little company continued touring the coastal towns east of Portland: Port Fairy, with a population of about 2500;[146] Warrnambool, population 2000;[147] before returning to Port Fairy,[148] and then Portland. They then embarked for Adelaide[149] to present a three week season.[150] Shortly after the Edouin's departure from the region the Lewis circus was performing at Warrnambool.[151]

Adelaide, capital of the colony of South Australia, had a population of 16 000 in the 1850s, and was increasingly visited by theatrical companies from other colonies in the aftermath of the gold rush period.[152] The Edouins opened at the Royal Victoria on 3 March 1958. To ensure a good reception, they sent their Portland reviews to the *South Australian Register* mentioning their being 'favourably spoken of in Portland'.

By this time, 'Mr. George Lewis's equestrians had crossed overland to Beechworth in north eastern Victoria where they performed at Mooney's Hotel.[153] On 17 May 1858, Lewis, giving his address at 26 Young Street Collingwood, was applying for a general theatrical license.[154]

Returning to Victoria by the end of June 1858, the Edouins were performing in the 'long room' of C. Emden's Junction Hotel in Kyneton, a small town of about 3500 people on the road to Castlemaine some 80 kilometres

---

144 *Portland Guardian*, 25 January 1858.
145 PROV, VPRS, 1189/P, Unit 823, Item E921.
146 *Banner of Belfast*, 29 January 1858.
147 *Warrnambool Examiner*, 2, 5, 9, 16 February 1858.
148 *Banner of Belfast*, 12 February 1858.
149 *Portland Guardian*, 22 February 1858.
150 *South Australian Register*, 3–23 March 1858.
151 *Warrnambool Examiner*, 24 February – 2 March 1858.
152 Philip Parsons, ed., *Companion to Theatre in Australia*, Currency Press, Sydney, 1995, p. 25.
153 *Ovens and Murray Advertiser*, 19 March 1858, p. 3.
154 PROV, VPRS, 1189/P, Unit 823, Item F4570; on 7 June 1858 license to 'George Lewis granted for 12 months for theatrical entertainments and exhibitions', PROV, VPRS 1189/P, Unit 827, Item 59/M5686.

CHAPTER THREE

north of Melbourne.[155] They were at the Victoria Theatre in Ballarat by 20 August.[156]

The Edouins and the Lewis troupe were only two of many such entertainment companies touring around the goldfield towns in the late 1850s. For example, the famous American performer 'Professor' Risley and his show was a competitor to Lewis around the gold towns.[157] There were also smaller groups. The young dancer Tilly Earl(e), later to marry Rose's brother John, made her debut at the Shamrock Hotel's Concert Hall, Sandhurst, in August 1958, performing a show with dancer Madame Strebinger and contralto Sara Flower. The popular ballad singer Charles Thatcher was another drawcard on the goldfields.[158]

Lewis's equestrians opened in Castlemaine's Market Square on 11 September, and travelled to Sandhurst three days later to lead a procession through the town.[159] By 9 October, Lewis and his equestrian troupe were located at Ballarat's Charlie Napier Theatre performing equestrian dramas that included *Mazeppa*, *Bosworth Field* and *Dick Turpin*. The stars were the juveniles 'Marie and Jessie' and the rider Harry Adams, as well as an Indigenous rider with the unlikely name of Alexander Alkanna Hernandez advertised as 'The aboriginal [sic], the Greatest Somersault Thrower and Rider in the world'.[160] Six months later when the great American rider James Hernandez (real name Mickey Kelly) had joined Lewis in Ballarat the New South Wales (Moreton Bay) 'native' had reduced his name to Alexander Alkanna.[161]

Rose Edouin's father again appears on the record as agent for a licence application by his son Charles of the Duchess of Kent Hotel, Ballarat. The licence is dated 3 September 1858.[162] In mid-October the 'Celebrated Edouin Family' travelled to Castlemaine where, at the New Criterion Hall, they opened on 18 October 1858. Advertisements mention the troupe as being 'the only Dramatic Company in the colony legally Licensed by Act of Parliament ...' and which was noted 'for its respectability and excellence'.[163]

---

155 *Kyneton Observer*, 29 June, 1 and 3 July 1858.
156 *Ballarat Star*, 20 August 1858.
157 See *Ballarat Star*, 2 November 1858; *Bendigo Advertiser*, 2 January 1859.
158 *Bendigo Advertiser*, 3 July 1858. For Thatcher see Hugh Anderson, *The Colonial Minstrel*, Cheshire, Melbourne, 1960.
159 Mackay, George, *Annals of Bendigo*, G. Mackay and Co., Bendigo, 1912, p. 50.
160 *Ballarat Star*, 6 October 1858.
161 *Ballarat Star*, 20 June 1859. Mark St Leon suggests that the name 'Alkanna' may have been the rider's pronunciation of 'Alexander'. See also Mark St Leon, 'Celebrated at first, then implied and finally denied ...', *Aboriginal History*, Vol. 32, 2008, p. 68.
162 PROV, VPRS, 1189/P, Unit 823, Item H7566.
163 *Mount Alexander Mail*, 18 October 1858, 22 October 1858. I have not found any official record of this claim.

They moved to the Adelphi Theatre, Mount Alexander Hotel, for two nights where they included a new vaudeville called *Port Curtis*, a topical piece dealing with a new gold rush in northern Australia.

Scarcely seeming to stop for breath, the Edouins returned to Melbourne and boarded a ship for Launceston. The first advertisement in the *Cornwall Chronicle* of 3 November announced 'The Edouin Family' for three nights at the Cornwall Assembly Rooms. Other members of the cast included Mrs Davis, Mr Shute and Mr Searle. Charles Edouin was billed as Stage Manager. The troupe shared the bill with vocalist Robert Farquharson, a Launceston favourite en route to India. Robert Farquharson Smith, baritone, was later to be a member of Australia's first large scale opera company managed by W. S. Lyster. Charles Edouin was also listed as pianist with a Mr Sharp, violinist. The Edouins were not the only juvenile performers in town: the Nelson Family from London were at the Theatre Royal.[164] This family consisted of two girls Sara and Carry, and a boy Alfred. They were managed by their father Sydney Nelson, a composer of popular songs – including 'Bonny Mary of Argyle'. The Nelsons arrived in Australia in 1852 and toured the colonies with their 'drawing-room entertainments' until 1859 before travelling to New Zealand and California.

From Launceston, the Edouins played two-night stands at nearby Evandale and Longford[165] before setting out on an overland journey to Hobart. According to the visiting actor Clarence Holt, who had travelled the route in 1854, the (convict-built) road to Hobart was quite smooth.[166] This must have been a welcome relief for the family after their experience of the rough roads of Victoria since arriving from England sixteen months before.

Back in Melbourne, George Lewis is reported by *Bell's Life in Victoria* of 13 November 1858 to be training horses free of charge at Coppin's Cremorne Gardens, an early amusement park and pleasure garden in the Melbourne suburb of Richmond. The Gardens were developed in 1853 by caterer James Ellis, former manager of London's Cremorne, who had arrived in Melbourne as a bankrupt in 1852. Attractions included an elaborate dancing rotunda, tight-rope performances above the ornamental lake and fireworks displays over a huge modelled and painted panorama.[167] By 1859 a small theatre, the Pantheon, had been added. A popular summer haunt, Cremorne Gardens

---

164 *Cornwall Chronicle*, 10 November 1858. Nelson's dates: 1800–1862.
165 *Cornwall Chronicle*, 20 November 1858.
166 Clarence Holt, 'Twice Around the World, or Recollections of an Old Actor', National Library of Australia: MS2244.
167 See Mimi Colligan, *Canvas Panoramas: Panoramic Entertainment in 19th Century Australia and New Zealand*, Melbourne University Press, Melbourne, 2002, Chapter 5.

CHAPTER THREE

were managed by actor-manager and politician George Coppin in partnership with actor G. V. Brooke from 1856 to 1859 and then by Coppin alone. Here Lewis and his circus were involved in the Cremorne Old English Fair. Again, George Lewis's seemingly callous attitude to children is evident. A letter critical of his behaviour was published in the *Argus* of 27 December 1858 protesting against the cruelty of equestrian performances when two little girls (possibly Mary and Jessie Wild) fell from their horses, one breaking her arm, but were forced to go on. The same letter praised an Indigenous rider, known as Aboriginal Sammy, who could leap many horses at once.[168]

The Edouin's engagement in Hobart (population 19 000) proved to be successful. They played at the Theatre Royal from 6 to 31 December 1858. They then toured the nearby towns of Richmond, Sorell and New Norfolk, before returning to Hobart to give a final performance on 24 January 1859 at the Royal. Their advertising included many favourable critiques from London and mainland newspapers.[169] On 17 December, they shared the bill with the popular soprano Madame Carandini and her fourteen year old daughter Rosina.[170]

The family returned to Melbourne in February 1859 and secured a place in J. R. (John Rodger) Greville's Dramatic Company for a tour of northern Victoria.[171] After a season at the Star Theatre in Beechworth (population 3000), they travelled to nearby Albury (population 500) just over the Murray River in New South Wales. Billed as 'The Edouins' "Celebrated Pantomime, Farce and Ballet Troupe"' supported by a 'fully organized Dramatic Company' they appeared at the Exchange Hotel Assembly Room in April 1859. Just as English provincial tours were often organised to coincide with visits to towns during market or fair times, the Edouin's season at Albury was timed to coincide with local events, in this case the local races. At a 'Grand Fashionable Night … with patronage by the Stewards of the Albury Races' the Edouins danced a Jockey Hornpipe dressed in 'the Winning Colours'. The review described the troupe as 'superior to any which has visited the town' and bemoaned the small audience.[172] After another season in Beechworth the Edouins returned to Melbourne, and for the next five years the family made this city their base with Rose as its most prominent member.

168 *Argus*, 27 December 1858. I have found no details of Aboriginal Sammy's life.
169 *Mercury*, 4, 17, 18, 20 December 1858.
170 Later, as Mrs Palmer, to be a popular concert soprano in Melbourne.
171 This tour was managed by Alexander Henderson. *Ovens and Murray Advertiser*, 19 March 1859. Henderson was later to partner Lydia Thompson who in turn employed Willie Edouin as comedian in her burlesques.
172 *Albury Border Post*, 9, 13, and 16 April 1859.

CIRCUS AND STAGE

An illustration of Mongo Mongo, an Aboriginal rider with Ashton's Circus in New South Wales. *Illustrated Sydney News*, 23 June 1855. Aboriginal Sammy and Alexander Alkanna performed similar feats for Lewis at Cremorne Gardens.
Newspaper Collection, State Library of Victoria.

Much later, in one of her several farewell speeches from the Calcutta stage, Rose addressed the problem of the maturing juvenile performer:

> By this time we were getting to awkward sizes, so we were taken to Melbourne to remain quiet and steady ... The next two years were the most difficult of my experience, for I not only had to learn, but to unlearn, a great deal. Of course what was pretty in a child became stupid in a woman; and always in ballets, &co., we had to act so much, that the difficulty was not to act, but to act less, but I flattered myself I mastered even that and played ... the leading business in nearly all the principal theatres in the colonies ...[173]

---

173 *Englishman*, 15 January 1874.

Chapter four

GEORGE IN ASIA

In an effort to expand his career, George Lewis decided in 1859 to take his equestrian troupe of five adults and four children to the British colony of Hong Kong. China was an exceptionally dangerous place at this time. The Taiping Rebellion was in full swing but by keeping to the ports entertainers had the protection of the British Concessions. Lewis and his troupe embarked on the 443 ton ship *Creole*. Apart from the Lewis troupe, the majority of the 165 passengers were Chinese gold miners returning home. Prominent among the Lewis company was the great Irish American rider James Hernandez 26, and Harry Adams 26, equestrian and clown. Adams had appeared with Lewis in Melbourne in 1854, and both Adams and Hernandez had been successful in the USA and Britain.[174] J. M. Wolfe, who gave his age as 30, was an actor who had performed in George's equestrian dramas on tours of the Victorian goldfields. There was also an 'A. Augustini' aged 18.[175] Circus names can be somewhat puzzling for the historian. Colonial performers often assumed the famous names of British artists – after all, how could people in Victoria or New South Wales verify that 'Pablo Fanque', 'Hernandez' or 'Christoff' were not the British or American originals? We have seen that the clown Tom Barry was *the* Tom Barry of London[176] but circus historian Mark St Leon has established that the 'Pablo Fanque' and 'Christoff' of Australia were nephews or brothers of the famous black British rope dancers.[177]

'Lewis's Great Australian Hippodrome' opened in Hong Kong on 15 December 1859 on ground behind the Government offices.[178] Somewhere on the journey Lewis had engaged the female rider Mlle Floretta Camille,

---

174 John Turner, *Victorian Arena: A Dictionary of British Circus Biography*, Lingdales Press, Formby, UK, 1995; playbill private collection.
175 PROV, VPRS 948 Outward Passenger List for *Creole*.
176 See chapter one.
177 Mark St Leon, *Circus in Australia*, The Author, Penshurst NSW, 2007, p. 62. The two arrived in Australia in 1854; see PROV, VPRS 947, Inward Passenger List for *Champion of the Seas*.
178 *China Mail*, 2 January 1860.

'First Lady Rider of the Day', and three little girls 'Jessie Gardoni, Little Ella and the Infant Augusta'.[179] Lewis charged $HK3 for reserved seats and $HK2 for 'second seats'. The advertising mentions how the troupe had been 'hailed and welcomed' by the people of Hong Kong.[180] Apart from the occasional amateur 'Hong Kong Garrison Theatricals', there was not much entertainment in the small colony.[181] During the Lewis season the troupe performed to audiences from both the military and navy and colonial officials. There were special day performances for local Chinese at half-price.[182] The latter would be compradors, Chinese who helped European trade with the Imperial government. One wonders if Chinese 'coolies' were permitted to attend such performances.

The *Overland China Mail*, of 30 December 1859, gave a favourable review of the 'Circus of Mr. Lewis' which has 'obtained a large and well deserved share of patronage, the tent being crowded on some nights and usually well filled':

> Mr. Hernandez accomplishes equestrian feats with ease and grace. He personates several characters with much humour, and his leaps might do for Astley's. Mr. Adams makes a capital clown both as regards word and gestures, and is a good mimic. Lilliputian Tom goes bravely through his gymnastic feats and Mdlle Camille is a great attraction in this part of the world, where actresses and lady riders are so rarely seen.

The paper noted that the Governor's wife Lady Robinson was to attend the performance, thus allowing ladies to attend the entertainment. The Governor himself promised to be present at Lewis's Benefit on 2 January.[183] The troupe was to perform in nearby Macao on 9 January.[184]

Lewis stayed in Asia for the next fifteen months, probably touring north to Shanghai and then to India. He and his company arrived in Calcutta in early October 1860. Soon advertisements appeared for 'Lewis's Great Australian Hippodrome and Mammoth Amphitheatre on the Maidan … just arrived from China'. It was only three years since the 'First War of Independence', otherwise known as the 'Indian Mutiny', had taken place. The old East India Company had been replaced by direct rule from London. Calcutta was now the capital of West Bengal with the British Viceroy in charge. The Maidan was a park-like space between Chowringhee Road and the river Hoogli. The

---

179 *Hongkong Recorder*, 15 December 1859.
180 *Hongkong Recorder*, 17 December 1859.
181 *Hongkong Recorder*, 15 November 1859.
182 *Hongkong Recorder*, 24 December 1859.
183 *Hongkong Recorder*, 31 December 1859.
184 ibid.

CHAPTER FOUR

The five houses in Chowringhee that formed the nucleus of the Grand Hotel.

Chowringee Road showing the Maidan and buildings on the site of what later became Lewis's Theatre Royal. From Montague Massey's *Recollections of Calcutta over Half a Century*, Thacker, Calcutta, 1918, plate following p. 98. State Library of Victoria

area also contained Fort William, a major British defence structure, and the Botanical pleasure park of Eden Gardens.[185] According to advertisements, Lewis was given special permission by the British authorities to erect his huge tent on the Maidan. Lewis's show opened on 15 October. The cast included James Hernandez; Madame Birch 'Australia's Star and Gem of the Circle'; Pauline Annette; Jessie Gardoni; Little Ella; The infant Augusta; 'Professor Lewis and his Fairy Pupils; Lilliputian Tom'; Mr J. M. Wolfe 'the celebrated Shakespearean Jester'; 'The Brothers Leopold and Austin Shangahae [sic] (The Chinese Tom Thumb)'.[186] It is probable that the 'infant Augustine' and 'Austin Shangahae' are the same person. In India, where the local typesetters might have had difficulty with English, the advertisements for amusements sometimes contain mistakes with names and numbers of cast members.

Lewis's agent Henry Birch arrived in early November, advertised not only as 'the eminent London and Australian Tragedian' but as an equestrian playing Richard III in *Battle of Bosworth Field, or, the Death of White Surrey*.[187] During this season Lewis held special performances for charity.

---

185 Now Eden Gardens Cricket Stadium.
186 *Englishman*, 10 October 1860.
187 *Englishman*, 5 November 1860. Henry Birch had arrived for Lewis in 1854. He later acted with tragedian Clarence Holt's dramatic company around the Victorian country towns during in the late 1850s.

Lewis's Great Australian Hippodrome and Mammoth Amphitheatre.

HAVING ARRIVED FROM CHINA PER "FIERY CROSS,"
Will open on Monday evening next, Oct. 15th, 1860.
ON THE MAIDAN,
FIRST APPEARANCE IN CALCUTTA OF
THE GREAT HERNANDEZ,
(THE STAR RIDER OF THE WORLD,)
SUPPORTED BY
The most Powerful and Talented Troupe of Male and Female Equestrian Artistes of the Age.
A SPLENDID STUD OF HIGHLY TRAINED HORSES
AND ARABIAN PONIES.

Open every evening during the stay of this Distinguished Troupe, with a magnificent Programme of Arena Wonders.
Introducing.
Mr. James Hernandez.
Madame Birch.
(Australia's Star and Gem of the Circle.)
Mamlle Pauline Aniette.
Jessie Gardoni.
Little Ella.
The Infant Agustine.
Professor Lewis and
(His Fairy Pupils.)
Lilliputian Tom,
Mr. J. M. Wolfe.
(The Celebrated Shaksperean Jester)
The Brothers Leopold.
Austin Shanghae.
(The Chinese Tom Thumb.)
or
Wonder of the Celestial Empire.
and
A Host of other Celebrities.

The Hippodrome will be open for inspection, this evening Saturday from 8 till 10.
The Refreshment Saloons and Ladies' retiring apartments, will be under the direction of Mr. Wilson, Auckland Hotel.

First Class Reserved Seats,
7 Rupees.
First Class Unreserved Seats.
5 Rupees.
Second Class Seats,
3 Rupees.
Promenade 1 Rupee.
Doors open at 7½, to commence 8½ precisely.
NOTICE.
The Box Office.
Will be open on Friday, Saturday and Monday next, from 11 till 4, for the Sale of Tickets for Reserved Seats, which must be secured previous to the commencement of the performance, to prevent inconvenience to those Ladies and Gentlemen, who may feel disposed to honor the Hippodrome with their presence.

J. M. WOLFE,
Acting Manager.
Wilson's Hotel. 3808

LEWIS' AUSTRALIAN HIPPODROME.
ERECTED ON THE OPEN SPACE.
At the Back of the Raffles Intitution,
AND IMMEDIATELY FRONTING THE
SAILOR'S HOME.

Will give Six Representations only, viz.
On Thursday 21st instant, Friday 22nd,
Saturday 23rd, Monday 25th, Tuesday 26th, Wednesday, 27th.

The above company consists of twenty male, female, and infant artists, eight highly trained horses, a troupe of Dogs and Monkeys.
The band attached to the Hippodrome will perform several selections from popular operas during the performances.

PRICES OF ADMISSION.
First Class Seats............ $2
Second do do $1
Children under 10 Years of age Half Price.
First Class Seats, can be selected between the hours of 10 A. M. and 4 P. M. from to-morrow.
Doors open at 7.30 P. M. Performance will commence at 8 precisely.
Singapore 20th November, 1861.

Left: Lewis's first advertisement in Calcutta, published in *Bengal Hurkuru*, 15 October 1860.
Microfilm, National Library of Australia

Above: Advertisement for Lewis's Hippodrome in Singapore. *Straits Times*, 30 November 1861.
Microfilm, National Library of Australia

CHAPTER FOUR

> Mr. Lewis of the Hippodrome is making a worthy return for the liberal support which is accorded to him by the Calcutta public. We have been informed that he divided one half the gross receipts of the crowded attendance ... under the patronage of His Excellency the Viceroy and Lady Canning ... between the Calcutta Alms Houses and the Orphan Free School.[188]

This amounted to 498 rupees to each.[189] A few weeks later the children of the orphanage were treated to a day at the Lewis circus. The *Englishman* showed a typical Anglo-Saxon attitude to race in the comment comparing one of Lewis's child performers, the 'dusky Austin Shanghai', with golden-haired and blue-eyed twins of a 'Staff Officer' in the audience: 'We never noticed a more striking illustration of care and breeding'.

The reviewer singled out the 'graceful direction of Madame Birch' of the 'horse *Black Diamond* waltzing'. 'Professor' Lewis himself also impressed with his 'feats of strength and agility'. On the last day of the Calcutta season an advertisement made much of the performance of *Napoleon*, a horse 'trained by Mr. Lewis since his arrival in Calcutta'. Also announced was the sale of the Hippodrome tent, some carriages, ponies and 'the celebrated Trained Horse "*Black Diamond*"'. After this successful season the Lewis Company left for Madras on 23 November.[190] From there the company might have had short seasons at Singapore and Batavia, where the Dutch East India Company officers would have been their main audience, until late March 1861.

This period in Asia probably influenced Lewis's later decision to move from equestrian circus to popular theatre. He could have learned the history of early British theatre in Calcutta: how the current entertainment in the city consisted mainly of circus and amateur theatre. Western drama had been introduced to Calcutta by the Russian linguist Gerasim Stepanovich Lebedeff in the late eighteenth century. Lebedeff translated two English plays into Bengali and Hindustani to be played by Indian actors.[191] Over the years most attempts at theatre catered for audiences from among the East India Company were short lived and were often played by British 'gentlemen actors'.[192]

Lewis arrived back in Melbourne on 15 April 1861 from Galle (on the island of Ceylon, now Sri Lanka) on the *Benares*. By this time Hernandez

---

188 *Englishman*, 2 November 1860.
189 *Englishman*, 6 November 1860.
190 *Englishman*, 20 November 1860.
191 Sudipto Chatterjee, *The Colonial Staged: Theatre in Colonial Calcutta*, Seagull Books, Calcutta, 2007, pp. 25–26.
192 See chapter seven.

had died and Adams had left the company, but Lewis had been joined by Mr and Mrs Birch and two Chinese boys aged eleven and five. The 'Gardoni or Wild' girls could still have been with him.[193] By June 1861, Lewis was performing at the Theatre Royal in Bourke Street with Christoff and the 'Chinese Tom Thumb'.[194] According to Mark St Leon, Christoff was George Christopher, a black rope dancer from London and a relative of the 'Great Christoff'.[195] Later in the month, Lewis was performing with Lilliputian Tom and Austin Shanghai (possibly the 'Chinese Tom Thumb') at the Prince of Wales Theatre, supported by Worrell's Circus.[196] This theatre in Lonsdale Street had been adapted, appropriately enough, from a horse bazaar. As well as equestrian circus performances it also showed drama and farce.[197] The American juvenile Marsh Troupe had also performed there in 1860.

Another voyage to Asia came at the beginning of September 1861. Lewis and a slightly different company left on the *Sea Nymph* for Batavia (now Jakarta, Indonesia) accompanied by the children Mary and Jessie Wild and Austin Shanghai (all under twelve), and the adults Messrs Birch, Barlow, Raphael, Stebbing, Cousins and Mrs Cousins and infant. The *Argus* 'Shipping Intelligence' for 2 September 1861 records that eight horses were on board. The troupe had rehearsed at Lewis's house and stables in Balmain Street, Richmond.[198]

All the men were equestrians, including William Barlow[199] who also trained and exhibited dogs and monkeys, and Mr Cousins who was a clown. According St Leon, Reuben Cousins was the *nom d'arena* of John Bumpuss and Mrs Cousins, née Jane Kendall, was also known as Mlle La Rosiere, a skilled rider.[200]

After a season at Batavia where the famous 'Professor' Risley was also performing,[201] they sailed to Singapore where they gave some shows in November.[202] Finding that Hernandez had died suddenly in that colony during

---

193 PROV, VPRS 948, Outward Passenger List for *Benares*.
194 *Argus*, 13 June 1861.
195 Mark St Leon, *Circus in Australia*, The Author, Penshurst, NSW, 2007, p. 62.
196 *Argus*, 24 June 1861.
197 Ralph Marsden, 'The Prince of Wales Theatre' in *On Stage*, Summer 2006, pp. 16–18.
198 *Argus*, 31 October 1862: evidence in Breach of Contract case between Barlow and Lewis.
199 Not to be confused with Robert Barlow – a singer whose speciality was the 'Blue Tail Fly', he was very popular at Lewis's Astley's Amphitheatre in 1854.
200 St Leon, op. cit., p. 223.
201 Frederik, L. Schodt, *Professor Risley and the Imperial Japanese Troupe: How an American Acrobat Introduced Circus to Japan and Japan to the West*, Stone Bridge Press, Berkeley, California, 2012, p. 98.
202 *Straits Times*, 23 November 1861.

CHAPTER FOUR

Risley's season, Lewis paid for a headstone on the grave of his star performer before leaving for Hong Kong on 29 November.[203]

Lewis's Australian Hippodrome opened in Hong Kong in December. On Tuesday 14 January 1862, 'Lewis's Australian Hippodrome Company' appeared in a 'Grand Fashionable Night' under the patronage of the Governor of Hong Kong, Sir Hercules Robinson, later to be Governor of New South Wales, and Lady Robinson. Such patronage by governors was good for business. At least one of the silk playbills listing the performers and their acts that would have been presented to official guests has survived from this time.[204]

The performance started at 8.30 pm and was attended by the 'Band of H. M.'s 5th Regt. of Native Infantry'. The playbill is full of puffery and not much detail, but it describes, to some extent, what went on during the show. It opened with a 'Magnificent Eastern Pageant' with the 'principal Ladies and Gentlemen of the Establishment, richly Costumed and Mounted on Six Splendidly Caparisoned Chargers'. After this formal parade, Mr Barlow provided something of an amusing contrast with 'his celebrated trained dogs and monkeys'. 'Little Ella, the Australian prodigy, and child of wonder' appeared in a 'graceful and daring act' – she would have balanced and posed on her horse in what we know as 'bare-back' riding. Next came a gymnastic act, 'La Perche', with George Lewis holding a pole while Gabriel (or Gamboa) Raphael climbed to the top, where he performed various feats and poses. The next act, 'Scenes from Heathen Mythology' with Mr Barlow, is difficult to identify, but bare-backed rider Mrs Cousins with her 'Favourite Act of Daring Equestrianism' must have been exciting. Little Ella was back with her sister Jessie Gardoni in an equestrian and mime act called 'Donald and Jessie, or the Lovers of Caledonia' on 'two trained steeds'. Then Mr Raphael rode in, representing the 'Union of Nations, or England, Ireland and Scotland'.

After an interval of ten minutes Mrs Cousins and the two young girls rode on three horses as the 'Three Graces'. Then came 'Mr. G. Lewis and his Infant Wonder the admiration of the Australian Colonies' in 'Sons of Syracuse, or the Games of the Ancient Romans'. The 'Infant Wonder' was most likely Austin Shanghai and the performance would have included the 'Risley Act'. There was another ride by Mr Raphael billed as 'The Greatest Equestrian in the World'. Finally Barlow, leaving his dogs and monkeys outside the tent, returned as an equestrian Phaeton riding three horses simultaneously.

---

203 *Straits Times*, 30 November 1861. The article emphasised that Lewis had asked that his donation of $Singapore 150 be kept secret until his departure.
204 Playbill owned by the writer.

From Hong Kong the troupe sailed to Shanghai, opening on 15 February 1862.[205] Here they enjoyed 'very great houses' and 'considerable profit'. Lewis's admission charges were $3 (13/6d), $2 (9/-) and $1(4/6d).[206] The season and tour ended on 18 April. Some of his performers, including Mr and Mrs Cousins and the two girls left Lewis in Shanghai. Not being able to find replacements, he decided to 'break up' his troupe, selling his 'old tent'. He intended to 'show' at Point de Galle on the way back to Melbourne by steamer, but found that Barlow had sold his dogs and remaining monkey in Hong Kong. This decision led to a court case in Melbourne. Returning to Hong Kong, Lewis sold up the horses and other circus effects. He arrived in Melbourne from Galle on 10 July, accompanied by Austin Shanghai, William Barlow and Gabriel Raphael.[207]

William Barlow soon sued Lewis for breach of contract. The problem was that while Barlow had been contracted for eighteen months, Lewis had broken up his troupe after only about seven months. At the Supreme Court Barlow deposed that Lewis paid him £8 per week and board and lodging but, while continuing the board and lodging, ceased payment in April when he (Lewis) broke up his company. The court case was not without humour as the lawyers and judge referred facetiously to Barlow's trained dogs and monkeys. When, for example, Barlow spoke of an untrained dog he was asked if the others were trained. In his summing up, Mr Justice Molesworth suggested that there was apparently a mutual inclination to avoid a definite explanation, each party probably thinking that ultimately he would have the advantage of the other. The jury found for Barlow, but damages were set at only one shilling.

After this slight set-back, Lewis seems to have decided to stay in Melbourne for a time. He advertised a riding school from his property in Balmain Street, Richmond near Cremorne Gardens, where 'Ladies and Gents' could be 'taught Riding by Mr. Lewis and Madame Birch'.[208] Like many of the 'off Bourke Street' performers, 'Madame Birch' is a shadowy figure. She could be Elizabeth Birch, wife of Henry Birch, an equestrian

---

205 J.D. Haan, 'Thalia and Terpsichore on the Yangtze: A Survey of Foreign Theatre and Music in Shanghai, 1850–1865' in *Journal of the Royal Asiatic Society*, Vol. 29, 1988; *North China Herald*, 15 February 1862.
206 *Argus*, 31 October 1862. Much of the information for this section of Lewis's career comes from a report of a breach of contract case, *Barlow v Lewis*, held at the Melbourne New Court House on 30 October 1862.
207 PROV VPRS 947, Inward Passenger List for *SS Madras*.
208 *Argus*, 24 November 1862. A later reminiscence, most likely confused, described Madame Birch as 'Mrs Lewis'! J. Alex Allen, 'Coppin's Cremorne: Richmond in the 'Fifties', *Argus*, 8 April 1933.

CHAPTER FOUR

actor who had worked for Lewis since 1854. Again we have trouble with names. There were at least two performers named Birch in Melbourne during the 1850s and 1860s. For example, the above mentioned Henry Birch seems to have been Lewis's agent recruiting talent in Europe, and later worked for Lewis in India and China. This could be the same Mr Birch, an actor who toured the Victorian goldfields with Clarence Holt's Dramatic Company in the late 1850s. Finally there was a William Birch touring Australia, Japan, India and America from 1863 with a moving panorama entertainment, 'Mr. Birch's Holiday Trip'.[209]

Over the summer of 1862–1863 George Lewis found plenty of employment, appearing at Cremorne Gardens during its last days. George Coppin, the proprietor of Cremorne, was losing money and auctioned the property in March 1863. It was eventually used as a private mental asylum.[210] The weekly *Bell's Life in Victoria* of 20 December 1862 reported that 'Mr. Lewis has organised a small but effective corps for the display of equestrianism and gymnastics.' His riding school was apparently profitable – he had five horses: three for teaching riding and two performing circus horses.[211] In the *Argus* of 29 July 1863, Lewis was advertised to appear at the Theatre Royal 'for this night only' with his 'Mongolian Pupil' at the end of a four-week season by Burton's Great Circus. Henry Burton, who had managed a circus in eastern Australia since the 1840s was, together with Ashton's Circus, Lewis's greatest rival.

Lewis again left for Asia on 6 August on the 750 ton *Maori*, bound for Batavia. This time he was accompanied by the equestrians Mr and Mrs Cousins, Mr and Mrs Yeamans and the rope dancer John (or George) Christoff. After performing in Batavia he proceeded to Hong Kong. By February 1864 his troupe, billed as 'Australia's Hippodrome', was booked at the 'Cricket Ground every evening for one month'.[212] After this, the troupe probably played at Shanghai and Galle. Again the troupe broke up and Mr Lewis arrived in Melbourne on the *Bombay* from Galle on 13 June 1864.

---

209 Mimi Colligan, op. cit., 2002.
210 Mimi Colligan, 'Cremorne Gardens, Richmond' in *Victorian Historical Journal*, Vol. 66, No. 2, November 1995, pp. 122–136.
211 *Argus*, 24 November 1862.
212 *Hong Kong Daily Press*, 2 February 1864.

Chapter five

THE EDOUINS RETURN TO MELBOURNE

After nearly two years performing around Victoria and in South Australia and Tasmania the Edouin family returned to Melbourne. Their first appearance was in August 1859 at the Olympic Theatre on the corner of Lonsdale and Stephen Streets. This prefabricated iron structure had been imported from Manchester by George Coppin in 1854 and opened in 1855. Coppin had also taken over the Theatre Royal and adapted Astley's Amphitheatre to become the first Princess's Theatre. At the Olympic, Rose, now 15, and her siblings were still playing in *Frolics in France* and had added the pantomime *The Seven Castles of Christendom* to their repertoire.[213] Writing in the *Examiner* of 13 August 1859, Dr Neild referred to Eliza's death as their 'calamity' and noted their continuing undoubted talent.

The summer of 1859–1860 saw Rose, together with Julia aged nine, and Willie aged thirteen, performing at the Pantheon, a new small theatre in Coppin's Cremorne Gardens.[214] Fireworks shows were held between plays and the audience was encouraged to 'stroll into the cool gardens, with the pale statuary gleaming out from the dark foliage and the myriad stars shining overhead'.[215] The 'little family' were old hands of the London Cremorne Gardens where they had performed in 1850 as 'Les Petits Edouins'.[216] By 3 February 1860 Rose was showing her versatility by playing the Alfredo-like part of 'Billy Taylor' in a burlesque, or parody, called *Our Traviata*. The solid 40-year-old G. H. Rogers played 'Our Mary Ann', the Violetta role. On the same bill Rose took the role of the daughter in *The Willow Pattern Plate*. Neild's critique gives a feeling of the burlesque when he describes Rose Edouin:

---

213 *Argus*, 1–13 August 1859.
214 Coppin was granted a license for the Royal Pantheon Theatre for drama, fireworks etc. in October 1859, PROV, VPRS 1189/P, Unit 829, File L59/10818.
215 *Examiner*, 4 February 1860, p. 13 (part of Dr Neild's description of the performance of 3 February 1860).
216 See chapter two.

CHAPTER FIVE

The Olympic, Coppin's prefabricated theatre, c.1859. Engraving from letterhead.
Gustavus Vaughan Brooke Papers, MLMSS 7238, Manuscript Collection, State Library of New South Wales

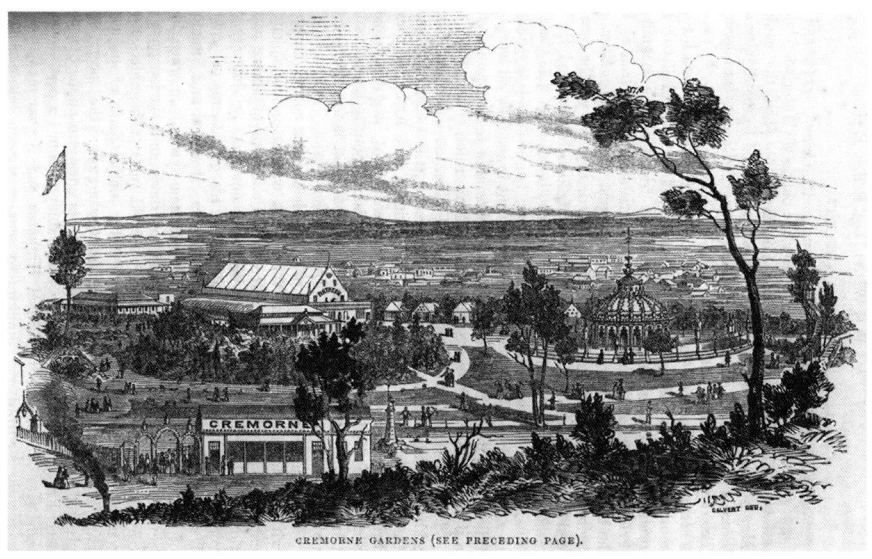

Cremorne Gardens' Pantheon Theatre. 1858. Detail of an illustration by Samuel Calvert in the *Illustrated Journal of Australasia*, April 1858, p. 145.
Private Collection

admirably made up and capitally played. Fancy the grotesque contrast presented by the small person of that clever little lady with the bulk of the pthisical [sic] Rogers ... Fancy the effect of a remarkably close imitation of Signor Bianchi's ungainly attitudes.

The opera *La Traviata* had recently been performed at the Royal with Eugenio Bianchi as Alfredo. Many years later, in 1877, Rose burlesqued the role of Lohengrin, again imitating the tenor who created the part at the first Australian performance of Wagner's opera. Nevertheless, Neild cautions her to work at her craft:

> I am glad to see Miss Rose Edouin so steadily advancing in her profession. She has an agreeable person, much natural intelligence, sufficient stage aptitude, and will make a really clever actress if she will only steadily persevere ... and avoid the besetting sin of youthful histrionists – the entertainment of a belief that they have mastered their art when they have acquired little more than its rudiments.[217]

While cross-dressing had been a requirement in the days of Shakespeare, when boys took the female roles, after the Restoration in 1660 women taking male roles and dressing in breeches became very popular.[218] By the 1860s 'breeches parts' were widespread, especially in pantomime and burlesque (at this period the word 'burlesque' was used in the sense of parody and extravaganza), hence Rose as Alfredo. Soon after, in late February 1860 at Cremorne Gardens' Pantheon Theatre, Rose played Romeo in a burlesque of *Romeo and Juliet, or, the Cup of Cold Poison*, to a cross-dressed G. H. Rogers as Juliet. Melbourne *Punch* published a full page caricature of the burlesque and a doggerel verse which included lines commenting on the absurdity of the mature G. H. Rogers playing Juliet and 16-year-old Rose playing Romeo:

> At Kremorne I seen it hacted
> Wensday night as ever ware
> Wich it maid me skreem with lafter
> Watchin them lovers rare
> For the ladi's five foot seven
> And the gent is fore foot sicks ...[219]

---

217 *Examiner*, 4 February 1860, p. 13. Rogers' dates: 1820–1872.
218 Rosamond Gilder, *Enter the Actress; The First Women in the Theatre*, George Harrap & Co Ltd., London, 1931, pp. 169–170.
219 Melbourne *Punch*, 23 February 1860, p. 36. One is reminded of C. J. Dennis's *Romeo and Juliet* parody in *Songs of the Sentimental Bloke*.

CHAPTER FIVE

Melbourne *Punch*'s absurdist view of little Rose as Romeo and G. H. Rogers as Juliet. 23 February 1860, p. 36.
Newspaper Collection, State Library of Victoria

In the same season Rose exchanged her trousers for skirts playing Princess Mignonette in the pantomime *Prince Dorus* with her siblings Julia and Willie dancing and clowning.[220]

Irish born comedian John Drew (ancestor of the American Barrymore family of stage and motion picture fame) was one of the many Americans who came to Australia during the gold rush. Drew attracted good audiences to the Pantheon Theatre with Rose as Jessie in *My Colonial Cousin*, a localisation by Varley, a Sydney playwright, of the Tom Taylor play *Our American Cousin*. Rose ended the season as the lead in the burlesque *The Nymph of the Lurleyburg*.[221] During the winter she appeared at the Prince of Wales Theatre in Lonsdale Street[222] where she made her first contact with *Hamlet*, taking the small part of Osric. The American tragedian McKean Buchanan played the title role.[223] She took another male part, that of Lemuel in *The Flowers of the Forest*, at the same theatre.[224]

In November 1860 the Edouins returned to the Pantheon at Cremorne, where they performed in the pantomime *Jack the Giant Killer*, with Julia Mathews, their colleague from the Royal Marionettes in London in the 1850s, playing Jack.[225] In March 1861, Rose, at the age of 17, took her first benefit at the Pantheon. During the year the Edouins toured back to Sandhurst.[226] Meanwhile their father's pseudonym, 'J. E. Jones', appears in the Melbourne Street Directory as proprietor of livery stables at Gertrude Street, Fitzroy.[227] In later years Willie Edouin, then a successful actor-manager in America and England, told how as a child he had worked as an ostler in his father's stables.[228]

Tours of the goldfields continued in early 1862. In the growing city of Sandhurst, Rose had the experience of playing Juliet opposite the popular actress Mrs Heir (formerly Fanny Cathcart) in breeches as Romeo.[229] By April the Edouins had travelled to Geelong for a season at the Theatre Royal under Greville's management. Among Rose's roles were Lurline in

---

220 *Examiner*, 25 February 1860.
221 *Argus*, 27 March 1860.
222 This theatre/circus building had been adapted from a hotel hall and horse bazaar. See Ralph Marsden, 'Marsh's Royal Lyceum Theatre', *On Stage*, Vol. 7, No. 1, Summer 2006, pp. 16–18.
223 *Truth*, 26 January 1906.
224 *Examiner*, 1 September 1860.
225 *Argus*, 26 December 1860.
226 Later called Bendigo.
227 *Sands and Kenny; Sands and McDougall Directories*, 1861–1870.
228 *Table Talk*, 29 April 1887.
229 *Bell's Life in Victoria*, 22 February 1862.

CHAPTER FIVE

the *Nymph of the Lurleyberg*, Selim in H. J. Byron's *Bluebeard* and she was announced to perform *The Lola Montez Spider Dance*![230] On 4 June they left Geelong on the *Havilah* for the city of Adelaide, now with a population of 18 000. On the opening night of a three-month season at the Victoria Theatre, Greville's Company consisted of the Edouins, Mrs Susan Wooldridge, William South, Shute, and Chapman. Charles Edouin Bryer conducted the orchestra.[231] Rose, the star, was lauded by the critics for the 'good taste' of her acting. The season ended on 27 September.[232]

For the 19-year-old Rose the year 1863 proved a successful one. She increased her repertoire with many new roles and was able to observe successful and experienced actors such as George Fawcett Rowe, Barry Sullivan, Fanny Cathcart, Marie Duret and Julia Mathews in plays and roles that she would make her own in years to come. Dr Neild noticed that she was much 'improved'.[233] In March she was supporting Marie Duret and Julia Mathews in *Flowers of the Forest* [234] and *Jack Sheppard* at the Princess's, playing Lady Trafford and Mrs Sheppard, while her 13-year-old sister Julia had the small part of Rachel in the latter play.[235] By April, Rose had the main role of Lurline in *The Nymph of the Lurleyburg* with Julia Mathews as her maid. Julia, John and Willie Edouin also had parts at the new Royal Haymarket Theatre.[236] Starring at the Haymarket at this time was the American comedian Joseph Jefferson. He had been in Victoria since 1862 and would stay until 1865.[237] Among the roles Rose played with Jefferson were Penelope in *The Hope of the Family*, Florizel in *The King of the Peacocks*, Smike in *Nicholas Nickleby* and Mary Meredith in *Our American Cousin*.[238]

A new member was added to the Edouin family on 22 April 1863 when Edwin Charles Bryer (known professionally as Charles Edouin) aged 30, married Elizabeth Louisa Naylor 21, at St Marks Church, Fitzroy.[239] An

---

230 *Geelong Advertiser*, 24 April, 9, 13 May 1862. Unfortunately reviews of these performances cannot be found.
231 *South Australian Register*, 9 June 1862.
232 *South Australian Register*, 27 September 1862.
233 *Examiner* 7 February 1863, p. 13.
234 *Bell's Life in Victoria*, 14 March 1862.
235 *Entr'acte and Playbill*, 20 March 1863.
236 *Argus*, 2 April 1863.
237 Benjamin McArthur, *The Man Who Was Rip Van Winkle*, Yale University Press, New Haven, 2007.
238 *Argus*, 11, 18, 25 April 1863.
239 Marriage Certificate. Lizzie had arrived, aged 16, as an assisted immigrant on the *Sea Park* on 20 March 1858 met by her actress aunt Mrs Avins of Moor Street Fitzroy; PROV, VPRS, Assisted Passenger List; see also May Maxwell, 'On the Boards in the Earlies', Frances Fraser and Nettie Palmer, eds., *Centenary Gift Book*, Robertson & Mullens for The Women's Centenary Council, Melbourne, 1934, p. 96.

English born actress, Lizzie Naylor was to specialise in character and soubrette parts. Her later stage name would be Mrs Edouin Bryer.

In May, Rose assumed a role that she was to play many times in her career: Zoë in Dion Boucicault's *The Octoroon*, with Joseph Jefferson and Dolly Green.[240] For the *Herald* critic, Rose 'acquitted herself most creditably. Her pathos at times was remarkably good, and she likewise vested the character with that feeling and despair which ... the Octoroon girl is supposed to possess when she is to be sold as a slave'.[241] Still studying her art, she went from lead to supporting character role when she played another slave, a black one this time, at the Princess's when in August 1863 she played Madge in local playwright George Fawcett's topical American Civil War play *North and South*. Rose's sister-in-law, Lizzie Naylor, played the wife of a Confederate officer and her brother Charles was in charge of the orchestra. John and Willie and were also in the cast.[242]

The strong part of Lady Gay Spanker in Dion Boucicault's comedy *London Assurance* was another role Rose added to her repertoire in this year.

Irish-English actor-manager Barry Sullivan[243] had been performing in Melbourne and Sydney since 1862. From March 1863 until February 1866 he held the lease of the Theatre Royal, Bourke Street. He evidently was impressed with Rose's performances at the Princess's Theatre, for by 17 October Rose had moved to the Theatre Royal as Desdemona to Barry Sullivan's Othello.[244] For the next ten months Rose took on more leading roles in Barry Sullivan's company at the Royal, continuing in diverse roles that laid the foundations of her adult career. These included acting Zepherina with the visiting London tragedian Charles Dillon (she had played the part of his son as a child in London) in *Belphegor the Mountebank*. Tilly Earl, soon to marry Rose's brother John, took the role of Belphegor's son.[245]

Shakespearean parts also presented themselves – from a Singing Witch in Sullivan's *Macbeth*[246] to Lady Anne in Sullivan's *Richard III*[247] and Regan with Sullivan and Mrs Heir in *King Lear*.[248] Rose completed the year in the

---

240 *Argus*, 1 June; *Examiner*, 6 June 1863.
241 Undated clipping in 'Newspaper Criticisms of Mrs GBW Lewis (Miss Rose Edouin)' [1 June 1863].
242 *Green Room or Theatrical Advertiser*, 15 August 1863.
243 Jean Gittins, 'Thomas Barry Sullivan', *Australian Dictionary of Biography*, Vol. 6, Melbourne, 1976, p. 219.
244 *Entr'acte and Playbill*; *Argus*, 19 October 1863.
245 *Argus*, 22 October 1863.
246 *Argus*, 7 November 1863.
247 *Argus*, 20 November 1863.
248 *Entr'acte*, 30 November 1863.

CHAPTER FIVE

breeches part of Feramorz the Troubadour (the King in disguise) in William Brough's 1857 pantomime adaptation of Thomas Moore's poem *Lalla Rookh*. Also performing were her siblings John (Harlequin), Willie (Clown), and Julia (Columbine) with Tilly Earle as Princess Lalla Rookh.[249] To give an idea of the level of the writing, the song Rose would have sung was Moore's 'The Minstrel Boy' but with Brough's new words:

> The minstrel boy through the town is known,
> In each quiet street you'll find him,
> With his master's organ – it is ne'er his own,
> And his monkey led behind him.[250]

During 1864, Sullivan cast Rose in smaller Shakespearean roles such as the Dauphin to Sullivan's *King John* (Julia took the important role of Prince Arthur) and as Hero in *Much Ado about Nothing*.[251] Meanwhile Julia, Willie and John were using their dancing talents in various interludes between acts at the Theatre Royal. At this time Rose and her unmarried siblings lived with their mother at 149 Fitzroy Street, Fitzroy.[252]

On 27 February 1864, Sullivan produced a play – *Leah the Forsaken* – that Rose would make her own in years to come. This melodrama was first staged in London in October 1863 with the star American actress Kate Bateman in the title role. It was broadly about the plight of the Jews in Eastern Europe before some emancipation was granted them in the eighteenth century. Sullivan's star in Melbourne was the English actress Louisa Cleveland.[253] At this stage Rose had the second female role of Anna, Leah's rival for her Christian lover. Tilly and Lizzie had small parts. Over the next few months Rose consolidated her acting experience by playing second female lead to Mrs Robert Heir, a sensitive and popular actress who, as Fanny Cathcart, had come to Australia with G. V. Brooke in 1855.[254] Rose might have learned much from acting with the experienced Fanny Heir and Louisa Cleveland, but was most likely frustrated in playing 'second fiddle'. Over the

---

249 *Argus*, 26 December; *Age*, 27 December; *The Victorian*, advertisement, 26 December 1863, p. 540.
250 William Brough, *Lalla Rookh; or, The Princess, the Peri, & the Troubadour: A Burlesque and Pantomime in One Act*, Lacy, London, 1858, p. 11.
251 *Entr'acte*, 30 January, 21 April 1864.
252 *Melbourne Street Directory*, 1864.
253 *Herald*, 27 February 1864.
254 Helen Van Der Poorten, 'Mary Fanny Cathcart' in *Australian Dictionary of Biography*, Vol. 3, Melbourne, 1969, pp. 369–371.

next few months Rose played several such roles: Josephine in *A Husband to Order*,[255] Mrs Selborne in *A Roland for an Oliver*,[256] Alonzo's wife in Sullivan's elaborate production *Pizzaro*, and Charlotte in *The Gamester*.[257] Long before the advent of theatre schools such as the Royal Academy of Dramatic Art Rose's early career was an example of how actors learned their art.[258] They learned most theatre skills by actual performance.

The return in June of George Lewis from a long circus tour of Asia[259] was an event that was to change, for good or ill, the career paths of all the Edouin family. About this time, Lewis began moves to form a drama company rather than a circus troupe. He approached various members of the Theatre Royal company. In the *Argus* of 18 July 1864 there was a rumour that there would be 'changes in the minor ranks of the company at the Theatre Royal. The Edouins ... take their departure at an early date, to seek a fortune in China, and Miss Tilly Earle accompanies them.'[260] Tilly Earl married Rose's brother John on 25 July.[261]

George Lewis hired a 414 ton ship, the *Catherine*, to take his newly formed 'Dramatic Troupe' to Shanghai. According to the ship's list the passengers were: George Lewis 44, Mrs Sarah Edouin 50, Miss Rose Edouin 20, Miss Julia Edouin 17, Charles Edouin 30, Mrs Elizabeth Edouin 25, William Edouin 22, John Edouin 23, Miss Tilly Earl 21, Miss Jenny Nye 21, W. B. Gill 23, Mrs W. B. Gill 35, J. B. Creswick 25, Thomas Andrews 25, and John McDonald 40.[262] Not recorded on the shipping list was Charles and Elizabeth's first child William Edwin born on 20 June just five weeks before the voyage to China.[263]

What made this group of players accept George Lewis's proposal to leave the relative comfort of Melbourne's foremost theatre and Barry Sullivan's direction for a tour of an unknown and war-torn country such as China? In Rose's case it could have been the promise of starring roles – and a possible

---

255 *Entr'acte*, 16 April 1864.
256 *Entr'acte*, 5 May 1864.
257 *Entr'acte*, 18 May 1864.
258 Christopher Kent in Martha Vicinus, ed., *A Widening Sphere*, Indiana University Press, 1977, p. 97.
259 PROV, VPRS Inward Passenger List, *Bombay*, 1864.
260 George Lewis's plans are mentioned in the Richmond *Australian*, 20 July 1864. Lewis had lived in Richmond when in Melbourne and he at one time 'had been candidate for council'.
261 Marriage Certificate, John William Bryer, 24, Teacher of Dancing to Matilda Earl, 21, 1864.
262 PROV, VPRS 948, Outward Passenger list, *Catherine*, August 1864.
263 Birth Certificate. Infant William appears on their return passenger list in 1865.

CHAPTER FIVE

romantic link with George. For the others, who were a minor part of the Royal company, here was a chance to take on better roles. For George Lewis the trip seems to be the result of his experience, through his circus tours of Asia, of what both the British in the Concession Ports and the Chinese comprador class wanted for entertainment. Having made money in China and India with circus entertainment for many years, he saw Asia as a new and untapped market for British theatre.

Chapter six

LEWIS MOVES FROM CIRCUS TO STAGE

Lewis's Dramatic Troupe left for China on 1 August 1864 and arrived in Shanghai in early October. It seems that Lewis's equestrian agent, Henry Birch, had arrived before the troupe to prepare the way. At this time, Shanghai was one of the five 'treaty ports' formed in China at the end of the First Opium War and Lewis aimed to entertain the small enclave of foreigners with a more 'professional' theatre than to which they were accustomed. Hitherto, the European population largely had to amuse themselves. Amateur dramatic companies, made up of merchants, officials and various visiting naval and military personnel, mounted plays several times a year. Some of the amateur male actors had to play female roles in popular farces and comedies. As the Taiping uprising had ended, the area was less dangerous than it was when Lewis visited with his circus in 1862. The European population numbered about 2100, including 160 females, plus 1050 military in the garrison. As well as the British, this international population included Americans, French and Portuguese.[264]

On 5 October, Lewis's Australian Dramatic Company opened an eight-week season at the Lyceum Theatre in Shanghai. This 'theatre' would have been what was known locally as a 'godown' – usually a warehouse adapted to seat up to 800 in pit and gallery.[265] There was a change of programme every second evening. The repertoire, consisting mainly of light pieces, included *The Maid and the Magpie*, *Rose of Castille*, *Faint Heart Never Won Fair Lady* and *Fra Diavolo*.[266] Rose Edouin's name does not appear in the advertisements so far gleaned from the Shanghai English language

---

264 J. D. Haan, 'Thalia and Terpsichore on the Yangtze: A Survey of Foreign Theatre and Music in Shanghai 1850–1865' in *Journal of the Royal Asiatic Society*, Vol. 29, 1988, p. 159.
265 ibid., p. 177.
266 *North China Herald*, 8 October 1864. This newspaper was a weekly and did not contain details of every performance.

newspapers. Nor does the news that on 19 November 1864, in the middle of his Shanghai season, George Lewis, widower, aged 46, married Rose Edouin, spinster, aged 20.[267] Lewis's star bare-backed rider Jane Bumpuss Cousins (La Rosiere) was one of the witnesses at the Shanghai Church of the Holy Trinity. Time was to show that it was a love match as well as a good show business move. While 26 years is a large age gap it was not unknown, particularly in the nineteenth century, for a man to have delayed marriage in order to make his fortune. Also George was not free to marry until he heard of his first wife's death. Then again, Rose, given her problems with her father, might have been attracted to an older man who promised support of her theatrical ambitions and who would be with her for life. Years later in India, she described this part of her career almost paraphrasing *Jane Eyre*'s 'reader I married him' statement:

> In 1864 Mr. Lewis engaged us to go to China, and – well, you guess, or rather know the result. I married him, and after a very prosperous season there we returned to Australia, but not to remain long, for in 1867 we started for India, and 1874 finds us still here.[268]

If we can believe the sparse newspaper reports of the early part of the tour, the female stars of this part of the tour appear to have been Tilly Earle, young Julia Edouin and Lizzie Naylor, rather than Rose. The troupe drew 'tolerable houses'. An idea of their repertoire and personnel can be seen in one of the advertisements for J. B. Creswick's Benefit: *Aurora Floyd*, *Household Fairy* and *Aladdin the Wonderful Scamp*: 'C. Edouin, Musical Director and Manager, Henry Birch, Agent.' There is mention of Janet Gill's (mother of comedian Willie Gill) benefit as Mrs Malaprop in *The Rivals* and Tilly Earl's benefit as the Wonderful Scamp in *Aladdin*.[269] The *North China Herald* of 19 November 1864 stated that the 'Hit of the week was the prison scene from *King John* with Julia Edouin and Mr Birch … the acting was perfect, Miss Julia Edouin doing fullest justice to the character of Prince Arthur, and indeed taking the house by storm'. Also that Tilly Earl's 'fame is well established in Shanghai'.[270] By 26 November the temperature in Shanghai had fallen to freezing point. An advertisement in the *North*

---

267 Marriage Certificate, Public Record Office UK. Miscellaneous Foreign Registers and Returns 1852–1888, R.G. 33/12, 29; Bridget S. Everett Papers Manuscript Collection, State Library of Victoria; *Bell's Life in Victoria*, 30 July 1864. I am yet to find any details of his first wife.
268 *Englishman*, 15 January 1874.
269 *North China Herald*, 26 October 1864.
270 *North China Herald*, 19 November 1864.

China Herald on 3 December gives an idea of the climatic conditions: the hall would be 'Thoroughly warmed with splendid stoves' while Lizzie Naylor and gentlemen amateurs were to play in the farces of *Capital Match* and *Take That Girl Away*. On 9 December there was a benefit for Mr Birch to a large audience 'but many ticket holders were prevented from attending because of the cold'.[271] By 17 December the troupe had left, most likely for the south, along with their rivals the Christy's Minstrels. It is so far not known where they went after this visit to Shanghai but Lewis's Australian Dramatic Company returned there in March 1865.

They opened at the Lyceum on 23 March with the comedy *The Serious Family*.[272] The next performance mentioned in *Shanghai Commercial Record* was that of 27 March. It included a farce by W. B. Gill, one of the actors from Melbourne, *Which is Which?* and, extraordinarily, *Camille* starring Rose in the title role of the 'fallen woman'. It was her first mature leading role. Hitherto most of her roles had been in burlesque and pantomime, second leads and ingénue parts. The *Record* of 5 May 1865[273] was most disapproving, commenting that the play was:

> singularly unfitted for the powers of the performers. Miss Rose Edouin acted with her usual ability but as the heroine is a character almost impossible to render, we must not object where we cannot praise.

Rose does not appear to have repeated this role in the remainder of her career. Perhaps this unfavourable review frightened her. She was certainly to play other 'fallen' characters – for example Gilberte in *Frou Frou* and Mercy Merrick in the *New Magdalen*. Her next Shanghai review was more favourable. In the drama *Flowers of the Forest* she and her fellow players Lizzie Naylor and J. B. Creswick were described as acting 'with power and well restrained manner'.

After a tour south through other treaty ports, a journey of some 1100 kilometres, the Company opened in Hong Kong on 24 February 1865 to 'glowing reports'.[274] From Hong Kong they travelled to Singapore and then to India and Batavia. From there they embarked on the *Douglas*, arriving in Melbourne on 25 July 1865. The performers Jenny Nye and Willie Gill, and Willie's mother Janet, returned on other ships.

---

271   *North China Herald*, 10 December 1864.
272   My source for the rest of Lewis's tour of China is J. D. Haan, op. cit., pp. 226–231.
273   Quotations from this newspaper paper appear J. D. Haan, p. 227.
274   *Bell's Life in Victoria*, 29 April 1865.

Rose as a child. From the cover of *Souvenir of Mrs. G. B. W. Lewis' Professional Jubilee Testimonial Benefit, Theatre Royal October 3rd 1902* (see p. 156).
Theatre Programme Collection, State Library of Victoria

Left (top): Rose's mentor, Samuel Phelps, *carte-de-visite*, 1850s. Private Collection

Left (bottom): George Lewis around the time that he arrived in Melbourne, detail from a composite *carte-de-visite*, Melbourne, c.1855. Reproduced in the *Age* in the 1930s.
Newspaper Collection, State Library of Victoria

Opposite page: Playbill for *A Midsummer Night's Dream*, with Rose playing Puck, December 1855. Victoria and Albert Museum Archives

Sadler's Wells.
LESSEES. — MESSRS. GREENWOOD AND PHELPS

UNDER THE MANAGEMENT OF
MR. PHELPS.

MONDAY, November 26th, TUESDAY, 27th, WEDNESDAY, 28th, and THURSDAY, 29th, 1855.

The Performance to commence with SHAKESPEARE'S Play of The

MIDSUMMER NIGHT'S DREAM

WITH NEW SCENERY, DRESSES AND DECORATIONS.

Theseus (Duke of Athens) Mr. HENRY MARSTON
Egeus (Father to Hermia) Mr. LUNT
Lysander } (in Love with Hermia) { Mr. FREDERICK ROBINSON
Demetrius } { Mr. BELFORD
Philostrates (Master of the Revels to Theseus) Mr. HAYWELL
Quince (the Carpenter) — Mr. J. W. RAY
Snug (the Joiner) Mr. BARRETT
Bottom — (the Weaver) — Mr. PHELPS
Snout — (the Tinker) Mr. LEWIS BALL
Flute — (the Bellows-mender) — Mr. C. FENTON
Starveling (the Tailor) Mr. MEAGRESON
Hypollyta (Queen of the Amazons, Betrothed to Theseus) Miss ATKINSON
Helena (in Love with Demetrius) Miss MARGARET EBURNE
Hermia (Daughter of Egeus, in Love with Lysander) Miss J. MARSTON
Oberon (King of the Fairies) Miss ELIZA TRAVERS
Titania, (Queen of the Fairies) — Miss C. PARKES
Puck, or Robin Goodfellow, Miss ROSE EDOUIN
Fairy Attendant. — — Miss FOOTE
Peasblossom } { Miss FRAMPTON
Cobweb } (Fairies) { Miss SHARP
Moth } { Miss GREY
Mustardseed } { Miss WHITE
Pyramus, Thisbe, Wall, Moonshine, Lion, Characters in the Interlude, performed by the Clowns.
Other Fairies attending their King and Queen, Attendants on Theseus and Hypollyta, &c.

SCENE—ATHENS, & A WOOD NOT FAR FROM IT

To be followed with a Laugable Interlude, entitled A

Pleasant Neighbour

Sir George Howard, — Mr. HAYWELL
Thomas, — Mr. C. SEYTON
Christopher Strap, — (a Cobler) — Mr. J. W. RAY
Lady Elizabeth Howard. — Miss C. PARKES
Nancy Strap, — — Mrs. H. MARSTON

On FRIDAY, THE WIFE.

On SATURDAY, for the First Time these Two Years,

KING LEAR.

HAMILTON of BOTWELLHAUGH
AND
THE COMEDY OF ERRORS
Will be Repeated in the course of Next Week.

BOXES—First Circle, 3s. Second Ditto, 2s. Pit, 1s. Gallery, 6d.
PRIVATE BOXES to be had on Application to Mr. AUSTIN, Jun., at the Box-Office of the Theatre, from 11 to 3. And at Mr. SAMS' Library, St. James's Street; Mr. MITCHELL, Royal Library, Old Bond Street; Mr. ANDREWS, New Bond Street; Mr. EBERS, Bond Street; Mr. ALLCROFT, Bond Street; at the Carlton Library, 12, Regent Street; and CAMPBELL, RANSFORD, and CO., New Bond Street. Bill Inspector, Mr. WILCOX.
☞ **HALF-PRICE, TO BOXES ONLY, AT NINE O'CLOCK.**
Children under Three Years of Age cannot be Admitted. All Children Entering the Pit, must Pay the Full Price of Admission
Doors Open at Half-past Six. The Performances to Commence at Seven.
APPLICATIONS relative to THE BILLS of the THEATRE to be made to Mr. GREENWOOD, at the BOX-OFFICE
JOHN K. CHAPMAN & COMPANY, Steam Machine Printers, 5, Shoe Lane, & Peterborough Court, Fleet Street.

Photograph taken c.1857 of Julia, Rose, Willie and Eliza in *Frolics* in France, from *Souvenir of Mrs. G. B. W. Lewis' Professional Jubilee Testimonial Benefit, Theatre Royal October 3rd 1902*. Theatre Programme Collection, State Library of Victoria

Main Road in Ballarat East, showing the Victoria Theatre in Ballarat where the Edouins performed in 1858. Drawing and lithograph by F. Cogne, 1859.
Accession no. H1850, Pictures Collection, State Library of Victoria

The Theatre Royal in Bourke Street, Melbourne, c.1861, a few years after the Edouins' debut.
Accession no. H20742, Pictures Collection, State Library of Victoria

The Haymarket Theatre in 1862, while Rose was getting good roles.
Accession no. 30328102131686/23, Pictures Collection, State Library of Victoria

Coppin's Princess's Theatre, adapted from Lewis's Astley's Amphitheatre, in Spring Street, Melbourne, after Lewis had left Melbourne, c.1862. Photograph by Charles Nettleton.
Accession no. H88.22/2, Pictures Collection, State Library of Victoria

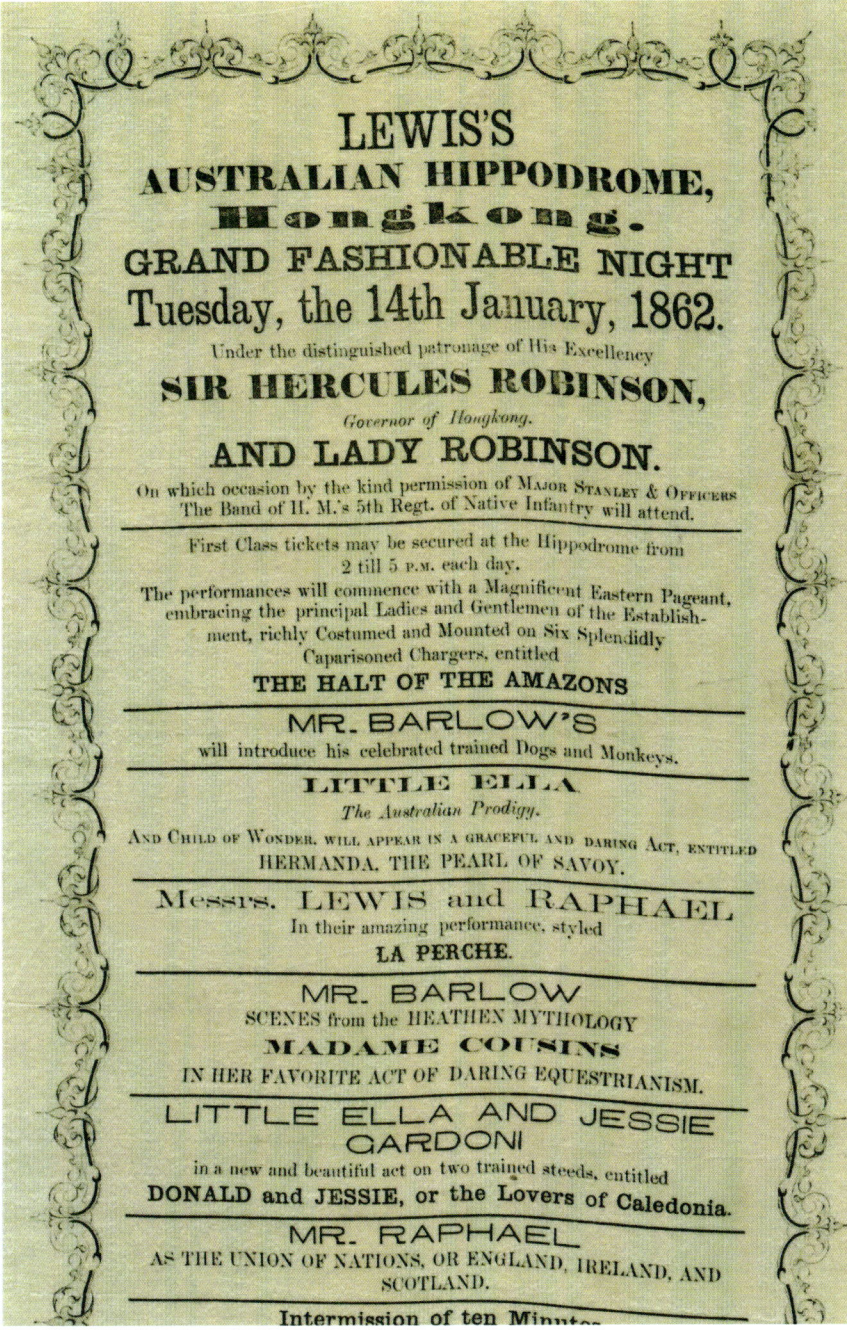

Detail of Hong Kong silk playbill, 1862.
Private Collection

Edwin Adams, American tragedian with the Lewises, c.1862.
19th Century Actors and Theater Photographs Collection, Washington State University

Frederick Appleton, perhaps Rose's best leading man in India, 1860s. *Carte-de-visite* Album.
Accession no.1992.079. p.5a, Performing Arts Collection, Arts Centre Melbourne

Rose warmly dressed for winter in China, 1864. *Carte-de-visite*.
Private Collection

Rose, the young actress, c.1864. *Carte-de-visite*.
Accession no. H34244, Pictures Collection, State Library of Victoria

Joseph Jefferson and Rose Edouin in *Our American Cousin*, c.1864. Photographs of Actors and Actresses. Accession Number PXA 362 Vol. 6, No. 12, p. 4, State Library of New South Wales

Louisa Cleveland, as Leah the Forsaken, at the Melbourne Theatre Royal in 1864. Rose would have worn a similar costume in India.
Emma Nelson's Family Album. Private Collection

Rose's 'little father' Charles 'Teddy' Edouin and his wife Lizzie Naylor, c.1864.
Emma Nelson's Family Album. Private Collection

Actor Manager Barry Sullivan of the Theatre Royal, who cast Rose in some important roles. Emma Nelson's Family Album, 1860s. Private Collection

Marian Dunn (Mrs. Marcus Clarke) as a young actress, c.1865.
Private Collection

Four Edouins: Rose, Willie, John and Julia, 1860s.
Accession no. H10470, Pictures Collection, State Library of Victoria

Home from Asia: a motherly looking Rose with the infant George (in dark frock) and baby Lucy May, just before leaving for India in 1867. *Carte-de-visite* Album.
Accession no.1992.079. p. 26, Performing Arts Collection, Arts Centre Melbourne

CHAPTER SIX

The remainder of the year was marked by the birth of Rose's first child George, on 29 September.[275] The address given for the birth, Hong Kong Cottage, 416 Carlisle Street, St Kilda, could be an indication that the house was named in commemoration of the profits gleaned from the Asia tour. Records show that George Lewis bought land on St Kilda Road on 17 November 1865. It was perhaps with some of these Asian profits that Charles Edouin became licensee of the Imperial Hotel on the corner of Bourke and Spring Streets where he advertised that there was a piano in a private room for entertainments.[276] Deciding that his theatrical destiny lay in a different direction from that of the Lewises, Rose's brother, nineteen year old Willie Edouin, left for Hong Kong with Mr and Mrs William Birch (not to be confused with the equestrians) on 29 November by the *Golden Horn*. Willie was not to see his family in Australia again.[277]

In the meantime the father of the Edouins, still calling himself John E. Jones, had a female companion at his livery stables at Fitzroy.[278] He had formed a de facto relationship with London born Isabella Jane Wing, 28 years his junior.[279]

By 21 April 1866 Rose had returned to the stage when she, together with Julia and Lizzie, spoke the orations at the Brooke Memorial Fund at the Princess's Theatre on 21 April. G. V. Brooke, who had left Australia in 1861, had been on his way back in 1866 Australia for a season with Coppin when his ship founded in the Bay of Biscay and he drowned.[280]

While her siblings and their wives performed in ballets and farces at the Princess's Theatre, Rose seems to have concentrated on looking after her baby and by July she was pregnant again. This did not stop a return to the stage some months later. On 29 November, she played Peg Woffington in Charles Reade's *Masks and Faces* with Julia as Kitty Clive, and the Enchanter in the extravaganza *Princess Spring Time*.[281] Moving to the Haymarket Theatre in early December, Rose gave several performances in the title role of Dion Boucicault's *Arrah-na-Pogue*. On 20 December, after she had played Nell

---

275 Birth Certificate.
276 *Bell's Life in Victoria*, 16 November 1865, p. 1. This hotel still exists on the site.
277 Nilanjana Banerji, 'Edouin, Willie', in *Oxford Dictionary National Biography online*.
278 Sands & MacDougall Melbourne Directories 1866–1870.
279 Isabella Jane Wing, born November 1838, Shoreditch, London. Information from her great-great-granddaughter.
280 Lurline Stuart, 'Fund-raising in colonial Melbourne: the Shakespeare statue, the Brooke bust and the Garibaldi sword', in *La Trobe Library Journal*, Vol. 8, No. 29, April 1982, p. 6.
281 *Era*, 27 January 1867.

Gwynne in *Court and Stage,* Rose said farewell to the stage in a valedictory address written for her by Dr Neild including the lines:

> So when I thought to change my busy life,
> And play no other part save that of wife,
> The quiet duties of a home to fill,
> Believe me, but the old love lingered still![282]

The 'fatherly' Dr Neild wrote an article in his weekly theatre page regretting her retirement and giving us a picture of Rose at 22.[283]

> Mrs. G. B. W. Lewis, whom we have better known for I cannot tell how many years as Miss Rose Edouin, said farewell to the public on Thursday night. I should not like to regard this as a genuine farewell, but I have good reason for believing that it is. I can only regret the loss the Melbourne stage must suffer by the absence of a lady whose merits are so great, and whose personal and good qualities are so many. Her cheery, joyous, hearty manner always seemed to me a specific for bad spirits; it did one good to see her pleasant bright face, and to hear her real, unforced, unstagey laugh. There is nobody who can quite fill the place she leaves, and I could almost feel angry with her for deserting us. Nevertheless I am glad to know she has reached that material success which gives her the option of quitting the stage or remaining upon it; and I trust she will enjoy for many years to come the solid happiness of a domestic life she has so deservedly earned.

It is likely that Dr Neild knew of her pregnancy, but his prediction of a 'domestic life' for Rose was to be contradicted by subsequent events.

Rose, aged 23, gave birth to her first daughter Lucy May on 27 April 1867 at her new house Shanghai Villa on St Kilda Road, South Yarra.[284] After acquiring land on St Kilda Road in 1865, George had become something of a pioneer developer on what later became one of Melbourne's premier thoroughfares.[285] The naming of the first house as 'Shanghai Villa' again indicates his appreciation of his Asian tours. The house (designed by architect Peter Conlon) was sometimes described as a cottage but its dimensions

---

282 *Argus,* 30 November 1866; *Age,* 21 December 1866.
283 *Australasian,* 22 December 1866, p. 1202.
284 Birth Certificate colony of Victoria 1867.
285 See Miles Lewis – Melbourne Mansions Database on line University of Melbourne. www.fmpro.abp.unimelb.edu.au/fmi/iwp/cgi?-db=mmdb

CHAPTER SIX

were quite sizeable. There was a large drawing room and dining room and, as well as four bedrooms, there were three servant's rooms, brick stables and coachouse. Over the years the Lewises filled the house with opulent Chinese and Indian furniture bought on their Asian tours.[286] Peter Conlon had been Lewis's neighbour during his time at Cremorne Gardens. The Lewises' neighbours now included Edward Henty, Victorian pioneer and his wife at the mansion, Offington, and Thomas Moubray a former mayor of Melbourne at his mansion, Armadale. Despite Rose's quiet domestic life on semi-rural but well-to-do St Kilda Road George Lewis had made arrangements to take his reconstituted 'Burlesque and Dramatic Company' to Calcutta. On 20 July 1867 they left on the 1292 ton iron clipper ship *Underley*, bound for Calcutta. The list comprised Mr & Mrs Lewis (and the children Lucy and George), Mrs Edouin (Sarah), Miss Edouin (Julia), Mr & Mrs Chapman, Mr & Mrs South, Mr (Henry) Birch, Mr Allen, Mr Haygarth, Mr Stoneham, Mr Compton, Miss Melville, Miss (Waddy) Deering, Mr (Ollie) Deering, Mr Douglas and Mr Hunter.[287] At this time, Rose's brother John and his wife Tilly Earl were happily employed as dancers in Melbourne theatres.[288] They and her brother Charles, busy as licensee of Edouin's Hotel, and his wife Lizzie opted not to go to India.[289]

So, instead of settling down to 'domestic bliss', Rose would be acting and touring throughout Asia, south eastern Australia and England for the next 40 years.

---

286 The drawing room measured 20 by 33 feet and the dining room 20 by 22 feet: Inventory in *Argus*, 11 April 1882 when the house was sold.
287 PROV, VPRS 948, Outward Passenger List, *Underley* October 1867.
288 John Spring, 'Computerised Listing of Melbourne Public Performances, 1850–1869', Monash University, 1981.
289 R.K. Cole Collection of Hotel Records, State Library of Victoria.

Chapter seven

LEWIS'S GRAND DRAMATIC BURLESQUE AND BALLET COMPANY IN INDIA

Although the British residents of Calcutta were the main focus of his venture to India, Lewis was possibly aware of the strong traditions of Indian theatre dating back thousands of years. From his time in Calcutta in 1860 he would have heard of the introduction of Western drama in the late eighteenth century and the growing popularity, among Bengalis educated in English culture, of Shakespeare and other English dramatists. Most Western theatre was performed in the private homes of the wealthy zamindars and bhadralock classes (land-holders and tax collectors for the British), some of whom had built proscenium theatres in their homes. Dwarakanath Tagore (grandfather of the poet Rabindranath Tagore) built such a theatre in his Jorasanko palace in north Calcutta in the 1830s.[290]

Foreign entertainers from opera companies to minstrel shows flocked to Calcutta during the days of the British occupation or 'Raj'. Performers often visited Calcutta on their way to or from tours in the British colonies. During the ascendency of the British East India Company, before the Mutiny of 1857, there had been various attempts at establishing an English theatre both amateur and professional. But apart from the moderate success of actress-manager Mrs Esther Leach and her actress daughter Mrs Anderson, James Barry and others at the San Souci Theatre during the 1840s, there had been few regular seasons in Calcutta.[291] A feature of Barry's management in 1848 was a performance of *Othello*, with a Bengali, Baishnab Charan Addy,

---

290 This summary of pre-Mutiny theatre in Bengal is based on Sudipto Chatterjee, *The Colonial Staged: Theatre in Colonial Calcutta*, Seagull Books, Calcutta, 2007.
291 Denis Shaw, 'Esther Leach, "The Mrs. Siddons of Bengal"', in *Educational Theatre Journal*, Vol. 10, No. 4, December 1958, pp. 304–310. Leach's dates: 1809–1843. Also see Sudipto Chatterjee, op. cit., p. 63.

in the title role. Unfortunately, responses from the Calcutta Anglophone press were grudging and racist.[292]

As well as the English theatre there was what has been called a 'renaissance' of Indian theatre. Part of the nineteenth century 'Bengal Renaissance', Michael Madrhusudan Datta, Dinabandhu Mitra, Giresh Chandra Ghosh and others had written and performed dramas in Bengali, sometimes influenced by Western drama. Ghosh (1844–1911) was later to acknowledge Mrs Lewis as something of a mentor during the mid-1870s.[293]

At first the Lewises had little competition and were hailed by the Calcutta press as being the first to bring good professional theatre to Bengal. At the time of the Lewises' arrival a troupe of Japanese acrobats appeared, passing on quickly to other regions of India.[294] The famous English soprano Anna Bishop had performed at the Calcutta Town Hall some months before the Lewis Company arrived,[295] and in 1867 an Opera House was being constructed, sponsored by a group of local enthusiasts on a subscription basis. An opera company, led by the impresario Augusto Cagli, toured between Melbourne and India during this time. During and after the Lewis regime there were other drama and opera companies such as that of Mr and Mrs English at the Corinthian Theatre from 1875.[296] When the Lewises returned to Australia for the first time in 1871 one of their comedians, Willie Gill, took over the Lewis Theatre for a season.[297] Then there was a visit by the popular British comedian Charles Mathews to English's Theatre in 1875–76.[298] In the late 1890s, the Australian-based Brough Company gave some seasons that introduced the plays of Oscar Wilde to India.[299]

One of the 'regulars' who was more than just a visitor was the English born minstrel-show proprietor Dave Carson. He had arrived in Calcutta in the early 1860s and was among the first foreign entertainers to set up in Calcutta after the 1857 first war of independence and the establishment of the British 'Raj'.[300] Carson's touring company performed at the Town Hall

---

292 See Sudipto Chatterjee, 'Moor or Less, Othello Under Surveillance, Calcutta, 1848', at sia.stanford.edu/india/Othello%20Paper%20Stanford.doc
293 I am indebted for this information to Sudipto Chatterjee who is translating Ghosh's autobiography.
294 *Times of India*, 28 September 1867, p. 2.
295 Richard Davis, *Anna Bishop: The Adventures of an Intrepid Prima Donna*, Currency Press, Sydney, pp. 248–255.
296 S.K. Mukerjee, *Story of Indian Theatre*, K.P. Bagchi & Company, Calcutta, 1982.
297 *Australasian*, 23 April 1870, p. 531.
298 *Englishman*, 21 December 1875, p. 2.
299 *Englishman*, 7 December 1897, p. 2.
300 The Amusement pages for the period 1862–1876 of the *Indian Daily News, Bengal Hurkaru*. Carson had appeared in Melbourne with the San Francisco Minstrels

and sometimes at the Opera House. Carson was cashing in on the popularity in the English-speaking world of the American 'blackface' minstrel-shows where from the 1840s white men made up with burnt cork parodied the African slave in American society. By the 1850s the genre was also popular in England and Australia.[301] As well as the parody and racist elements it amounted to a show containing revue, vaudeville and burlesque. Possibly appealing to the lowest common denominator among the British inhabitants, one wonders how it was received among the Bengali people.[302]

After returning to Melbourne in 1865, George Lewis claimed to have made a 'small fortune' in China. Now calling himself George Benjamin William Lewis, his baptismal name, and remembering his successful time in India in 1860, he set his 'money-making' sights there. Lewis's first dramatic company in Calcutta consisted of about 21 artists from Melbourne, including Rose's mother Sarah Bryer, her younger sister Julia Edouin, and a few people from Lewis's circus company including Austin Shanghai, the young acrobat from China. Also in the party were the Lewises' two children George aged two years, and Lucy May aged five months, both Australian born. Of course, many of the actors were English: theatre folk who had been attracted to Melbourne by the Victorian gold rushes of the 1850s. Rose Edouin, aged only 23, was soon listed in the advertisements as 'Mrs. G. B. W. Lewis', billed as the 'Directress' and star.[303] From this point I will refer to George Lewis as 'Lewis', 'George', or 'G. B. W.'

After a journey of about four weeks, Mr G. B. W. Lewis's Dramatic and Burlesque and Ballet Company arrived in Calcutta from Melbourne in early September 1867. Acquiring access to rent free land on the Maidan, along Chowringhee Road,[304] he had a prefabricated corrugated iron theatre erected 'close to the Ochterlony monument'.[305] The theatre measured about 40 by 100 feet and claimed to hold 800 people.[306] It was to be 'roofed with sheets

---

during the late 1850s and early 1860s, see John Spring, 'Computerised Listing of Melbourne Public Performances, 1850–1869', Monash University, 1981.
301 Robert C. Toll, *Blacking Up: The Minstrel Show in Nineteenth Century America*, Oxford University Press, New York, 1974; Richard Waterhouse, *From Minstrel Show to Vaudeville*, New South Wales University Press, Sydney, 1990.
302 I have not yet been able to obtain translations of the Bengali press. Mukerjee, p. 36; The Carson company deserves close study for its place in Calcutta theatre and the Bengali reaction to it.
303 *Englishman*, 7 September 1867, p. 1, list of performers in advertisement.
304 *Era*, 12 September 1869, p. 10.
305 Montague Massey, *Recollections of Calcutta for Over Half a Century*, Thacker Spink & Co, Calcutta, 1918. Writing 51 years later, Massey remembered it as being a 'wooden theatre', p. 11
306 *Englishman*, 17 September 1867, p. 2.

CHAPTER SEVEN

of corrugated iron …' to make it 'impervious to rain'. Such theatres were available from English iron foundries like Bellhouse & Co. of Manchester, as seen in George Coppin's Olympic Theatre imported to Melbourne in 1854. Where Lewis obtained his theatre is not known. The *Bengal Hukaru* reported that it was approached by a 'broad flight of steps' from the top of which there was a good view of the 'ample and imposing' stage. Inside it contained a proscenium, pit, boxes and a gallery and would have been fitted out to look like a nineteenth-century English provincial theatre with gilt plaster ornamentation and red velvet seats.[307] Rain and mud was a problem for the first few nights until Lewis installed a board-walk to the theatre.[308] Initially, prices were quite high – from two to seven rupees – but these were soon lowered to one to five rupees. A few seats under the gallery could be had for one rupee until Lewis closed the area because of bad behaviour among the audience. Nevertheless, the London *Era* pointed out that these prices (up to ten shillings) were far higher than those in London, where the highest price was about seven shillings.[309] At this period, with little competition, Lewis could charge what he liked.

From the beginning the company was viewed by the newspaper critics as provincial. The *Bengal Hukaru* bemoaned that there was a kind of double provincialism in the fact that Mr Lewis had formed his company not even from the English provinces but 'from Australia'![310]

Lewis's first Calcutta theatre was called 'Lewis's Royal Lyceum'. After a successful opening, the company suffered a disastrous set back when a severe November cyclone flattened the building and destroyed most of the costumes and scenery.[311] Refusing help from the Calcutta community, Lewis

---

307 *Indian Daily News, Bengal Hurkaru*, 14 September 1867, p. 2.
308 *Indian Daily News, Bengal Hurkaru*, 18 September 1867, p. 3.
309 *Indian Daily News, Bengal Hurkaru*, 12 September 1869, p. 10.
310 *Indian Daily News, Bengal Hurkaru*, 14 September 1867, p. 2. This was true: Melbourne was a provincial city but a very prosperous one, capital of the colony of Victoria with a population of half a million (the central Municipality of Calcutta had a similar population of the British residents numbering about eleven thousand) and still, in the 1860s, living on the wealth generated by the Victorian gold rushes of the 1850s. By the 1860s Melbourne possessed three large theatres – the Royal, Haymarket and Princess's (most able to hold up to 3000 patrons) – as well as a growing number of small halls where moving panoramas and music-hall type entertainments were held. These theatres attracted successful performers from the British Isles and the USA and not always from the provinces. The American actors Edwin Booth, Laura Keene and Joseph Jefferson were on the way to stardom when they visited Australia, and the Irish tragedians G.V. Brooke and Barry Sullivan had only recently found their niche in the British provinces when they enjoyed long seasons in Melbourne.
311 *Indian Daily News, Bengal Hurkaru*, 3 November 1867, p. 3.

was able, within eight days, to erect another theatre and the company played to appreciative audiences until the end of the cool season in March 1868. It is clear that young Mrs Lewis – she was 23 – dominated the acting and the choice of plays. Plus, of course, she was 'Directress', stage managing and rehearsing the actors whether she was in the play or not. In the first season Rose and some of her fellow cast members played in all genres. In the early seasons there was a performance three times per week, usually Monday, Wednesday and Saturday. In later seasons they sometimes played every night except Sunday. By then, Rose might only appear twice a week.[312] Her energy must have been prodigious: I have calculated that she was pregnant at least three times while in India, often playing 'principal boys' some months into her pregnancies, and thus probably making a very buxom 'boy'![313]

At the conclusion of their first season in March 1868, and despite the prospect of intense heat on the plains of India, the company went on tour. Travelling by trains, recently introduced to India, they toured the military stations such as Dinapore and Allahabad and on to Delhi. Between March and mid-April 1868 the company had two- or four-night stands at Jamalpore, Dinapore, Benares, Allahabad, Cawnpore, Lucknow, Delhi and Meerut. On 17 March 1868, at the beginning of the tour while at Jamalpore, Lucy May, Rose's ten month old daughter died from convulsions and teething problems.[314] It was perhaps asking too much of an infant to be transported from a Melbourne winter and a cool season in Calcutta to the unremitting heat of the Indian plains. Two year old George was evidently more robust. No doubt grief-stricken, the Lewises retired to Simla for the summer where in June 1868 another son, William, was born. This infant, however, lived only twelve months. He died on 25 June 1869 from bronchitis.[315]

According to the London *Era*, the Calcutta municipal authorities required the Lewis theatre to be dismantled after each 'cold' season. In September 1868, the new 'much improved' theatre was 150 feet by 60 feet wide and could hold 800 people.[316] Back in Melbourne a local daily reported

---

312 Survey of advertisements and reviews in the *Englishman*.
313 Ecclesiastical Records of Bengal; births in colony of Victoria. Rose possibly had at least two pregnancies during her time in India: two births are recorded in India, those of William in 1868 and Victoria May in 1869. The Lewis grave in Melbourne commemorates six children including two unnamed infants, a son and a daughter.
314 Ecclesiastical Records Bengal, India Office, British Library, Burials at Mooltan, 17 March 1868, Lucy May daughter of George Benjamin William Lewis. Gentleman.
315 Ecclesiastical Records Bengal, India Office, British Library, Burial Certificate William Lewis, son of George Benjamin Lewis, Theatrical Manager, N/1/128 folio 162.
316 *Englishman*, 6 October 1868, p. 2.

that Lewis's takings in India were £200 – £250 per night.[317] These types of sums would have grossed Lewis up to £3000 for a three month Calcutta season. The Trieste-born musician Alberto Zelman, later to be important on the music scene in Melbourne, was Lewis's musical director with Charles Edouin as orchestra leader.[318]

And so it was that between September 1867 and March 1870 the couple and most of their company remained in Bengal, spending the summers from early 1868 touring or staying at Simla.[319] Rose Lewis's second daughter, Victoria May, was born in Simla in 1869.[320] Not long before this birth, Rose received the news that her eldest brother Charles had died of 'heat exhaustion' during the rail journey across the plains of India after the company's tour.[321]

But the 'show had to go on'. A playbill for the 1869 Calcutta production of *The School for Scandal* gives us an insight into the way the Lewis productions were 'marketed'. The bill, dated 10 February 1869, was souvenired by Emma Nelson, a Melbourne actress in the 1872–1874 India and China seasons.[322] The playbill is a single printed piece of paper folded into the shape of a fan. It would have been distributed at the performance of *Richard III* two days previously. As well as giving the cast lists for the Sheridan play *School for Scandal* and the farce *My Uncle's Intended*, the playbill urged patrons to book at the Great Eastern Hotel for Mrs Edouin Bryer's benefit on 10 February 1869. She played Mrs Candour to Rose's Lady Teazle with Henry Birch (the old equestrian actor from the Calcutta circus season of 1860) as Sir Peter.

Between 1871 and 1875 they returned to Melbourne via Bombay and China during the following summers. From 1871 Bombay was a type of 'off Broadway' place for the Lewises to 'try-out' the productions they were to present in Calcutta.[323]

Although its predominantly London repertoire was primarily aimed at British members of the colonial public service, Lewis's theatre attracted many educated Bengalis, noted for their critical knowledge of Shakespeare. A 'Calcutta letter' in the Bombay *Times of India*, while discussing the city's amusements, went on to comment, somewhat condescendingly, on theatre criticism in the Bengali press:

---

317 *Argus*, 26 November 1868, p. 5.
318 *Englishman*, 2 October 1868.
319 From 1871 to 1876 the Lewises had two breaks of eighteen months from India.
320 Ecclesiastical Records, Bengal, India Office, British Library, Vol.1 Folio 56: Baptism 10 August 1869, Victoria May. This child was to die of scarlet fever in Melbourne in 1876.
321 *Australasian*, 10 July 1868, p. 722.
322 After being inherited by her grandson Keith Davies, the programme is now in the State Library of Victoria Theatre Programme Collection.
323 *Times of India*, sample of advertisements 1871–1876.

It is amusing to notice some of the criticisms in the native papers on our theatricals. They are mostly confined to Shakespearean plays. The tone is by no means complimentary to our theatrical troupes, as their performances are very severely handled, and in many respects, I must confess, with a certain decree of justice. Shakespeare has been studied by our Baboos in their educational courses at the universities or colleges, and they regard everything below Shakespeare as something scarcely worth notice. They are themselves paying considerable attention to dramatic literature; several new plays have recently been published, of which the native press speaks highly. They say that if they were translated into English and placed on our London boards they would create a sensation.[324]

So, unlike the British who were prepared to 'make allowances' for the provincial standards of the Lewises, British-educated Bengalis expected more than the odd pantomime and burlesque interspersed with, for instance, an unevenly acted *Hamlet*. None of the critics liked the company's first 'leading man', tragedian John H. Allen, an American who since the mid-1850s had gained mild success in his home country[325] but received mainly unfavourable reviews of his performances in Melbourne. His Richard III at the Bourke Street Theatre Royal in 1866 was described as ranting 'so much as to elicit an expression of dissatisfaction from a few of the more critical of the audience'.[326] The mediocre Allen was probably the only 'tragedian' in Melbourne at the time willing to travel to Calcutta.

During their sojourns in Calcutta, the Lewises tried to join in with the life of the city by donating proceeds to 'worthy' causes such as the Native Hospital at Howrah and Famine relief.[327] Lewis was also involved in the Calcutta Freemasons' Lodge.

The character of critical comment in the press and the success of Lewis's venture seem to have varied in relation to the personnel of the different companies he brought to India. All, however, agreed that Rose Edouin, Mrs G. B. W. Lewis, was a superb actress having 'grace', versatility, and 'good taste' – the latter despite her appearing in burlesque and pantomime in 'breeches' parts. By 1870 her versatility was almost legendary. One newspaper

---
324 *Times of India*, 11 January 1868, p. 3.
325 He had been sometime lessee of New York's Bowery Theatre in 1859, see John Norton Ireland, *Records of the New York Stage*, Bradstreet Press, New York, 1867, p. 599.
326 *Argus*, 12 May 1866.
327 *Englishman*, 28 March 1870, p. 2; *Englishman*, 28 February 1874, p. 1.

CHAPTER SEVEN

described her ability to play 'from High Tragedy down to Burlesque with equal skill and success'.[328]

The two related genres of pantomime and burlesque were among the most popular forms of stage entertainment in the nineteenth century. Based on the old forms of the Italian *commedia dell'arte* and fairy tales and stories such as *Jack and the Beanstalk*, *Cinderella*, *Robinson Crusoe* and *Aladdin*, the Christmas pantomime appealed to adults as well as children. For adults there was political satire, lavish and spectacular production, leggy chorus girls (sometimes called Amazons) and a Principal Boy played by a curvaceous actress attired in doublet and hose. Most pantomimes had excessively long titles such as *Lalla Rookh: or The Princess, The Peri, and the Troubadour* and *Jack the Giant Killer: or, Harlequin King Arthur and the Knights of ye Round Table*. Excruciating puns were featured in the dialogue such as:

Morgi. Such dirty weather gives the Turkish sailors work-some.
Ali. On the Black Sea the Turks must find *it-urksom*.[329]

By the mid-nineteenth century, pantomime form consisted of an 'opening' based on a fairy story, a transformation scene, and a 'Harlequinade', in dance and mime, featuring the characters of Harlequin and Columbine, Pantaloon and Clown.[330]

As well as pantomime, there were similar forms called extravaganza and burlesque. These were based on myths and legends rather than fairy tales and were put on at Easter or other times of the year. Burlesque, while retaining the dreadful puns, did not have *commedia dell'arte* connections, and often parodied and satirised serious plays and opera such as in *Lor! Sonnambula* and *Romeo and Juliet, or the Cup of Cold Poison*. In the late nineteenth century, the 'Principal Boys' and chorus girls of pantomime and English burlesque evolved in America into an entertainment of less 'good taste' featuring 'bump and grind' and strip-tease.[331]

During the first four Lewis seasons, between 1867 and 1870, the personnel of the Lewis company remained fairly constant but with additions or replacements when an actor proved unsuitable. For instance, J. H. Allen was

---

328 *Indian Daily News, Bengal Hurkaru*, 27 October 1869, p. 2.
329 E.L. Blanchard, *Harlequin and the Forty Thieves, with local annotations by Mr Frank Edwards*, Azzopardi, Hildreth & Co., Melbourne, 1877, p. 30.
330 David Mayer, *Harlequin in his Element: The English Pantomime*, 1806–1839, Harvard University Press, Cambridge, Mass. 1969, chapter two, pp. 19–74.
331 'Burlesque' in Phyllis Hartnoll, ed., *Oxford Companion to the Theatre*, Oxford University Press, Oxford, 1983, p. 119.

not a good foil for the brilliant acting of Rose Lewis.[332] After a disastrous *Hamlet,* where he was accused of 'rant' and of having no idea of the play, Allen was replaced for the 1868–1869 season by Frederick Charles Appleton from Melbourne. Appleton's Hamlet was seen as original and refreshingly free of 'rant'.[333] Two of Rose's siblings, actor and dancer John Edouin aged twenty-eight, and Charles Edwin Bryer aged thirty-five who was to lead the orchestra,[334] had arrived for the 1868–1869 season together with their actress wives, soubrette Tilly Earl, and Elizabeth (later known as Mrs Edouin Bryer after the death of her husband in 1869) who specialised in soubrette 'character' roles. Also arriving for the beginning of the 1868–1869 season was the young comedian Willie Gill, with his actress mother Janet, who had performed with the Lewis Company in China and who later found success in America.[335]

Rose's repertoire was remarkably varied and wide-ranging. Melodrama in the nineteenth century often abounded with strong female roles: *Leah the Forsaken,* Miami in *Green Bushes,* Zoë in *The Octoroon* and Lady Isabel in *East Lynne* together with comedies such as *The Lady of Lyons, The School for Scandal* and *London Assurance*. She also took the leading roles in the Boucicault Irish dramas *The Colleen Bawn* and the *Shaughraun* and seems to have excelled in all these widely different roles.

There were several 'orientalist' productions of pantomimes in the Lewis repertoire such as *Lalla Rookh* (based on Thomas Moore's poem), *Aladdin, Ali Baba and the Forty Thieves,* and *Blue Beard*. All these pantomimes were part of a general nineteenth-century interest by Europeans in the spectacular and exotic 'otherness' of the East.[336] All originated in the London theatre at the heart of the metropolitan power. In London these pantos and burlesques, with female characters clad in diaphanous and revealing costumes, might sexually titillate the audience, often, of course, more from the fertile imagination of the designers than from reality. There were, perhaps, also some self-congratulatory elements in the thought that many of the exotic lands depicted were now part of the British Empire. From the descriptions in the reviews there was certainly much of this in the Lewis productions. In

---

332 *Australasian*, 4 June 1870, p. 722: letter from Willie Gill saying sarcastically: '"The great American tragedian", J.H. Allen has exhausted himself as circus clown, and has left Mauritius for England'.
333 In 1882 Appleton became the first actor to obtain a B.A from the University of Melbourne. University of Melbourne Archives.
334 *Englishman*, 21 October 1868, p. 1
335 Kurt Gänzl, *William B. Gill: From the Goldfield to Broadway*, Rutledge, New York, 2002.
336 Edward Said, *Orientalism, Routledge & Kegan Paul*, London, 1978; reprint, Penguin, 1991.

CHAPTER SEVEN

Calcutta there was the added element of British hegemony, where Indians in the audience saw strange representations of themselves. The pantomime tradition of 'localising' the play script also tried to 're-imagine' the text for the local audience of British civil servants often at the expense of local Bengalis, sometimes at the expense of the civil servants themselves. Lacking a full text of the Calcutta versions of the pantomimes and burlesques, for example William Brough's *Lalla Rookh, or, the Princess the Peri and the Troubadour*, we have to rely on a long quotation in one of the reviews where there is a cruel sketch of a 'babu' (played by Mrs Edouin Bryer in male attire) giving, as part of the localisation of the play, a welcoming address to the representative of the Duke of Edinburgh, then on a tour of India. The 'fun' was supposed to be in the 'babu's' obsequiousness and mistakes in his English. The offensive speech included lines such as:

> My present address to your Highness will convince to what standard we have attained by your well-known perseverance. We have also attained a high standard and *pucka* knowledge of the arts sciences and chewing *betel*.[337]

At an earlier burlesque performance of H. J. Byron's *Beautiful Haidee*, based on an oriental episode in Lord Byron's *Don Juan*, there were derogatory 'hits' at Dr Chakrabarty (called Dr Chuckerbutty in the play) and a Mr Sconce that were supposedly taken in 'good part' by the people who were 'sent up'. Dr S. G. Chakrabarty is a good case: we might wonder why the first London-trained medical practitioner in India should be the 'butt' of ridicule. He had graduated from the University of London, returned to Calcutta in 1850 having gained his degree with honours, and went on to become an expert in the public health of the city.[338] Pantomime and burlesque were famous for their satire and parody of current events whether it be in London, Melbourne or New York.

Rose Lewis displayed her versatility in many ways other than tragedy and comedy and appearing in 'male' roles. She often played the ethnic 'other' in many of the plays available to her from the London or New York stage. The 1845 play *Green Bushes*, by the English writer Buckstone, had a 'powerful' part for her in the half French, half American Indian girl Miami the huntress, who loved and hated fiercely an English settler who betrayed her.

---

337 *Indian Daily News, Bengal Hurkaru*, 27 December 1869, p. 2. (One can almost hear the perpetuation of such parodies in the work of Peter Sellers and recent BBC comedies).
338 David Arnold, *Science, Technology and Medicine in Colonial India*, Cambridge University Press, Cambridge, 2000, p. 64.

Another 'American' play, this time by the Irish playwright Dion Boucicault, was *The Octoroon*, first performed in New York in 1859. Rose played Zoë an 'octoroon', the illegitimate daughter of a part-African slave and a white judge in the American 'South'. Zoë loves a gentleman planter and takes poison rather than submit to the slave-owner villain who had bought her after her father's death.

In *Leah the Forsaken*, an 1859 drama by the American Augustin Daly based on a play by the Austrian writer Hermann Salomon Mosenthal, the heroine was a tragic Jewess betrayed by her Christian lover and persecuted in her German village. It was Rose's most popular and admired role while she was in India. A reviewer of one of Rose's performances stated that 'the whole force of the piece rests upon the exertions of the heroine alone.'[339]

Playing the 'other', was, of course, one of the tasks of an actor – villains, heroes – characters different from the real person playing the part. Nevertheless, the three plays just mentioned required careful acting to convey another culture from that of the actress and her usual string of English heroines. However, perhaps Rose's most 'other' character was that of Monee, a Bengali *ayah*, in this case, a lady's maid, in the London playwright Tom Taylor's 1860 comedy-drama *Up at the Hills*. The Lewises produced it several times in 1869 and 1870. The play tells the story of military men and civil servants in a hill town above Calcutta. The characters include a rich young widow, her childhood sweetheart, a wise old military wife and a caddish embezzling Major who wants to marry the young widow for her fortune but is having an affair with Monee an Indian maid or ayah who loves him passionately. Monee is not really a 'powerful' part for Rose Lewis: the girl is submissive both to her lover and her mistress. The often racist Calcutta press noted that such a plot was unlikely and that it was obvious that the playwright had never visited India. The dénouement that the villainous British Major, having been foiled in his evil intentions towards the widow, announces that he is engaged to Monee (though possibly going to his death on the North West frontier) was seen as improbable by the critic. The implication is that, despite much evidence to the contrary, such an alliance could never happen in India.[340] A similar opinion about the likelihood of a white gentleman contemplating such an alliance with an octoroon was repeated in a review of Rose's performances as Zoë and Monee some weeks later. The critic comments on the failure of *The Octoroon* in the USA because

---

339 *Englishman*, 27 November 1871.
340 These alliances have been documented by William Dalrymple in *White Moguls*, Harper Collins, London, 2003.

of the race question, and states that similarly *Up at the Hills* will not achieve success in India: 'It is only where ignorance is bliss that such dramas will enjoy full repute':

> In the States the idea of an alliance between an Octoroon and a planter is even more disagreeable than that of the matrimony of a Major and an Ayah in Bengal. Mrs. Lewis undertook the somewhat invidious role of both these interesting heroines; doubtless her part on Saturday last, was as much the more congenial to her as it was acceptable to the audience. Zoë's part is a very good one, light, gay, serious, passionate, and eminently tragic, it gives good scope for all an artist's excellencies. Yet somehow ... though it would be difficult to find fault with Mrs. Lewis's acting, the character did not seem to suit as well as some of her roles in the more legitimate drama. The fact is Mrs. Lewis's talents are of a higher order and result from a more subtle ... intellect than that of which the exigencies of sensation demand the exercise – or more correctly speaking perhaps – the sacrifice.[341]

The review in the *Bengal Hurkaru* makes some flippant remarks about the fact that Mrs Lewis had recently been 'up at the hills' with her children and had perhaps based her interpretation of the role on her own experience with ayahs.[342] As we have seen, reviews in the English language Calcutta press indicate that a strong proportion of local people formed the audience. What did they make of the bizarre mix of the Lewis repertoire? Was Dr Chakrabarty insulted or merely amused at his treatment by the Lewis company? Further, what did the Bengali audience make of the drama *Jessie Brown*, a play which dealt with the 'Indian Mutiny', or the moving panorama of the Cawnpore massacre of British women and children featured in *Lalla Rookh*?[343]

In early 1870, after more than two-and-a-half years in India and their third season in Calcutta, Lewis announced that he had decided to end his connection with the sub-continent and return to Australia. He had evidently had made sufficient profits to finance the building of investment properties on Melbourne land which he had bought in 1865. The Lewises could at last settle down to enjoy an easy life after all those years of travelling. Rose had been on the road since the 1850s while George's travels had commenced in the 1830s.

In early March Lewis advertised his Lyceum Theatre for sale: 'New corrugated iron ... &c, &c ... Extensive Stage Scenery, Machinery,

---

341 *Englishman*, 18 October 1869.
342 *Indian Daily News, Bengal Hurkaru*, 11 October 1869, p. 3.
343 I have, up to now, been unable to access any reviews from the Bengali newspapers.

Properties &c. &c'.[344] Ever the businessman, however, he encouraged Willie Gill, his 'low' comedian, to continue the performance of 'British theatre' in Calcutta. Together with a Calcutta businessman, a Mr Sultana, Gill planned to open a theatre on the Maidan in October 1870. At his benefit just before the end of the season, Gill gave a speech full of rhetoric praising 'Lewis's bold venture' before which:

> no such thing as a regular dramatic season has been inaugurated ... I purpose presenting to your notice an entirely new dramatic company, complete in every detail, which shall be located on the Maidan, henceforth to be remembered as the spot upon which Mr. Lewis's under management, a taste for the British drama has been sown, which I trust will never be eradicated while the English tongue resounds throughout Chowringee ...[345]

In view of the Lewises' plans, the title of the final play of the season might have had a particular relevance: it was T. W. Robertson's comedy *Home*, with Rose, however, in the role of Mrs Pinchbeck, a home-breaking adventuress. After this farewell performance at Lewis's Lyceum on 31 March friends and admirers joined the company for a supper on the stage of the theatre where Rose was presented with a silver salver and tea and coffee service inscribed with the words:

> to Mrs. G.B.W. Lewis on the occasion of her departure from Calcutta at the termination of her third theatrical season ... as a token of regard from a few of those who have admired her untiring energy and versatile talent as well as learned to esteem and respect her in private life. Calcutta April 1870.[346]

Together with their two children, Rose's mother and sister and the widowed Elizabeth Edouin Bryer, the Lewises arrived back in Melbourne in May 1870 on the steamship *Malta*. Other members of the company including Appleton, Stoneham and Walton travelled back with them. Julia, Appleton, Stoneham and Walton found work at the Adelaide Theatre Royal.[347] John Edouin and his wife Tilly Earl had left Calcutta for England where they hoped to work in the London theatres.

---

344 *Englishman*, 10 March 1870, p. 1.
345 *Australasian*, 23 April 1870, p. 530.
346 *Englishman*, 2 April 1870.
347 *Era*, 18 July 1870.

Chapter eight

MELBOURNE AND INDIA

The Lewises stayed fifteen months in Melbourne from May 1870 to August 1871. Most of this time would have been spent relaxing in their stylish house on St Kilda Road. Rose was pregnant, and though other pregnancies had not prevented her from taking roles, she did not appear on the Melbourne stage in 1870. Her fifth child, Benjamin, was born on 16 October but lived only one day.[348] Grief-stricken and possibly ill, she did not return to the stage until June 1871, playing Lady Teazle in *The School for Scandal* at the Theatre Royal, Melbourne.[349] Given the probable animus toward her father, Rose most likely did not make contact with John Edwin Jones (his livery stables were now at 1 Napier Street, Fitzroy) or with his common-law wife Isabella.[350] Isabella was already the mother of Rose's half-siblings: Blanche, born about 1868; Charles Edwin, born 1869; and Herbert Ernest, born 1871. J. E. Jones (John Edwin Bryer) was the informant.[351]

Back in Calcutta, Willie Gill was true to his promise to provide a theatre on the old Lewis site. He called the 'new' building the Olympic Theatre. This opened in early October. But although some critics liked the 'capital actors' – Harry Power, T. S. Bellair and Gill himself – the venture failed.[352]

In early 1871 an actor new to Melbourne, John Burdett Howe, had been engaged by George Coppin as a tragedian at the Theatre Royal.[353] Howe opened on 11 March 1871 as Hamlet with Julia Edouin playing Ophelia. Dr Neild noted some faults in Howe's reading of the part but also called his Hamlet 'distinguished'. Neild found Julia Edouin 'not very impressive' but

---

348 The baby, Benjamin, was buried at Melbourne General Cemetery on 17 October 1870.
349 *Argus*, 14 June 1871.
350 Sands and McDougall Melbourne Directories 1871–1875.
351 The informant on the birth certificate was J.E. Bryer (Rose's father) and he described himself as the father of Herbert Ernest.
352 *Era*, 27 November 1870.
353 J. Burdett Howe, *A Cosmopolitan Actor: His Adventures all over the World*, Bedford Publishing Company, London, 1888, pp. 186–209. Howe's dates: 1829–1908.

nevertheless 'pleasing'.³⁵⁴ Julia also played Lady Anne to Howe's Richard III.³⁵⁵ Lewis was impressed by Howe's performances. Howe was not by any means a great actor but knew the repertoire and could sing. He was versatile, able to play comedy as well as tragedy and sing Irish songs between acts. Howe recounted that George Lewis met him in a Collins Street restaurant and signed him as 'leading man' for a season in Calcutta.³⁵⁶ Howe later rather regretted this engagement. Coppin had contracted him as a 'first-class star' initially for only four weeks, but, as Howe reflected in his memoir, 'before I was honoured by Mr Coppin with a renewal of four months at a certainty, I had accepted an offer made me by Mr Lewis ... who (as he himself informed me) had no intention of returning to India until he saw me in my various roles at the Theatre Royal, Melbourne.'³⁵⁷

In the meantime Rose's brother, calling himself John Bryer, and his wife Tilly had been performing in Manchester and London. By March 1871, however, John and Tilly were listed in the UK census of March 1871 as tobacconists no doubt 'resting between engagements'. By August, they were in New York, employed with brother Willie Edouin in Lydia Thompson's company at Wallack's Theatre.³⁵⁸ The 'failed' actor-manager of Calcutta W. B. Gill also turned up in this troupe.³⁵⁹

Lewis's new company was, of course, led by Rose. On this journey, the Lewises had left their son George, aged six, at Mr Stacy's school in Melbourne but took two-year-old Victoria May with them. As well as Julia and Mrs Edouin, and Mr and Mrs Howe, there were thirteen other actors and theatre workers. These included actors Mr and Mrs J. Robert Taylor, Florence Norman and Emma Rogers, Edward Shafto Robertson, Charles Bennett, Myles Fenton, Tom Andrews, Edward Kitts and Tom Lewis, scenic artist David Garrick, and stage machinists Quinn and Philip Touzel.³⁶⁰ All were more or less prepared to perform everything from farce to tragedy.

A real tragedy occurred during the voyage. Their light comedian, a young man named Edward Shafto Robertson who had come to Australia for his

---

354 *Australasian*, 18 March 1871, p. 338.
355 *Argus*, 25 March 1871.
356 J. Burdett Howe, op. cit., p. 189.
357 J. Burdett Howe, op. cit., p. 186.
358 *Argus*, 1 August 1871; *New York Times*, 17 August 1871; Kurt Gänzl, *Lydia Thompson*, Rutledge, New York, 2002.
359 Kurt Gänzl, *William B. Gill: From the Goldfield to Broadway*, Rutledge, New York, 2002.
360 PROV, VPRS 948, Passenger List of SS *Avoca*; *Englishman*, 15 September 1871, p. 1.

CHAPTER EIGHT

health and had been acting small parts at Coppin's Theatre Royal, Melbourne, fell down an open deck hatch. He died three days later from a head injury. Robertson was a brother of playwright T. W. Robertson and actress Madge Kendal. According to Howe's memoir *A Cosmopolitan Actor*, the accidental death cast shock and gloom among the company.[361]

After disembarking at Galle, Ceylon, the company boarded the steamer *Deccan* for the trip north to Calcutta. The 'Lewis Dramatic and Burlesque Company' opened its fourth Calcutta season at the Opera House in Lindsey Street in September 1871. In his memoir, Howe described the Lindsay Street theatre as a 'charming little house'. Lewis had secured a site on Chowringhee, the thoroughfare beside the Maidan, and was building a new, more substantial venue.[362] Howe, worrying about the prevalence of cholera in the city, stayed with the Lewises and the rest of the company at the Great Eastern Hotel, their usual residence when in Calcutta.

On the opening night, 16 September 1871, Howe and Julia Edouin were successful in the old comedy *Not Such a Fool As He Looks*. Lewis's speech after the National Anthem mentioned his plan to build a new theatre and the sad loss of Robertson.[363] Howe mentions the 'crowded house' and the presence of Lord Mayo, the Viceroy and the two grandsons of 'the notorious Tipoo Sahib' and various 'native princes and potentates' at the opening.[364] Rose made her first appearance for the season on 22 September as Medea in a version of Euripides' play. The *Englishman*'s critic of 25 September 1871 praised her performance:

> From earnest loving appeal to passionate scorn and hate, her play of features was a perfect study in itself, and clad as she was in the classic garb of ancient Greece, her every movement was marked with a picturesqueness and a grace which was highly artistic.

The paper noted that Howe had little to do but did that well.

For the next three weeks the company played mainly comedy and farce, including the play made famous by Joseph Jefferson, *Rip Van Winkle*, starring Howe. The theatre was open on Mondays, Wednesdays, Thursdays and Saturdays. Following the municipal requirement that the Theatre was to be 'torn down' after each season, Lewis had this time made arrangements for a more permanent theatre to be built. As described by the Calcutta

---

361 J. Burdett Howe, op. cit., p. 189.
362 *Englishman*, 16 September 1871, p. 1.
363 *Englishman*, 18 September 1871.
364 J. Burdett Howe, op. cit., pp. 198–199.

correspondent in the *Era* of 26 November 1871, the new theatre was situated at 16 Chowringhee 'behind the old Calcutta Club'.[365] Measuring 132 feet long by 60 feet wide, it could seat 800. Inside:

> The proscenium, or space between the footlights and the curtain, is occupied by two upper boxes, and by doors leading behind the scenes. The proscenium is ornamented with four Corinthian columns, one at each corner. Besides these two proscenium boxes there are … two boxes on each side of the house near the stage, and the Viceroy's box in the middle of the dress circle. The dress circle is supported by iron pillars. It is reached by a double staircase, and seated for three hundred people. The theatre is entirely lighted by one large sun, consisting of gas jets about eight and a half feet in circumference.

Howe's description of the building of the new Lewis theatre on Chowringhee is helpful in understanding the workings of the construction:

> The very day after Lewis had secured the ground, over eighty workmen were on the spot, all with 'plant' to commence operations, most of them Hindoos, with of course European foremen and architect. The old mansion was torn down as if by magic, and in four days the foundations were being laid. Huge iron pillars and rafters arrived by the dozen, and in less than three weeks the roof was on. The decorations and scenery were all being painted at the Opera House, so that when the roof was on, they were carted to the theatre, and everything was ready to open on the fourth week.[366]

Lewis's Theatre Royal, Chowringhee, opened on 21 October 1871 with the 'slight comedy' by Buckingham, *The Silver Lining*, with Howe and Rose as leads. On 26 October, Rose took the role of Aurora Floyd in the melodrama based on Mary Braddon's novel of the same name. Soon after the opening Howe was struck down with what he feared was cholera, then endemic in the city, but he recovered in a few weeks to play Othello on 1 November. Julia played Desdemona with Rose as Emilia. The production was praised for its lavishness, especially Rose's ruby velvet gown – this must have been very uncomfortable in the pre-cold season heat. The reviewer noted that Howe took a 'modern' approach in his make-up, choosing Edmund Kean's

---

365 I have calculated that this theatre must have been part of what is now the Oberoi Grand Hotel, 16 Jawaharlal Nehru Drive.
366 J. Burdett Howe, op. cit., p. 200.

brown face rather than black face. Not quite approving, the reviewer was not pleased with Howe's naturalism.[367]

In sharp contrast to the tragedy of *Othello*, Rose next starred in the burlesque *Joan of Arc* – probably the London extravaganza by William Brough first performed in 1869. Here Rose emulated what she must have heard about Lydia Thompson's troupe of Blondes in New York, where buxom chorus girls, all 'Blonde', were a great attraction. Her brother Willie would have reported this by letter. However, with her ability to train juveniles, she assembled a troupe of small children all under three feet tall, and all with blonde wigs, parodying Lydia's titillating chorus. After praising the scenery, costumes and the songs, the reviewer continues:

> The great hit, however, in the burlesque was the manoeuvring of the Lilliputian army of Amazons – averaging in height from one foot to three – under the command of Mrs. Lewis … [who] looked perfectly dashing as Joan of Arc in her golden helmet and coat of mail …[368]

Rose played several performances of *Leah* in November and again the critics spoke of her excellence in this 'heavy' role: 'We have never seen this lady act better'. However the critics did not like Mr Herbert, whose acting was 'too constrained and unnatural' in the role of the heartless Christian lover and they wished Howe had played the part.[369] Rose would have had to carry the company all the more during this first part of the season, with Julia ill for ten days with a fever. As well as Shakespeare, the season continued with a varied repertoire of comedy, burlesque and melodrama including *The Irish Emigrant*, *Colleen Bawn*, *Marble Heart*, and *Meg's Diversion*. In early December 'a Grand Production of *Macbeth* was performed with Locke's music and a choir of 100 Voices'.[370] Rose and Howe were praised for their performances as the tragic couple:

> In the strong scenes, Mrs. Lewis was very powerful notably, when she screwed her wavering Lord's courage to the sticking point … Altogether her rendering of the part was thoroughly artistic.

Of Howe, the critic noted initial disappointment in his performance, saying 'his voice is against him', but then added:

---

367 *Englishman*, 2 November 1871; *Daily News*, 3 November 1871.
368 *Daily News*, 6 November 1871.
369 *Englishman*, 29 November 1871, p. 2.
370 *Englishman*, 11 December 1871, p. 3.

he quickly warmed up to his part as the play proceeded and made a complete success of it ... We understand that Mr. Howe has not had the benefit of seeing this part acted by any of the Western models ... if so, his conception of this character is simply wonderful.

The strength of the acting of Howe and Rose was not seen in the supporting roles and ensembles: 'The entire success of the performance ... was due to Mrs. Lewis and Mr Howe ... The banquet scene would, but for Mr Howe's acting, have been an unmitigated burlesque'.[371]

After acting and singing as Rob Roy in the old musical version of Scott's novel (Rose played Helen Macgregor), and giving a charity performance of *Not Such a Fool As He Looks* over the Hooghly river at Howrah, Howe was glad to rest while the company prepared for the pantomime.

From the detailed advertising, *Alibaba, or, Harlequin Abdalla* appears to have been quite lavish, including the many scenes of the traditional pantomime.[372] Rose played Abdalla as a 'lisping swell of the period, in a gorgeous dress of yellow and gold.' Rose trained four children to perform as her comical (and camp) bodyguards 'who follow after the style of their leader, and lisp and twist their moustaches with a *nonchalance* that is perfectly irresistible.' Political comment was present: 'several excellent local "hits" are here introduced, in which some recent events are handled rather smartly'.[373]

The post-pantomime season continued with comedies such as *London Assurance*, the melodramas *Black Eyed Susan*, *The Octoroon* and *Leah the Forsaken*, and the popular *Macbeth*, Rose and Howe receiving good reviews. There seems to have been only one performance of *Frou Frou*, a new melodrama based on the French by Meilhac, with Rose in the 'heavy' role of an unfaithful wife, Gilberte. The work called for a child to play the heroine's son – a part played in Calcutta by Rose's own six year old son George who had joined them from Melbourne.

Previewing a benefit performance for Rose of *London Assurance* at the end of January 1872, a writer acknowledged her role as 'more than an ordinary directress. She directs her company by her own example, and if all the members of the Company acted as well as their Directress, there would not have been the thin houses ... we have seen'.[374]

---

371 *Englishman*, 11 December 1871, p. 3.
372 *Englishman*, 23 December 1871, p. 1.
373 *Englishman*, 30 December 1871, p. 3.
374 *Englishman*, 27 January 1872, p. 3.

CHAPTER EIGHT

The season ended on 30 March with the, by now, usual practice of Rose playing Mrs Pinchbeck in *Home*. This time she appeared with two amateur performers, Captain H. Cowper and Mr Donald Creton. Howe left for England in March. The Lewises and their two children returned to Australia on the *Baroda* arriving in Melbourne on 5 May. Julia and other members had made their way home by other ships.

Chapter nine

INDIA AND CHINA

After just over eight weeks in Melbourne, probably enjoying their home life at Shanghai Villa, the Lewises embarked on 17 July 1872 for India on the steamer *Bangalore* bound for Bombay. They planned to spend four weeks in Bombay before proceeding to Calcutta. Lewis's contacts in Bombay must have indicated that a season there would be profitable. This proved problematical as they had chosen a very hot time of year. The company found the old Grant Street Theatre to be inadequate for their requirements. Nevertheless, they played to appreciative audiences. Apart from Rose, Julia, and their sister-in-law Mrs Edouin Bryer, Robert Lawrence (their leading man) and his wife Tasmanian-born Carry George,[375] it was largely a new company. There were two young women from Melbourne who had been engaged to play small parts, Emma Nelson and Caroline May (the latter might have been a relative of the Edouins, as Sarah's maiden name was May).[376] The male members of the troupe included George Anderson, Mr McLennan, Dorwyn (musician), and Parker (mechanist). This group was joined in Bombay by 'character' actors Mr and Mrs J. Robert Taylor and Emma Rogers, Tom Andrews, G. H. Leonard and Charles Herberte from previous seasons in Calcutta.[377]

On the opening night, 19 August 1872, Lewis spoke from the stage telling the audience that if the four-week season was successful the company would perform in Bombay annually.[378] In this short season the company

---

375 This couple were to be the grand-parents of twentieth century Melbourne actress Lorna Forbes.
376 Tasmanian-born Emma Nelson, a young aspiring actress, was with the company until 1874. Some of her memorabilia in the form of a Lewis programme and many *cartes-de-visite* of members of the company, was passed to her grandson, the late Keith Davies, who made them available to the author in 2004. Unfortunately this collection has no photograph of Rose. Emma's friend Caroline May, aged 25 died at Rangoon in 1874.
377 PROV, VPRS 948, Outward Passenger List of *Bangalore*; cast list for first performance, *Times of India*, 19 August 1872.
378 *Times of India*, 21 August 1872.

CHAPTER NINE

performed a selection of plays from the previous season in Calcutta, such as *School*, *The Colleen Bawn*, *The Octoroon* and *Leah*, and, as Lewis had engaged an 'Irish' comedian, Peter Mansergh for some performances of the comedy-dramas *Grist to the Mill* and *Handy Andy*.

In the review of the final performance of *Leah*, Rose was favourably compared to the creator of the part, Kate Bateman. Lewis addressed the audience telling them the season had not 'been as successful as he could have wished' and that he hoped that 'arrangements could be made for a new theatre or renovation of the present one.'[379]

Within two weeks the company had travelled by train across the plains to Calcutta. One wonders about the thoughts of Mrs Edouin Bryer, whose husband Charles had died on a similar train journey three years previously. For the first time since 1867 a theatre did not have to be re-erected. Lewis's Theatre Royal of 1871 had survived on the opposite side of Chowringhee. The *Englishman*'s theatre critic was happy with the re-paint and the removal of some of the 'tawdry decorations' of the previous year.[380] However, he was not happy with the casting of the opening play *An Unequal Match* by Tom Taylor. Rose was not to appear until 19 October so the company had a chance not to be outshone by their 'directress'. While the critic liked Carry George in the main role of Hester, he was disappointed with the performance of George Anderson ('a good stock-actor'), believing that the leading man, Robert Lawrence, should have taken the part, and he referred to the miscasting of the previous season. The reason for Rose's non-appearance was not given; she usually performed soon after the opening. She eventually appeared as Peg Woffington in the Tom Taylor play *Masks and Faces*. This part, based on the life of a Restoration actress, conveys the continual demands on a star actress – to which Rose perhaps related. Yet whatever had prevented her from appearing earlier, she threw herself into a vigorous round of burlesque with *Little Snow White* (Rose as Prince Golden Heart) and *The Very Last Days of Pompeii*, a 'send-up' of the Bulwer Lytton novel with Rose as Glaucus, another breeches, or tights and toga, part. The arrival of the English-born low comedian, J. L. Hall and his wife the former Emily Wiseman (from the Wiseman Family touring company, one of the Edouin's rivals around the goldfields) added some old fashioned clowning to the repertoire.[381] This couple had recently left the Dave Carson company.[382] Before joining the

---
379 *Times of India*, 16 September 1872.
380 *Englishman*, 30 September 1872.
381 *Englishman*, 19 December 1872.
382 *Australasian*, 29 March 1873, p. 403.

Halls in the panto of *Goody Two Shoes* on Christmas Eve, Rose gave one of her strong characterisations as Lady Isabel in the melodrama based on Mrs Henry Wood's novel *East Lynne*.

Meantime, Julia had made a 'hit' as Little Em'ly in an adaptation of Dickens's *David Copperfield*.[383] By and large Julia remained the soubrette, the sweet dancer of the company – but was she tired of this? Now 23, she was being courted by an overseer of an indigo plantation, English-born William Forbes Grahame, twelve years her senior, so she might have been thinking that there was a life beyond the theatre, that of settling down on an Indian plantation. When Rose played the knock-about character Naomi Tighe in T. W. Robertson's comedy *School*, for example, Julia was relegated to the 'laughable farce' *My Son Diana*.[384] In 'Theatrical News From Calcutta' (dated 2 January) in the *Australasian* of 1 March 1873 there are intimations of dissatisfaction in the company.

Although the correspondent described the company as an 'excellent working one' having just 'finished 12 nights of *Goody Two Shoes*' and observed that 'the troupe is considered much superior to the last Lewis brought over' he adds that 'some members of the company should be given more opportunities'. There is also a mention of 'female jealousies'. Was this about Rose's dominance of the company? The writer mentions Julia's forthcoming marriage and that the 'Lewises and the Bryers are strongly against the match, which, from all I can hear, makes the little lady [Julia] more determined to ratify her choice by matrimonial ceremony.' A *carte-de-visite*, dated 29 December 1872, has survived in the family album of Emma Nelson.[385] It shows a serious looking Julia seated with a bearded thirty-eight year old William Forbes Grahame leaning on her chair in a proprietorial pose. However, Julia stayed with the company until the last night of the season, 29 March 1873. She married Grahame on 9 June 1873 at St James's Church, Calcutta.[386]

By this time the Lewises and their company had left for China. Rose's mother Sarah stayed in Calcutta, perhaps to keep watch on the Lewis Theatre Royal, as another season was planned to open in September. The company arrived in Hong Kong and opened at the City Hall on 20 May with Rose playing the 'romping schoolgirl' Naomi Tighe in *School*. She performed with

---

383 'A letter from India', *Australasian*, 28 December 1872, p. 819.
384 *Englishman*, 22 November 1872, p. 1.
385 Davis family album in private hands.
386 Marriage Certificate, Ecclesiastical Records, British Library, India Office. Did Julia play the part of Kitty Clive, one of Peg Woffington's rivals in the farewell performance before the Lewises left for China?

some local amateurs in the cast and might have been disappointed when the local regimental band refused to provide music for the play.[387] The company played on Tuesday, Thursday and Saturday. In Hong Kong, Rose's repertoire was a mix of farce, burlesque, pantomime and melodrama. Her performance in her old role from the Pantheon Theatre in Melbourne Princess Lurline in the 'fairy comedy' *Nymph of the Lurleyburg* was hailed as 'very fine'.[388] More recent additions were Mrs Ormonde in *My Wife's Daughter*, and Mrs Doctor Savage in *Playing With Fire*.[389] Roles more familiar to Rose were as Eily in *The Colleen Bawn* and Zoë in *The Octoroon*. The critic of the *China Mail* of 2 June thought that this latter part was 'unworthy of the high dramatic abilities of Mrs. Lewis'. When she essayed her 'powerful' role of Leah on 7 June the Hong Kong critic thought that it was a 'foolish part' yet 'one of her best … [played with] great power' despite her 'slightly stagey manner'.[390] Her last three performances were liked by the paper.

On 11 June, she played the sympathetic role of Esther Eccles in *Caste* and the same night played the toga role of Glaucus in *The Very Last Days of Pompeii*, a parody of Bulwer-Lytton's novel *The Last Days of Pompeii*, which the *China Mail* of 12 June described it the 'best piece played by the company'. Rose's final performance was of Lady Gay Spanker in Boucicault's *London Assurance*, billed as the first appearance of the play in the colony.[391] The Lewis troupe left Hong Kong on 14 June to perform at Shanghai, and returned in August for a further season.[392]

Some of the problems and tensions of a touring company, when there is insufficient time for rehearsal, were reported during this 'Farewell' season in Hong Kong:

> It is to be regretted that the performance of Saturday evening was so far below what this company is capable of presenting and the more so … that the failure should have been connected with so spirited a piece as the popular burlesque of *Black-Eyed Susan* … The singing was wretchedly bad, Mrs. Lewis – who can do better – continually wandering into the wrong keys … Our critique is somewhat a harsh one, but is justifiable, for the performance was disgraceful to a company who can and should do better, and whose efforts it has been our pleasant duty on several

---

387 *China Mail*, 21 May 1873.
388 *China Mail*, 26 May 1873.
389 Advertisements and reviews in *China Mail*, 21 May, 4 June 1873.
390 *China Mail*, 9 June 1873.
391 *China Mail*, 14 June 1873.
392 *China Mail*, 7 August 1873. I have as yet been unable to access a Shanghai newspaper for their season there.

occasions to praise. Mrs. Lewis as William did not impress ... and alone deserves commendation for the excellent horn-pipe danced with Susan (Miss Jennie Nye).[393]

This review is the most unfavourable critique found during research for this biography. At first glance one wonders if Lewis had not paid his advertising account but it has a ring of truth and some of the performances are praised. However, Lewis's anger was expressed in the next *China Mail*, when instead of the usual large advertisement, a terse notice stated that there would be a performance that night and that details could be found in the rival newspaper *Hong Kong Times*.[394] Soon after this upset, the company left to return to Calcutta.

On 29 June 1873, Rose's mother Sarah Elizabeth Bryer died suddenly in Calcutta of 'fever and senile decay'.[395] Thus ended the life of one who was later described as being a 'belle' of Brighton. She was 63. Her life had not been easy: she had suffered being a deserted wife and had seen two of her children, Eliza and Charles, and two grandchildren, William and Lucy May, predecease her. Perhaps she had been a hard task mistress. Yet she had trained her talented children to be successful, hardworking show people. Julia was away on her wedding trip and Rose was somewhere on the China coast. By 1873 some telegraphic communications had reached China but most were unauthorised[396] so Rose may not have known of her mother's death until she returned to Calcutta in early September.[397]

A letter written on 14 July from Calcutta to 'Call Boy' of the *Australasian*, published on 27 September 1873, mentions the Lewises as 'still in China doing very well'. They were probably in Shanghai. The company arrived back in Calcutta on 9 September from Hong Kong by *SS China*.[398] Rose would have ten days to deal with her grief and prepare the company for the 20 September opening of Lewis's Theatre Royal. Advertisements promised new actors from London and Australia.

Rose did not appear until 29 September taking a new role for her, Rudiga in *The Woman in Red*. This drama, adapted from the French, was not unlike *Leah The Forsaken* or *Green Bushes* in that its main protagonist is a tragic

---

393 *China Mail*, 11 August 1873.
394 I have been unable to access this newspaper.
395 Bengal death certificate, Vol. 114 Folio 116.
396 D. R. Winseck and R.M. Pike, *Communications and Empire*, Duke University, 2007, pp. 118–122.
397 Daniel R. Headrick, *Invisible Weapon: Telecommunications and International Politics, 1851–1945*, OUP, New York, 1991, p. 36.
398 *Friend of India*, 18 September 1873.

female outsider. Rose might have seen the famous actress-dancer Madame Céline Celeste who had visited Melbourne in 1866 in the role. Yet soon Rose was playing comedy in T. W. Robertson's *Play*.[399]

Another letter written to 'Call Boy' on 13 October and published in the *Australasian* of 6 December reported that the expected actors had not arrived' and lists a repertoire not very new: *Black Sheep*; *Brother Bill and Me*; *Meg's Diversion*; *A Family Failing*; *Play*; *Wait and Hope*; *The Huguenot Captain*; *Loan of a Lover* etc. Rose made a hit in late October as the eponymous lead in the 1869 extravaganza *Columbus*, then back to drama on 1 November as Jane in *The Orange Girl*.[400] A week later she was playing Romeo in *Romeo and Juliet* with Carry George as Juliet. Again, the review mentions, patronisingly, Indians in the audience. When reviewing Rose's performance as Romeo, the critic discussed the practice of actresses playing male roles and remarked that her Romeo was 'manifestly a buxom lady playing a man's part with considerable cleverness'. The critic also noted that some 'babus' present seemed 'bewildered by changes to the text' (and, possibly, to the gender of the person playing Romeo).[401] A few months later Rose was criticised along the same lines for her role as Azael in *Azael the Prodigal*:

> Mrs. Lewis is wrong, we think, in undertaking these male characters. It is all very well ... for a hideous, bony muscular woman; but ... she is the very reverse of this, and is essentially feminine and graceful in appearance, voice and manner.[402]

Years later, a souvenir programme distributed at her Jubilee benefit attempted to discuss and justify her assumption of male roles:

> It has been frequently remarked why Mrs. Lewis so often portrays male characters and prefers men's recitations. It is easily explained, she was trained to it from infancy – her first success as the "infant Grimaldi" [a famous English clown], her second, "Puck" ... for three years at Saddler [sic] Wells she never wore petticoats, for if you think for a little, all the Shakespearian children are boys ... Then, arriving at maidenhood fell to her lot such parts as Romeo, the French Spy, Azael, etc, and nearly all the farces of that time ... [had characters who] donned pants. A critic

---

399 *Englishman*, 4 October 1873.
400 *Englishman*, 3 November 1873.
401 *Englishman*, 10 November 1873, p. 2. Females playing male roles in Shakespeare was widespread in nineteenth century in England and USA.
402 *Englishman*, 19 January 1874, p. 3.

once speaking of a performance of hers in male character, remarked – "That she was always manly, and never unwomanly".[403]

A 'Call Boy' letter written on 11 November, published in the *Australasian* of 20 December 1873, reports that the company was in difficulties and that, yet again, this was to be the last season. There was competition from opera and circus companies and the Lewis company was playing every night instead of every other evening. Their plays included *The School for Scandal*, and Shakespeare was still being tried with *The Merchant of Venice*, *Romeo and Juliet* and *Macbeth* in which on 17 and 22 November Rose took the role of Lady Macbeth. This repertoire was interspersed with Rose as the very feminine statue Galatea in the W. S. Gilbert burlesque *Pygmalion and Galatea*.

Reviews over the years almost invariably praised the performances Rose Lewis's versatility. For instance, she could play Lady Macbeth one night and Aladdin the next. This flexibility was sometimes a liability, as when a critic half expected her very dramatic Lady Macbeth to perform a minstrel-show-like 'break-down' dance at the end of the first Act:

> the only thing which prevented us from being properly thrilled by Mrs. Lewis's elocution was the knowledge that the lady on the stage apparently so earnest, was perfectly capable, if necessary, of finishing her speech with a cheerful 'breakdown'.[404]

Still in late November, 'Call Boy' reports 'Lewis's company playing every night with a repertoire including *Green Bushes*; *The Corsican Brothers*; *Pygmalion and* Galatea and *East* Lynne'.[405]

In the lead-up to the Christmas pantomime, Rose played Miss Kitty in *The Little Mother*; Princess Zeolide in W. S. Gilbert's *Palace of Truth*; Tiddy Dragglethorpe in Watts Phillips' *Lost in London*; Peg in *Masks and Faces*; and Eily in *The Colleen Bawn*. As well, during this time, the energetic Rose was training little 'cherubs' (possibly the children of colonial officials) for the pantomime *Little Tommy Tucker* and was, of course, playing Tommy Tucker herself.[406]

The panto having finished by 12 January 1874, Rose took her 'benefit' playing the comedy part of Mrs Oakly[407] in *The Jealous Wife* (the old eighteenth-

---

403 *Souvenir of Mrs. G. B. W. Lewis' Professional Jubilee Testimonial Benefit, Theatre Royal October 3rd 1902*, Miller Printing Company, Melbourne, 1902, pp. 9, 10.
404 *Englishman*, 24 November 1873, p. 2.
405 *Australasian*, 7 February 1874, p. 179
406 *Englishman*, 22 December 1873.
407 This is the correct spelling from the playscript although many critics wrote 'Oakley'.

century play based on an episode in Fielding's novel *Tom Jones*) then donning tights and toga to play the burlesque role of Glaucus in *The Very Last Days of Pompeii*. At the end of this performance, no doubt having changed quickly into an elegant dress with fashionable bustle, Rose gave an address. She had initiated some correspondence with the *Englishman* about its unfair criticism of her company, so the paper was at pains to show impartiality and print this address: 'We take the opportunity of reprinting from our contemporary the *Daily News* ... The account it contains of the fair artiste's career well deserves a place in the history of the drama.' After thanking her audience Rose commenced 'a brief narrative of my career' and tells them, rather archly, that she was born in 1844 – 'Now it is not too difficult to guess how old I am'. Mentioning how her elder brother, who was in the 'Theatre' arranged for herself and her sister [Eliza] to perform a 'Dutch Dance' during one of G. V. Brooke's productions at the Marylebone Theatre. She goes on to describe her success in 1855 as Puck in Phelps's *A Midsummer Night's Dream* and other successes in pantomime. Then she indicates some regret at having to leave London and perhaps lays some blame on her father. Rose also mentioned their success around the Australian colonies for a few years.

Thanking her audience again, she explains something of her self-driven energy in the 'arduous tasks I have imposed upon myself – almost labors beyond my power fraught as they are in this country by so many difficulties'. She then refers to the deaths of her babies, her brother, and her mother, and perhaps her sister's marriage, and her hope of a quiet life in Melbourne:

> Though Calcutta has not been all pleasure to me, having put me to so many griefs here I am happy to say I have always received great kindness both from the public and the press, except perhaps here during this season, when the *Englishman*, with its satirical and meaningless notices ... did not, I think, give the Theatre or the company fair justice. But this is a diversion. Though this is the last season I shall appear before you, yet when settled quietly at home, I shall ever turn my thoughts to ... the many kind favours I have received at your hands ... So with many heartfelt thanks, I beg to retire, wishing you all health happiness and a regretful farewell.[408]

There was still more than two months of the season left and Rose had a dozen more roles to play, but she felt her benefit performance was an appropriate

---

408 *Englishman*, 15 January 1874.

place to make a farewell speech. The 'farewell' was often a theatrical ploy to fill more seats in the house. For example, Calcutta theatregoers might tell their friends that soon Mrs Lewis would be gone forever and that they must see her last performances among them. Yet we can see some sincerity in her speech: the continual stage work since childhood and her confession that it is self-inflicted, the sadness, and the wish for quiet 'at home'.

Soon, of course, there were the anti-climaxes of her appearances in *Azael the Prodigal*, as Naomi in *School* and the wicked Mademoiselle Marco in *The Marble Heart*.[409] On 29 January Rose turned 30. In one of the few writings on Indian theatre that mention Rose she takes on an almost mythical status. She is referred to as a 'Mrs. Lewis' and how her productions and her theatre influenced the 'renaissance' of Bengali drama. We could get the impression that she was an old woman. She was certainly experienced, having started so young, but when she finally left India in 1876 she was just 32.

Her roles continued throughout February: Lizzie in *Play*, Nell in *Nell Gwynne*, the Prince in *Cinderella*, Galatea in *Pygmalion and Galatea* and Lilian in *New Men and Old Acres*.[410] Rose and Lewis had to contend with a controversy after their production of *Pygmalion and Galatea* was coupled with another W. S. Gilbert burlesque, *The Happy Land*, written with Gilbert A'Beckett and first produced in London in 1873. In Calcutta, in 1874, the Viceroy Lord Northbrook walked out after just a few minutes insulted by the localised 'satire'.[411] There are many instances in theatre history where performances were banned by politicians because of a perceived 'insult' and *The Happy Land* is notable example. It had caused trouble in London, where it satirised Gladstone and his colleagues, and in Calcutta, and later in Melbourne in 1880, where it ridiculed Victorian premier Graham Berry. The play is about three politicians who visit Fairyland and attempt to explain earthly politics to the fairy locals.[412] G. B. W. disclaimed any responsibility for the 'insult', implying that this lay with the actor G. H. Leonard. Next day Leonard wrote to the *Indian Daily News* accusing Lewis of trying to 'injure me by informing the public of Calcutta that whole affair emanated from me'.[413] The problem was serious enough for Rose to write a letter in reply the next day:

---

409 *Englishman*, 26 January 1874.
410 *Englishman*, 9 February 1874.
411 *Englishman*, 19 February 1874.
412 See Veronica Kelly, 'The Banning of Marcus Clarke's *The Happy Land*: Stage, Press and Parliament', in *Australasian Drama Studies*, Vol. 2, No. 1, pp. 71–111.
413 *Indian Daily News*, 10 March 1874.

CHAPTER NINE

I will admit that the words spoken by him at rehearsal were not disapproved of by me. I submit the lines for the perusal of the readers ... and simply ask them – are they the words spoken at night? "What does the King of India think of that? Oh they have no King it is governed from England, and the English Monarch sends an honorable gentleman there to represent her." Then followed some political allusion when the question was asked – "What does the hon'ble gentleman say to that? Oh he doesn't say much because it's below his notice, he tries to please in other places" "Does he succeed?" "Pretty well, but even he can't give satisfaction everywhere – there was a famine down there and he gave a very *handsome* sum in aid of the relief fund, just as the Monarch he represented, but the aboriginals were not satisfied – they never think that he has other claims on his bounty – 'tis true, some of the very big aboriginals gave more, but not what they ought, considering that the loss of the people by famine would have ruined their estates: besides their bread and salt does not cost them so much as it does in England". When I heard the lines, I did not think them brilliant (locals rarely are), but I did not think they were meant as an insult to His Excellency but rather a *rub* against the selfishness of the natives whose duty it is to succour such distresses while; on the part of the European community it is *charity*.

Significantly in the same letter Rose asserts that she alone had management of stage direction – 'Mr. Lewis has nothing to do with stage management.'[414]

Toward the end of February Rose was reported as being ill.[415] Perhaps she was pregnant. But on 4 March, however, she was well enough to play the role of the vivacious Polly in T. W. Robertson's *Caste* with Carry George. The Lewises gave the proceeds of the performance to the Indian Famine Fund.[416] There were great contrasts in Rose's two final roles of the season: the 'breeches' part of William in a burlesque of *Black Eyed Susan* for the Benefit of Misses May and Nelson on 5 March, and two days later as Leah in *Leah the Forsaken*. The *Englishman*'s critic of 9 March 1874, possibly with excessive nostalgia, compares Rose's interpretation with that of Kate Bateman, the famed creator of the role:

---

414 *Indian Daily News*, 11 March 1874.
415 Call Boy, *Australasian*, 2 May 1874, p. 563.
416 *Englishman*, 5 March 1874.

> In common with Miss Bateman she has been from childhood before the foot-lights, is an equally well-trained actress … but unlike Miss Bateman, whose genius has yielded one solitary but perfect flower, *Leah*, Mrs. Lewis's talent has been frittered away in the representations of a multiplicity of characters … When Mrs. Lewis thus concentrates her powers into one channel … she may then cross the gulf that yawns between obscurity and fame, and soar above the mere grace and cleverness that she has exhibited in *Leah*.

For the rest of her career Rose was unwilling or unable to take this advice – versatility remained her 'stock-in-trade'.

A few days later the company at 'loggerheads and at law' broke up. The Lewises and Rose's sister-in-law Lizzie Bryer returned to Melbourne, arriving on 4 May. The *Era*'s Calcutta correspondent described the 1873–1874 season as the 'weakest' to date.[417] Yet Lewis was reputed to have made £80 000 in India.

Rose had her 'quiet time at home' for some months. On 16 November her brother John Bryer and his wife Tilly Earl arrived on the *Northumberland*.[418] They had been playing with Lydia Thompson's company in America and London but it is possible that John was already ill with tuberculosis.

Meanwhile, by 1873, the Indian National Theatre was gaining some ground. Under the heading 'Amusements in India' the *Australasian* reports that:

> among the advances in the direction of native amusements the latest phase of educated Bengalese progress is the very successful establishment of a National Theatre in which vernacular plays are put upon a small stage … this "National Theatre" is a genuine adaption of European modes to native dramatic literature.

According to a Melbourne weekly, in April 1873 plays were staged at a private house in Chitpur Road in the 'native town of Calcutta'.[419] In October 1873, amid much celebration, the foundation stone of the Great National Theatre was laid in Beadon Street in what was known to the colonial authorities as the 'black town' north of the 'white town' around Chowringee. The *Englishman* reported that 'the spot was filled with a large number of educated natives' and that a 'European band, with flags bearing the inscription 'The laying of

---

417 *Era*, 19 April 1874.
418 *Weekly Times*, 21 November 1874, p. 9.
419 *Australasian*, 26 July 1873, p. 115.

CHAPTER NINE

the foundation stone of the Great National Theatre' played along Beadon Street.[420] By March 1874 performances at the Great National Theatre, Beadon Street, were being advertised in the *Indian Daily News*.[421] From this time the theatre of the Bengal renaissance was established.

---

420 *Englishman*, 3 October 1872.
421 *Indian Daily News*, 14 March 1874; Chatterjee, op. cit., pp. 117ff. The Minerva Theatre, built in 1894, is on the site of the Great National Theatre.

Chapter ten

EMPLOYING THE WILLIAMSONS, 1875–1876

By the middle of 1875, Rose's 'quiet time' at home was over. Young George was at nearby Mr Bernard Stacy's South Yarra College[422] and in late April the Lewises and six year old Victoria May sailed to Sydney on the *City of Adelaide*,[423] probably to negotiate with James Cassius Williamson about a season in India. At the time Williamson and his then wife Maggie Moore were busy at the Queen's Theatre with their smash hit *Struck Oil*, a play set during the American Civil War, where Williamson played an old (Pennsylvania) Dutchman with Maggie Moore as his daughter.[424] By 13 July the *Era*'s Melbourne correspondent (probably Dr Neild) was reporting that 'Mr. Lewis has prepared another company [for India] with the Williamsons'.[425] Meanwhile, in Bengal on 31 July, Frances Mary Grahame was born to William Forbes Grahame, indigo planter, and his wife Julia Lucy, née Bryer, of Naurthpore. The child was baptised at St John's Church, Calcutta.[426]

Lewis let his house on St Kilda Road and made his will, dated 6 August 1875.[427] The Lewises left Melbourne for Bombay on 10 August on the *Pera*. With them was a troupe of 14 males including W. G. Carey (a New South Wales born actor who was the new leading man), John Edouin and Rose's ten-year-old nephew George Bryer, and 13 female artistes including Tilly Earl and a new actress the Baronne de Sers, a Sydney born young woman supposedly married to a man styled 'Baron de Sers'. 'With the sanction of

---

422 Wesley College Archives. Information from Andrew Lemon.
423 *Argus*, 28 April 1875.
424 Ruth Vasey and Elizabeth Wright, compliers, *A Calendar of Sydney Theatrical Performances 1870–1879*, Australian Theatres Studies Centre, School of Theatre Studies, University of New South Wales, 1986, p. 136.
425 *Era*, 19 September 1875.
426 Baptism Record, 1 September 1875 [Bengal Volume 153, p. 9].
427 He appointed Rose, Elizabeth Edouin Bryer and Willie Edouin as executors, with Rose and their children as beneficiaries.

her father', the Baronne de Sers had made her debut at the Victoria Theatre in Sydney in June 1874.[428] Also on the steamer was George Benjamin Allen's musical troupe of 47, led by soprano Alice May.[429]

The Lewis Dramatic and Burlesque Company opened at the Bombay Grant Road Theatre on 9 September 1875, where they were to play until 23 September. The first production was the burlesque *Ivanhoe*. Tilly Earl, fresh from the experience of playing in the USA and England with Lydia Thompson's company, was one of those singled out for her amusing performance of Wanibi that 'made the audience in love with folly'.[430] Critics also approved the use of music from *Mam'zelle Angot*, the dancing of sisters Jessie and Ruth Grey, and several other 'pretty girls with undeniable legs'.[431]

Rose did not appear until 13 September when she starred in *Led Astray*, Boucicault's 1874 adaptation of the French drama *La Tentation*, the first of three plays advertised as 'Modern Society Dramas'. *Led Astray* was followed by *True as Steel* and Wilkie Collins's 1873 play (shortly to be published as a novel) *The New Magdalen*. Was Rose trying to take the advice of the critic from 1874 and concentrate on serious roles? She did not play burlesque while in Bombay. As Mercy Merrick in *The New Magdalen* she played a character that society had forced to become a 'fallen woman' and whose chance to 'redeem' herself involved impersonating another young woman. As usual, Rose was hailed for her acting as 'a perfect mistress of her art', but 'La Baronne de Sers' playing her wicked foil obtained a very unfavourable review:

> The Baroness de Sers had a very unpleasant role to fulfil, and, she did her best to look hateful and malicious … She possesses many personal gifts and when thoroughly trained will be a very superior actress … It was a severe ordeal for a *debutante* – and the Baroness was little more – to have to sustain a part which no art could succeed in making other than unpleasant not to say repulsive.[432]

Why did the Lewises engage the Baroness? On the one hand they may have been impressed with her title; on the other, perhaps Rose thought the

---

428 *Times of India*, 15 September 1875; Vasey and Wright, op. cit., p. 118. De Sers had played a supporting role in *East Lynne*.
429 PROV, VPRS 948, Passenger List of *Pera; Argus*, 9 August 1875. For an account of Alice May's life see Adrienne Simpson, *Alice May: Gilbert and Sullivan's First Prima Donna*, Routledge, New York, 2001.
430 *Times of India*, 10 September 1875.
431 *Friend of India*, 25 September 1875, p. 884.
432 *Times of India*, 18 September 1875.

contrast in acting ability would enhance her own role and continue her dominance of the company.

In the midst of all this 'society' melodrama, real tragedy struck Rose and her family. The next day her brother John died from Pulmonary Phthisis (tuberculosis), aged 35.[433] John had been nursed by his wife Tilly. Rose was advertised to play Leah on the day after her brother died. The 'show went on'[434] despite the death in the family, Rose, in her grief, possibly bringing more pathos to the role.

The last two nights of the short Bombay season were taken up with New South Wales born W. G. Carey playing the title role in *Othello*, with de Sers as Desdemona, and with Rose's benefit on the last night, 22 September, Rose performing as Peg Woffington in her beloved *Masks and Faces*. The critic of the *Times of India* of 23 September found Carey's Othello 'exceedingly good' but was disappointed in the small house for a rare performance of Shakespeare. Rose's benefit, however, had a large house with numbers of Indians, 'the stage appreciating Zoroastrian [Parsee] was there in force and had brought his wife and daughter; there was also the educated Hindu' in the audience. In his farewell speech Mr Lewis promised to bring 'two stars of the first magnitude' when he returned to Bombay.[435] Lewis was referring to J. C. Williamson and his wife Maggie Moore.

The company returned to a different Calcutta theatre scene from that which they had left in 1874. Then the main rivals for audiences were Cagli's Opera or the various touring circuses on the Maidan. After the Lewises' seeming retirement a meeting was held in the Town Hall and a 'theatrical committee' was formed to raise funds for a theatre season. Others, led by a former 'utility player' of Lewis's company George Anderson, built a new theatre, the Corinthian, on Dhumatollah Street, not far from the Opera House and the Lewis's Theatre Royal. A company from London led by a Mr and Mrs English arrived for the 1874–1875 season.[436] By the time of the Lewises return for the 1875–1876 season, the Corinthian Theatre housed the Alice May company with their offerings of English operas, interspersed with some performances of Gounod's *Faust*.[437] The Opera House was occupied by English's Comedy and Burlesque Company, and with the promise that the famous English comedian Charles Mathews would perform in December.

---

433 Ecclesiastical Records Madras, Vol. 49, p. 312; 'John Edouin dies of consumption in Calcutta', *Australasian*, 30 October 1875, p. 565.
434 *Times of India*, 24 September 1875.
435 ibid.
436 *Friend of India*, 18 September 1875, p. 865.
437 Mr Dangle, 'The Rise and Fall of the Calcutta Stage', *The Theatre*, 1 August 1881, p. 90.

CHAPTER TEN

The Corinthian Theatre in Calcutta, a rival to Lewis's Theatre Royal. *Indian Charivari*, 11 December 1874.
British Library

Nonetheless the Lewises' advance advertising promised two American actors, James Cassius Williamson and Maggie Moore, as part of the company for a 'limited number of nights' who 'have lately proved themselves the most successful Stars who have visited Australia'. Those who read the Australian newspapers would have noted the huge success of the couple in Melbourne, Sydney and Adelaide. Of course Rose was, as usual, giving 'her assistance and superintendence to the company ... and Mr Lewis [was] to spare no expense in producing on the Stage of the Theatre Royal the newest and most successful pieces of the Modern Stage, not omitting some established favorites'.[438]

The pattern of the Lewises' earlier seasons in Calcutta and Bombay was more or less followed in their final ones: the Calcutta season opened with the *Ivanhoe* burlesque allowing Rose a few days before launching into her 'heavy' melodramas and clever pantomimes. She played Armande, the almost erring wife in *Led Astray*, the pure Parthenia in the 1851 drama *Ingomar the*

---

438 *Englishman*, 1 September 1875.

Barbarian and the haughty Pauline in Lord Lytton's 1838 play *The Lady of Lyons*,[439] thus fulfilling Lewis's promise of playing a mix of old and new plays.

With the prospect of the Prince of Wales's visit to India there was hope that the influx of his entourage and other visitors would enhance the takings in the three theatres, but by 9 October the *Englishman's Weekly* commented on the small houses in all three theatres. The 'Lewis Troupe, with the exception of the of their opening night, when they had quite an ovation [are] subsisting chiefly on expectation … [the Lewis Company] … is said to be a fairly strong one … without any conspicuous talent, barring of course, the versatile manageress herself'. Rose played Mercy Merrick in *The New Magdalen* on 19 October again with the 'Baroness' de Sers who was, by this time, more competent in the part of the 'villainess'.

On 15 November the Williamsons arrived in Calcutta in order to open in *Struck Oil* on 20 November. The front page of the *Indian Daily News, Bengal Hurkaru* of 19 November 1875, advertised the three theatres across the front page for their performances on 20 November. Two of the theatres, interestingly enough, were directed by women: English's Theatre, Directress Mrs E. English, with a varied programme of farce and a piece by Farnie with music by Alfred Plumpton a British conductor who performed in Australia; Lewis's Theatre Royal, Directress Mrs G. B. W. Lewis, with the 'first appearance in Calcutta of Miss Maggie Moore and Mr J. C. Williamson; and the Corinthian Theatre, Director G. B. Allen with Miss Alice May's English Opera Company in Offenbach's *Genevieve de Brabant*. This was a full 'menu' for the relatively small European community of Calcutta.

The reviews of all three performances reported fair houses, but the Williamsons and their play *Struck Oil* received the most glowing reports.[440] The critic of the *Daily News* was impressed by the skill of the two actors.

> We have to notice simply a most admirable performance, such as has not been seen for many years in Calcutta, if indeed, we might not absolutely say, such as was never before witnessed in this city. And if we proceed to analyse the whole it will be found that the success depends upon the happy combination of two elements – a striking drama – no pun intended – and an admirable exposition of its characters and incidents … Mr. Williamson steps out of himself into the Dutchman, and Mrs. Williamson so transforms herself from a lady into a gawkish, mischievous, rollicking girl.

---

439 *Australasian*, 18 December 1875, p. 787.
440 *Indian Daily News, Bengal Hurkaru*, 22 November 1875; *Englishman*, 23 November 1875.

CHAPTER TEN

The *Englishman*'s review referred to the high expectations of the public and that the house, though a good one, should have 'been crowded ceiling to floor … praise is always more difficult than censure. To describe the excellence of Saturday's performance in adequate terms would probably be impossible …' As well as devoting much space to Maggie's acting, which the critic particularly liked, he admired Williamson's highly realistic rendering of John Stofel as the happy Dutchman … [which] combined irresistible humour with great pathos, while as the crazy Dutchman, he was quite a psychological study, and in the more painful parts, there was a weird grandeur about his acting that was most impressive'.

In their five-week season the Williamsons presented *Struck Oil*, *Kerry*, *Little Nell* and *Rip van Winkle*. They were supported by the Lewis company except for Rose. Her name was still at the head of advertisements as 'Directress'. It would be interesting to know her opinion of the American couple. Did she admire Maggie's accomplishments? How did they get on? Was she jealous of the large houses and the unanimous critical approval? Or did Rose take an opportunity to rest a while? In December Rose had to start rehearsing the pantomime that would interrupt the Williamson season for a week or two. G. B. W. must have been happy with the box-office results. In a letter dated 30 December 1875, Williamson wrote to actor Henry Edwards in America about the poor houses at Lewis's Theatre Royal before their arrival, 'However, we pulled business up immediately and [ran] *Struck Oil* two weeks', a thing hitherto unheard of in Calcutta.[441]

The huge success of the Williamsons did not stop Rose's new pantomime opening on 27 December. *Harlequin Blue Beard or, the Heathen Chinee and the Fairy of the Rippling Waters* had been sent by her brother Willie Edouin from Lydia Thompson's company in London. This was another orientalist/racist romp with Rose as the Prince Selim.

The Williamsons had been playing continuously since the middle of November and may have been grateful for the break. J. C. Williamson found time to visit Charles Mathews at English's theatre. It was in Mathews' dressing room that Williamson met the Prince of Wales.[442] However, with the opening of the Charles Mathews season at the Corinthian Theatre, the Lewises seemed to be facing stiff competition. Mathews was one of the most popular comedians on the English stage. He was returning to London from a successful tour of Australia and was engaged to play in Calcutta by

---

441 Ian G. Dicker, *J.C.W.: A Short Biography of James Cassius Williamson*, Elizabeth Tudor Press, Rose Bay, NSW, 1974, p. 67.
442 ibid.

English's company.⁴⁴³ But although the critics applauded his performances even his season was not a financial success.⁴⁴⁴

The Lewis pantomime was a critical success. After discussing the varying merits of both pantomime and burlesque, the review compliments Lewis for an especially well-made panto, from the performances led by Rose who showed 'grace and nameless charm' as Selim, through Madame de Sers as Sister Anne to Tilly Earl as Fatima – who looked 'charming and played with rare and humorous intelligence. She has gained in *chic* and *verve*'. The scenery and great stage effects of rippling fountains by the scenic designer Mr Pitt were also singled out for praise.⁴⁴⁵

The Williamsons returned to Lewis's Theatre Royal for three farewell nights after the close of the pantomime. Their final performance was in the last two acts of *Struck Oil* and *The Fool of the Family* on 12 January 1876. The Calcutta weekly, *Friend of India*, of 15 January 1876, reported the farewell performance: 'Of the excellence of the acting it would be superfluous for us to speak … Mr. Williamson's splendid impersonation of the crazy Dutchman, John Stofel, and … Mrs. Williamson's brilliant rendering of the part of his daughter Lizzie'.⁴⁴⁶ Williamson gave a short speech. However, the Williamson's plans did not accord with Lewis's promise to bring back two stars to Bombay. They left for London via Bombay on 13 January without playing in that city.⁴⁴⁷ In Calcutta, the Lewis Company had to play until 29 January and then proceed to Bombay via Allahabad and the 'show towns'. After some success in London and the provinces, Williamson soon returned to Australia to found the theatre management firm, J. C. Williamson's, which lasted until 1974.

After the excitement of the Williamsons the Lewis Company returned to their old repertoire for the last two weeks of the Calcutta season. W. G. Carey resumed his place as 'leading man' in the Charles Reade drama *Hard Cash*, Rosa Cooper played one of Rose Lewis's roles as Lady Isabel in *East Lynne*, and Tilly took the part of Polly in *Caste*.⁴⁴⁸

On 17 January Rose returned as Eily in *The Colleen Bawn*, where her young nephew George Bryer played a servant. Rose played Leah for the last time in Calcutta on 21 January. The notice in the *Indian Daily News, Bengal Hurkaru* commented that it was Mrs Lewis's 'great impersonation …

---

443   *Indian Daily News, Bengal Hurkaru*, 21 December 1875. Mathews' dates: 1803–1878.
444   *Bristol Mercury*, 8 January 1876 (quoted from *The Times*).
445   *Englishman*, 29 December 1875.
446   *Friend of India*, 15 January 1876, p. 57.
447   *Englishman*, 11 January 1876.
448   *Indian Daily News, Bengal Hurkaru*, 19 January 1876; review of *Caste*, 22 January 1876.

CHAPTER TEN

A caricature of the Lewises in *Indian Charivari*, 4 February 1876. This is the only image yet found depicting Rose in Calcutta. It was attached to a farewell complimentary verse in this *Punch*-like weekly.
British Library

and a favourite one ... and has always drawn a large audience but when it is known that this is Mrs. Lewis's last appearance in this character ... it will be a "bumper".

The Lewis Dramatic and Burlesque Company gave their last performance on 29 January 1876. The programme consisted of 'W. S. Gilbert's charming mythological comedy' *Pygmalion and Galatea* and the Examination scene from *School*.[449] The *Indian Daily News, Bengal Hurkaru* of that date took the opportunity to remark briefly on the history of Lewis's reinvigoration of theatre in their city, how before his arrival in 1867 there had been few professional theatrical performances. The critic applauded Lewis's courage when his first theatre was destroyed by a cyclone, and how he did not accept the help that would have been available:

> Every season he has produced such novelties as have been within the range of the possible in Calcutta ... How ably he has been supported by Mrs. Lewis ... [who] has been almost a slave to her profession: a most cheerful and willing one certainly; yet there are few players who have worked so hard.[450]

---

449 *Indian Daily News, Bengal Hurkaru*, 31 January 1876.
450 *Indian Daily News, Bengal Hurkaru*, 29 January 1876.

The review in the *Indian Daily News, Bengal Hurkaru* two days later first acknowledged Rose's skill in the part of Galatea: 'Mrs. Lewis showing all that naïve simplicity and innocence which makes the character so interesting and amusing, by the quiet satire upon social life and human nature generally'. The review described Lewis leading Rose on to the stage at the curtain and then proceeded to report Lewis's farewell speech. Allowing that the reporter may not have given a verbatim account, the speech seems rambling and rather self-justifying. For example, after congratulating himself for being independent and not relying, like his rivals on subscriptions of up to 'Rs. 40 000', Lewis declared that he had not made a profit from the season 'Indeed he had lost – a little'. Before the arrival of the Williamsons he had been losing 'Rs. 2 000 per week'.

Another theme in the speech was the respectability of his company:

> He had tried to do his best for his patrons and friends, and had always made it a duty to bring a respectable company and to keep it so, as he studied respectability as well as talent … He had endeavoured to bring the best available talent and he was proud of having introduced to the Calcutta public two such artists as Mr. and Mrs. Williamson … Yet though they were an undoubted success he did not double the prices or charge extra.

The problem from 1874, when the Viceroy had left the performance of the *Happy Land*, obviously still rankled with Lewis:

> Still his Excellency took no offence; but he thought it hard that a manager should suffer for the faults of a member of his company. However he felt some compensation in the fact that though the Prince of Wales had not an opportunity of giving his patronage to the theatre during his late visit, His Excellency the Viceroy had bestowed and was well pleased, [Mr Lewis] thanked him heartily – farewell.[451]

The paper also reported that Lewis had sold his interest in the Theatre Royal. On 31 January, the Parsee Operatic & Dramatic Troupe opened at Lewis's Theatre in the 'Ever fresh, Ever New Opera of *Indur Sabha*'.[452]

Taking the train to Allahabad where they played six nights, and then on to Bombay, the Lewis Company opened in that city at the Grant Road Theatre on 8 February with Rose as Eily in *The Colleen Bawn*. The *Times of India* of 9 February, welcoming the company for its second appearance in

---

451   *Indian Daily News, Bengal Hurkaru*, 31 January 1876.
452   *Englishman*, 6 April 1876, p. 1.

CHAPTER TEN

four months, gave Rose a favourable review as Eily and praised W. G. Carey as the roguish Myles-Na-Coppaleen. Rose's second characterisation was as the statue Galatea in *Pygmalion and Galatea*:

> The statue Galatea, is played by Mrs. Lewis, and to the qualities of exact and careful acting must be added a wonderful power to pose herself, motionless for a long time, thus doing away with the real statue which several English theatres substituted for the actress whenever convenient. The splendid passage wherein Galatea describes herself as timidly expanding into life, the mortal and the marble still struggling, was beautifully rendered by Mrs. Lewis.[453]

The company continued playing every night, but an unpleasant incident occurred when George Lewis was assaulted by Henry Burton, one of his actors. According to the court report, Burton had attacked Lewis with a stick while the latter was watching a performance from the Dress Circle. Burton pleaded guilty, saying that he had been provoked by Lewis who 'grossly insulted a most respectable lady, called her by the vilest names, in the presence of nobody but his wife'. (One of the actresses must have complained to Burton). The Magistrate fined the actor 40 rupees.[454] Burton then sued Lewis for wrongful dismissal. Lewis counter-sued for the return of the passage money. Burton was ordered to pay Lewis £25 for the fare from Australia.[455] These incidents took on a tragic note a few weeks later when Burton died of smallpox, then rife in the city.[456]

Rose was performing her established roles such as Zoë in *The Octoroon* and Esther in *Caste*. She also worked hard drilling her chorus of child 'Amazons' in the burlesque *The Island of Jewels*, and the production of the 'Christmas Pantomime' *Harlequin Blue Beard* from 26 February. This was advertised as the 'only appearance of this season with Mrs. Lewis as Selim.' The newspaper reported a 'crowded house' for *Blue Beard* which was 'a piece perfectly bristling with witticisms and "local hits", and it is really astonishing how Mrs. Lewis can act so much, sing so often and dance … so well without showing any signs of fatigue'.[457]

On Monday 28 February, possibly while reading this favourable newspaper review, the Lewises received a telegram from Melbourne with horrific news. Their six-year-old daughter Victoria May, having survived being born

---

453 *Times of India*, 12 February 1876.
454 *Times of India*, 18 February 1876.
455 *Times of India*, 2 March 1876.
456 *Times of India*, 16 March 1876.
457 *Times of India*, 28 February 1876.

in plague-ridden India, had died from scarlet fever, probably at a boarding school in Carlisle Street, St Kilda.[458] In the Lewises' absence, a notice was inserted in the Melbourne *Argus* by Lewis's solicitor Henry Westley who managed the family's affairs in Melbourne. About this time Westley probably bought a large burial plot for the family at the Melbourne General Cemetery.[459] The Bombay newspaper of 1 March erroneously reported the death of 'Mrs. Lewis's son, a boy of seven' and went on to review the pantomime, Miss Benison having taken the part at short notice after Rose's 'domestic calamity'. Not surprisingly, Rose did not perform for ten days after (in the words of the newspaper) 'her heavy bereavement'. In her farewell speech in January 1874, she had mentioned the 'grief' that she had experienced in India. Then she was referring to the deaths of her infant son and daughters, her brother Charles in 1869 and her mother's death in 1873. Now she was leaving India with the knowledge that she also had lost her brother John and her only surviving daughter. Many people would have had a mental collapse at such grief, but the show business work ethic was strong in Rose's family and on 8 March she reappeared in the highly emotional melodrama *The New Magdalene*. The review refers to 'moistened eyes' among the audience. Probably many were moved with sympathy for the actress as well as for her portrayal. Yet the next night she played a humorous part in the comedy *The Serious Family*, followed next by Byron's burlesque *Esmeralda; or, the Sensation Goat*. Was this her way of coping? From the time of her sister Eliza's lonely death at Daylesford in 1857 she was used to performing despite grief. What of G. B. W. Lewis? Just after the news of Victoria's death he had to appear in court regarding Burton's attack. He was now 58. As *paterfamilias* both of his company and his children, he must have been affected.

During the time of Rose's mourning the company performed competently. *Black Sheep* by Palgrave Simpson was given at 'short notice' and W. G. Carey was praised for his performance of Mathias in the famous Henry Irving vehicle *The Bells*. Actresses such as Rosa Cooper and Agnes Benison and dancers Jessie and Ruth Grey perhaps gained a little more prominence with Rose prostrated at her lodgings.

Over the years there seems to have been a 'falling off' in the quality of the company, Mrs Lewis and a few other cast members excepted. There was

---

458   Death Certificate, dated 26 February 1876.
459   Victoria May was later singled out as a particularly treasured child (she was to be the only one apart from George Encyl to survive infancy). Under her name the Lewis grave carries the inscription: *She Is Not Dead But Sleeps In The Arms Of Jesus/Now Like A Dew-Drop Shrined Within A Crystal Stone/Thou Art Safe In Heaven My Dove/Safe With The Source Of Love/The Everlasting One.*

trouble during the 1874 season when dissatisfaction among the actors with the Lewis management caused some of the company to be at 'logger-heads and at law'. The *Era* Calcutta correspondent dubbed it the 'weakest season yet'.[460]

Nevertheless, some of the actors who experienced some success in Australia benefited from the tours of India. These included Carry George, who could play some of Rose's roles, and her husband Robert Lawrence. They were part of the 1873–1874 company. The 1875–1876 season saw another Australian-born actor, W. G. Carey, who later had a theatre in Calcutta, taking 'first leading man' roles. The sisters Ruth and Jessie Grey also had important careers in Australia in the late nineteenth century.

Meanwhile, Mr Lewis's farewell speeches in India increasingly had a querulous tone – there had not been sufficient profit – he had large expenses and so on. The troubles reached a climax in 1876 when after a successful farewell season in Calcutta and a gruelling tour to the hill towns and Bombay, Lewis accused some of the young women of his company of keeping unsuitable company with their followers (often called 'stage-door Johnnies'). At the Bombay farewell, he railed against these 'counter-jumpers' and apparently described the young women as being 'loose women' or, as the Calcutta *Statesman* primly put it, "*lâches*".[461]

Viewed from the twenty-first century, the content of the Lewis repertoire seems often racist, imperialist, orientalist and melodramatic but here the company was reflecting the popular taste and largely unquestioned attitudes of London and Melbourne. Reading the mainly London texts of the heavy melodramas and the atrocious puns of the burlesques and pantos can be very 'trying'. But this type of popular theatre can be seen as a transition from the formal stage play of the mid-century to the more natural acting style and realist drama of the late nineteenth century: the theatre of Sydney Grundy, H. A. Jones, Pinero, Ibsen, Wilde and Shaw.[462]

The Lewis company was only one of many entertainment troupes that visited Calcutta in the mid to late nineteenth century, but they were the first to stay for any length of time: nine years. They influenced Calcutta theatre in the form of their public purpose-built proscenium theatre itself and by their repertoire and production values. Considering that the company gave six seasons in Calcutta, three in Bombay and toured from Calcutta to Simla and

---

460 *Era*, 19 April 1874, p. 10.
461 *Indian Daily News, Bengal Hurkaru*, 6 April 1876, quotation from the *Statesman*.
462 The Brough company brought the dramas of Grundy, Jones and Wilde to India in the 1890s. See forthcoming book by Elisabeth Kumm of Melbourne.

back several times, together, with two sojourns back in Melbourne, there is little 'public memory' about this nine-year achievement in either Melbourne or India. A survey of works on the history of theatre in India scarcely finds any reference to the Lewis troupe.[463] S. K. Mukerjee and others mention the Lewis theatre only in passing. These works usually refer mainly to the fact that the Lewis Theatre building was used as a model by the new wave of Indian dramatists during the 1870s.[464] In both Australia and England, the Lewises and their time in India seem almost forgotten by theatre historians despite the fact that the Lewises managed an important theatre in Melbourne after their return from India and that Mrs Lewis became a 'star' 'as an old woman' in London's West End during the 1910s.

Astonishingly Florence Brough, in her memoir written in England in 1923, *My Life on the Stage,* when recalling the Australian based Robert Brough Company's visit to India in 1895, knew nothing of the Lewises' seasons. She believed that her husband's company with about thirteen players was the largest western theatre troupe to yet visit Calcutta (Lewis's seasons usually numbered about 21 players). Moreover the Brough troupe performed in the very theatre that Lewis had built, the Theatre Royal.[465]

Importantly, Girish Chandra Ghosh, often called the 'founder of modern Indian theatre', acknowledged his debt to the Lewises in his memoirs.[466] S. K. Mukerjee has pointed to the playwrights in the National Theatre and Great National Theatre groups of the 1870s using the pantomime form to parody the 'Raj'.[467] Perhaps the Lewis presentation of *Lalla Rookh*, or other localised pantomimes and extravaganzas where Bengalis are parodied, influenced Ghosh and his colleagues to 'turn the tables' on the British Establishment.

Utpal Dutt in his book on Ghosh mentions that Mrs Lewis was an 'admirer of Girish whose 1875 performance in *Sadhababar Ekadashi* [The Widow's Nuptials] she considered a masterpiece'. I have yet to find the source of this reference.[468] Dutt's statement that the Theatre Royal on Chowringhee was of

---

463 This is surprising as there are many advertisements and reviews in the Anglophone press in India and in Melbourne newspapers. Sudipto Chatterjee in *The Colonial Staged*, connects Giresh Chandra Ghosh with the Lewises.
464 S.K. Mukerjee, *Story of Indian Theatre,* K.P. Bagchi & Company, Calcutta, 1982, pp. 1, 7, 41, 53.
465 *Adelaide Advertiser*, 10–29 December 1923. I am indebted to Elisabeth Kumm for discovering this reference.
466 I am indebted to Dr Sudipto Chatterjee for information regarding the influence of the Lewises on Giresh Chandra Ghosh. It is interesting that Ghosh and Rose Edouin Lewis were born in the same year, 1844.
467 Mukerjee, op. cit., p. 35.
468 Utpal Dutt, *Girish Chandra Ghosh*, Sahitya Akademi, Calcutta, 1992, p. 13. Some historians have confused Mrs Lewis with an American actress of that name, possibly

CHAPTER TEN

Elizabethan design, however, is mystifying – in fact the theatre was the later proscenium style of a mid-nineteenth-century theatre. Perhaps something has been lost in translation.

The great and revered Indian actress Binodini Dasi, writing in her autobiographies, was aware of some Western influence on the new Indian theatre of the 1870s. She mentions 'Mrs. Lewis's theatre' but does not write in detail. Binodini was only eleven years old when she began her stage career in 1874 and perhaps Rose, with her own experience of juvenile performance and interest in teaching stage skills to children, would have appreciated the talent of the young girl. It would be interesting to know if Binodini and Rose ever met. At such times one wishes that Rose's diaries had survived. Binodini mentions that she was 'anxious to see the performances of any famous British actor or actress' who came to the city and that 'the proprietors of the theatres' arranged for her to see English plays.[469] A performance at the Lewis Theatre Royal may have been one of these.

In retrospect, Lewis's engagement of the Americans James Cassius Williamson and his wife Maggie Moore to play in *Struck Oil* and other plays in Calcutta was perhaps Lewis's most successful management coup. The Williamsons were very popular in Calcutta as the *Friend of India* and other newspapers asserted:

> The most successful hit of the season has undoubtedly been 'Struck Oil' at Lewis's … The playing of Mr. J. C. Williamson and Miss Maggie Moore, who sustain the principal parts, is of a higher order than we often witness in Calcutta.[470]

While Lewis made a fortune from his foreign tours, the remainder of his and his wife's careers cannot compare with that of the Williamsons'. Although G. B. W. Lewis became the first lessee of a new theatre in Melbourne – the Academy of Music, later known as the Bijou – with, as in Calcutta, Rose as 'Directress', their management skills were soon to be challenged. Would the theatregoing public of Melbourne remember the talented Rose Edouin after an interval of nine years?

Mrs Jefferys Lewis.
469 Binodini Dasi, *My Story* and *My Life as an Actress*, edited and translated by Rimli Bhattacharya, Kali for Women, New Delhi, 1998, p. 79.
470 *Friend of India*, 27 November 1875, p. 1061.

Chapter eleven

THE VICTORIAN ACADEMY OF MUSIC, 1876–1879

Arriving back in Melbourne in April 1876 after their bereavements and their last Indian seasons, the Lewises might have been expected to rest and recover their energies at Shanghai Villa. Rose Lewis was only 32 but had been almost continually 'on the road' for twelve years. G. B. W. was 58 but was to remain vigorous well into old age.[471] So, having noted the news in the *Australasian* of plans for the construction of a new theatre in Bourke Street to be called the Academy of Music,[472] George decided to become lessee of the new theatre. He probably thought that it would, after his managerial experience in India, be a good investment of whatever profit he had made in Asia.[473] It would also make a suitable showplace for Rose's talents. The venture was driven by Melbourne investor Joseph Aarons. A London born businessman, Aarons had arrived in Melbourne in 1852 in his early twenties. Since then he had been a furniture and fancy-goods importer, trade assignee, a city alderman, a justice of the peace, and government insurance broker. Aarons was to invest up to £45 000 in the building of the Victoria Arcade and the Academy of Music.[474] The licence was issued to George Lewis through his agent and solicitor Henry Westley.[475]

---

471 *Age*, 9 July 1938, a letter-writer in the column 'Melodious Memories' stated that 'he was a magnificent man – about 6 feet 3 inches tall – and even in his later years he lost none of his height by stooping.'
472 *Australasian*, 26 February 1876; a column in the *Otago Witness*, 14 June 1905, p. 60, mentions Lewis's negotiations with Joseph Aarons. Plans for a new Melbourne theatre to be called the 'Bijou' had been mentioned in the *Era*, 4 April 1875 promoted by a former lessee of the Princess's named Holmes but nothing seems to have come of this.
473 There is no record of his profits in Asia, just hearsay in the theatrical gossip columns.
474 *Men of the Time in Australia*, Victorian Series, M'Carron, Bird, Melbourne, 1878, p. 1.
475 VPRS 3991/P Unit 1136 File 2712; apart from public records and newspaper reports direct links between the Lewises and Melbourne theatrical people are lacking. But, interestingly, Westley was married to Alice Wiseman, sister of Fanny Wiseman, who

CHAPTER ELEVEN

Lewis was taking a risk in his ambition to run a theatre in Melbourne. The city already had three theatres, and one of them, the Princess's, was dark at the time of his new theatre's opening. The Prince of Wales Opera House, also known as just the Opera House, opened in August 1872 in Bourke Street opposite the Theatre Royal. The well-thought-of Indian-born Shakespearian actress Mrs (Mary Frances) Scott-Siddons, a great-granddaughter of Sarah Siddons,[476] was doing good business at the Theatre Royal, and the Opera House was showing a popular minstrel type show. Each of these theatres could hold up to 3000. There was a risk therefore that Melbourne theatregoers might not flock to yet another venue playing a mixture of music and drama. Rose, now billed as a 'comedienne', might have to struggle to show her versatility in 'serious' plays and to rival, say, Mrs. Scott-Siddons.

Meanwhile G. B. W. realised he would need to sell some of his properties and nearly all, except Shanghai Villa, were put up for sale in October. Foremost were the four houses of George's Terrace near the corner of St Kilda and Commercial Roads. Other property included land along St Kilda Road and in the relatively new suburb of Elsternwick. It seems only the Elsternwick land was sold.[477] This, together with Lewis's profit from India and mortgages on other property, evidently was enough to support the stock company and other expenses of the proposed theatre.

Melbourne audiences had not had much opportunity to see Rose since her days of playing mainly 'second leads' in Barry Sullivan's company in the mid-1860s plus a few performances during their visits from India. Since then, of course, she had gained the confidence and experience of being star and director of her own theatre company in India and China, where reviews of her performances were usually very favourable. Perhaps she and her husband were carried away with ambition based on her success in the non-competitive market of Anglophone theatre in Asia. Melbourne audiences had, however, from the 1860s become more discerning, with visits from London's West End and British provincial stars such as Ellen Kean, Céline Céleste, Louisa Cleveland and Mary Gladstane.[478] Rose had worked

---

as Mrs South had played in the first Lewis Company in Calcutta. The Wisemans were Rose's juvenile fellow performers from the 1850s, so it seems that here was connection that helped Lewis choose his solicitor.

476 One of the sons of Sarah Siddons had worked with the East India Company in Calcutta and his grand-daughter became the actress known as Mrs. Scott-Siddons.
477 See *Argus* classified advertisements 26 October 1876; see also similar advertisements in *Argus* 26 January 1882. I have not been able to check the results of any of these sales.
478 For Cleveland and Gladstane see Janette Gordon-Clarke, 'The Progress of the Stars: Actresses and their Repertories in Australia from the 1850s to the 1890s', Ph.D. Thesis, Department of English, Monash University, 2000, chapters 2 and 3.

with Cleveland, would have seen Ellen Kean and Céleste but most likely had missed seeing Gladstane while in Asia. Moreover the Lewises had left Melbourne on their last tour of India in August 1875 just before two great international actresses, Francesca Janauschek and Adelaide Ristori, albeit well on in their careers, had arrived to give drama seasons in Australia. Rose would have read about these great tragediennes in theatre newspapers and, as seen in her repertoire, sometimes aspired to playing similar roles. Critics such as Neild of the *Australasian* and James Smith of the *Argus* expressed hope that the latter actresses and their companies would further educate Australian audiences in 'high art'.[479] Rose's career was to be a struggle between her aspirations to the 'high art' of Shakespeare and melodrama and her natural talent for comedy and pantomime. In a sense it was a case of the clown wanting to play Hamlet (and she eventually did). So the Lewises went ahead and obtained the lease of a new Melbourne theatre.

The building of the Academy of Music started just after the Lewises arrived back from India. The architectural firm of Reed and Barnes was commissioned by Aarons to design the building with Joseph Reed as principal.[480] The firm had designed many of the city's most important public buildings, including the Melbourne Public Library (now the State Library of Victoria) and the Wesley, Scots and Independent churches, but the Academy of Music was to be their only theatre design. The building was erected in only five months from May 1876. It contained the Victoria Arcade of shops on the ground floor with the theatre above to the rear. Much was written in the press about the opulence of the interior decoration, both of the theatre and the arcade. Here Aarons' experience in the furniture and decoration business would have given him access to such objects as 'bronze statuettes on well made pedestals; large Japanese vases, filled with artificial flowers' together with stained glass windows, two organs, much gilt decoration and red satin and rep covered seats.[481] The *Age* critic was generally impressed with the theatre, praising the comfort of the stalls and dress circle, but he feared that the isolated upper circle, high up at the back of the family circle, would be 'given up to large-lunged boys' who would annoy the rest of the audience. He also amusingly disapproved of the decoration of the dome which was filled with '… a number of abominably fat cherubs … [which] suggest the idea that they have been fed up for some celestial baby show'.[482]

---

479 Tony Mitchell, *High Art in a Foreign Tongue: Adelaide Ristori's 1875 Australian Tour*, Australasian Drama Studies Association Academic Publications 1, 1995, pp. 129, 138.
480 Reed's stamped signature appears on the plans. See University of Melbourne Archives.
481 *Leader*, 11 November 1876, p. 18.
482 *Age*, 6 November 1876.

CHAPTER ELEVEN

An engraving of Ilma De Murska on stage at the Academy of Music on the opening night in 1876. The engraving shows the opulence of the theatre, including the 'abominably fat cherubs' in the ceiling. *Lorgnette*, 4 May 1889 p. 6.
State Library of Victoria

The term 'Academy of Music' was popular in the USA and elsewhere for theatres. For example a new theatre in provincial Ballarat had opened as the Academy of Music in 1875.[483] Sometimes the building could be the equivalent of an opera house or it could also be a playhouse. Generally, these buildings were not places for learning music such as the Royal Academy of Music in London. At a time when theatre-going was frowned upon by many religious groups, the title lent a certain air of respectability. Nevertheless, shortly before the opening, Joseph Aarons hinted that the Grand Salon, 125 feet in length and containing an organ, could be perhaps be used for teaching music.[484] However, within a few weeks of its opening the venue was being advertised as the 'Academy of Music or Bijou Theatre'.[485] From 1880 the building was to be known exclusively as the 'Bijou Theatre'.

The first performance, on Monday 6 November 1876 in the presence of the governors of Victoria, South Australia and New South Wales, was

---

483 Now known as Her Majesty's.
484 *Australasian*, 21 October 1876, p. 530.
485 *Argus*, 21 December 1876.

certainly musical: it was a concert by the great Austro-Hungarian (Croatian-born) soprano Ilma de Murska. De Murska and her ensemble had been touring Australia and New Zealand since 1875.[486] For the first weeks of performances at the Academy of Music the singer alternated with the Lewis Dramatic Company, led by Rose and the American tragedian and comedian Edwin Adams. De Murska would sing one night and the Lewis Company would perform, for example, T. W. Robertson's comedy *Home* the next.

On the opening night Rose's only duty, after the singing of the National Anthem by the entire company, was to deliver a long address written in seemingly endless verse by her old friend and theatre critic Dr Neild. Critics spoke fondly of Rose, praising her 'beautiful voice and elocution'. In view of later events the address had an ironic and prophetic ring to it:

> Another theatre, and wherefore pray?
> When we are told that two will hardly pay.
> Another theatre – the scheme's absurd,
> Two do not fill; then why erect a third?"

The more than 80 lines continue:

> And rising like a genius o'er the whole
> Aarons the life, the motor-spring, the soul;
> Does our house please you, attic though it be?
> For all that, is't not garnished daintily?
> A credit to our colony and city
> But in respect of architects indeed,
> We did not lean upon a broken Reed
> And then our manager is not a stranger.
> Although of late years, somewhat of a ranger,
> But now abroad no longer he will roam.
> Then, too, of me a little bit you know;
> I should not like to say how long ago,
> How many years have come and gone since I
> First heard your plaudits, when just so high …
> Other old friends in our good company
> Tomorrow night, and many nights you'll see
> And one, though not an old friend, all the same
> Has just earned from all of us that name,

---

486 Nada Bezić. 'Ilma De Murska', *Grove Music Online. Oxford Music Online.* 2009. http://www.oxfordmusiconline.com.ezproxy.lib.monash.edu.au/subscriber/article/grove/music/07815. De Murska's dates: 1834–1889.

CHAPTER ELEVEN

> For Edwin Adams is of world-wide fame,
> And, trust me, we will strive, in our employment,
> To make this house a house for your enjoyment.
> No place for dullness this, so let it be
> Or theatre or academy,
> The time pass so pleasantly within it
> That every hour shall seem but as a minute.
> Here will we teach at least heart-music, gentlest, best,
> That lulls the daily sorrows of this life to rest.

Well after 9.00 pm, the prima-donna De Murska commenced her concert which included the arias 'Casta diva' from *Norma* by Bellini and 'Una voce poco far' from Rossini's *Barber of Seville*. De Murska also sang duets with tenor Ferante Rosnati and basso Augusto Susini. The orchestra or 'small band' for the operatic selections was conducted by Alberto Zelman Senior who had conducted Lewis's orchestra in the first few seasons in Calcutta. The versatile English instrumentalist John Hill, to whom it seems De Murska was bigamously married,[487] accompanied her non-operatic songs on the piano and violin. Reviews of De Murska praised her 'extraordinary vocalisation' which 'caused the audience to rise to its feet in positive enthusiasm.'[488]

Advertisements for the Academy of Music indicated that, as in India, 'Mr. G. B. W. Lewis' was 'Lessee' while 'Mrs. G. B. W. Lewis' was 'Directress'.[489] Their first dramatic offering on 7 November (Melbourne Cup night) was *Home*. Neild, now writing under the new pseudonym 'Tahite' (in honour of Hattie Shepparde, an actress he had admired) in the weekly *Australasian* of 11 November, was not too impressed. This was a play Rose had often performed in India. He found the role of the 'adventureress' Mrs Pinchbeck too 'repulsive' a role for Rose, but was glad to see that she showed a 'finished manner, and that discerning aptitude, which her intelligence and her intimate familiarity with the requisites of effective acting suggest'.[490] Neild's colleague at the *Leader* (possibly James Smith) was also pleased with Rose's reappearance:

> Mrs. Lewis has that delightful quality of conveying an impression of ladylike ease and refinement. She possesses an attractive stage presence,

---

487 Harold Love, *The Golden Age of Australian Opera*, Currency Press, Sydney, 1981, p. 247.
488 *Leader*, 11 November 1876, p. 18.
489 *Age*, 6 November 1876.
490 *Australasian*, 11 November 1876, pp. 626–627.

a finished style of elocution, and a facility for adapting herself to the parts she assumes.[491]

The leading man American Edwin Adams was an internationally famous and successful actor who had come to Australia in July 1876. He had appeared at the Melbourne Royal, mainly as a tragedian in *Hamlet* and *Enoch Arden*, but, suffering from tuberculosis, was unable to complete his engagement. G. B. W. Lewis however, was able to secure Adams' services for four weeks, 'against the warnings of his medical advisors',[492] from 7 November. The *Leader* review noted that,

> comedy is not quite this gentleman's line. His health is at present somewhat enfeebled and though he lacks nothing that experience [and] natural talents … can supply, still there is an absence of that buoyancy and vitality that mars the general effect of his acting in such parts.

After playing in several performances of the comedies *Home* and *Extremes*, ill health forced him to announce his farewell performance. His talent as a tragedian was shown in the 1854 melodrama *The Marble Heart*, where he played the dual roles of an ancient Greek sculptor and a contemporary French sculptor. Knowing the actor's poor health, the review can be seen as quite poignant:

> Mr. Adams developed the fascinating interest in this morbid [Raphael] character with a remarkable power which affected his auditors much as the terrible realism of some of Edgar Allan Poe's weird stories enthrals the reader. The intensely emotional scene with the courtesan Mdlle. Marco [played by Rose] in which Mr. Adams depicted the passionate pleading of a lover, and the mad despair of a rejected suitor whose refusal was his death stroke, was a wonderful piece of acting.[493]

Adams returned to America and was dead within the year.

Not all Rose's reviews were favourable in this first season in Melbourne. The *Argus* critic thought her Mdlle. Marco too 'jolly looking a lady to realise one's idea of a cold hearted beauty who made havoc among her admirers', though he did concede that she did well in the speech where she 'defends her mercenary conduct by quoting the poverty of her early life'. In mid-December Rose had to speak similar sentiments of justification in the

---

491 *Leader*, 11 November 1876, p. 18.
492 'Our Melbourne Letter', *Brisbane Courier*, 18 November 1876. Adams's dates (1833–1877).
493 *Argus*, 4 December 1876.

CHAPTER ELEVEN

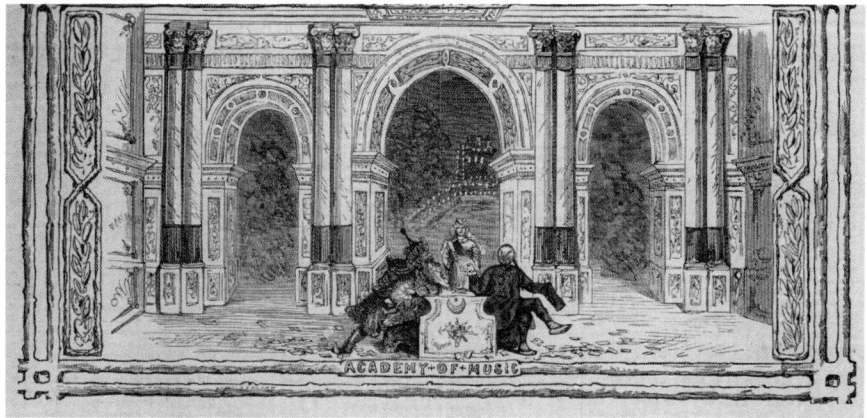

Rose (centre) as Selim, and Fred Thorne (right) in her brother Willie's hit role of 'Heathen Chinee', with W. H. Wallace as Blue Beard in *Blue Beard*. *Australasian Sketcher*, 20 January 1877. Newspaper Collection, State Library of Victoria

role of Mercy Merrick, former prostitute and impersonator in the Wilkie Collins play *The New Magdalen*. She had triumphed in this role in India but disappointed Dr Neild: 'Mrs. Lewis has a very wide range of ability, and her powers cover probably a larger area than most actresses ... but they do not comprehend amongst their best efforts the character of Mercy Merrick.'[494]

For the first two months of the season, the Lewises were waiting for several new players: Henry E. Walton, W. H. Wallace and Ellen Fitzwilliam. Lewis must have been reminded of the long wait for the arrival of the equestrians for his circus in 1854 after the opening of Astley's Amphitheatre in Spring Street. From the first night the company had numbered about twenty actors divided between people somewhat new to Melbourne – such as Flora Anstead, Nelly Daly, Kate Reeves, sisters Ruth and Jessie Grey, Kate Foley, Mrs W. Ryan, Harry Saville, Chas. Brown, A. Boothman, Wilson Forbes and Walter Carle – and those described under the heading 'Re-Appearance of the Established Favourites' – such as J. P. Hydes, Harry Daniels, E. D. Haygarth, Capt. H. M. Humphreys, Mr Flexmore and Rose's nephew and niece, Master George aged eleven, Miss Lily Bryer aged ten, and of course, 'Mrs. G. B. W. Lewis'.[495] The repertoire for the first months of the season was a blend of works performed in India such as *Home*, *The Marble Heart*, *The Serious Family*, *The New Magdalen* and *Harlequin Blue Beard*, and

---

494 *Australasian*, 23 December 1876, p. 818.
495 *Argus*, 7 November 1876, see list in the Academy of Music advertisement. Some of these actors had not yet arrived in Australia. Flora Anstead had appeared before at Melbourne's Theatre Royal.

pieces such as the 'new' 1874 American play *Saratoga* and the 1858 comedy *Extremes; or, Men of the Day*.

By the end of the year most of Lewis's expected players had arrived from London, and had been augmented by London comedian Fred Thorne. A British weekly had commented that 'Melbourne is a good field for English actors.'[496] Rose's greatest triumph in this first season was as Selim in the Christmas pantomime *Harlequin Blue Beard* with Fred Thorne in her brother Willie's famous role as the 'Heathen Chinee'. *Melbourne Punch* welcomed Rose's return 'albeit a little more motherly – still there is the old wicked dimple in the cheek – and her dancing is as charming as in days of yore.'[497] (Surely *Punch* was being too facetious: the idea of a 'motherly' Prince Selim is quite bizarre. Rose after all was only 34. But as we have seen in Calcutta she was by now a 'buxom' woman.)

Neild, who had been careful in his praise of Rose's acting, was at last enthusiastic for her abilities:

> Mrs. Lewis sparkles with good nature, and looks the handsomest, jolliest hero of extravaganza you could see. When she sings, her cheery voice reminds you of ever so long ago, when nobody was a more deserved favorite than she in this class of performances; when she dances you think of nothing but sparkling water. And she is full of fun, too, and helps out the humour of the situations delightfully.[498]

At the end of the panto season Neild continued his 'rave':

> Mrs. Lewis is, at this moment, the best exponent of the extravaganza "prince" you have seen in Melbourne for a long time past. For ease and jauntiness, the complete absence of all embarrassment, and the possession of a happy *degagée* no lady that I know at this moment, on the Australian stage, can go beyond her in burlesque. She is perfectly at home in it, and she preserves … a refinement of manner which tones all she does into a perfect propriety.[499]

These and later reviews reflect much of the criticism of Rose's performances while she was in India: that she shone in pantomime, burlesque and comedy but melodrama and tragedy, while proving her versatility, were not where her strengths lay. Yet she persisted with strong roles such as Mercy Merrick,

---

496 *Aberdeen Weekly Journal*, 24 May 1877.
497 Melbourne *Punch*, 4 January 1877, p. 4.
498 *Australasian*, 30 December 1876, p. 851.
499 *Australasian*, 20 January 1877, p. 61.

CHAPTER ELEVEN

William Creswick, c.1880. Detail from *The Shakespearian Advertiser*.
Accession no. H2000.180/1, Pictures Collection, State Library of Victoria

and Mdlle. Marco. Advertisements for the Academy of Music show a certain ambivalence about how to describe Rose's theatrical talents. Early advertisements call her 'The Charming Comedienne and Versatile Actress'; later publicity described her as 'The Charming Versatile Actress'.

After her triumph in *Blue Beard* she appeared as Lydia Languish in *The Rivals*. Here Rose's performance was described as 'pleasing' while the recently arrived Mrs Fitzwilliam as Mrs Malaprop scored very favourable reviews.[500] Mrs Fitzwilliam (Ellen Chaplin, 1822–1880) had a good reputation for

---

500   *Australasian*, 10 February 1877, p. 178; *Argus*, 9 February 1877.

playing 'old woman' and comedy roles at London's Adelphi and Haymarket Theatres.[501]

After a successful four-week season in which Rose played on the same night not only the gentle popular comedy *The Two Roses* but also *Aladdin*, the Melbourne correspondent of the *Era*, probably Dr Neild, commented on how the name Bijou was increasingly being used to refer to 'this pretty house'. He also reported that the lavish costumes for *Aladdin* had been bought by the Lewises on their last visit to China in 1874.[502]

Rose probably needed to rest after the four-week season of *The Two Roses* and *Aladdin*, so she must have been relieved when George engaged Giulia and Eduardo Majeroni for a four-week run. This Italian acting couple had visited Australia with the great Italian actress Adelaide Ristori in 1875 and decided to settle in Australia. Giulia Majeroni was Ristori's niece. Unlike Ristori, they could act in English. They had performed a month's season at the Theatre Royal in November–December and by March 1877 were looking for another theatre. They opened to extremely favourable reviews in the 'grand emotional drama' *The Living Statue*, translated from the Italian. The Majeronis were supported by the actors of the Lewis Dramatic Company.[503] All, except Rose. Toward the end of this season, however, Rose appeared in the Majeroni's benefit performance of the first three acts of the 'beautiful historical play' *Queen Elizabeth*. This was by nineteenth-century Italian dramatist Paolo Giacometti and had been translated into English. The English version had been played in Melbourne by Mary Gladstane in 1873 and the Italian version by the Ristori Company in 1875. Curiously, in a serious drama Rose played a breeches part: the supporting role of 'King James the Sixth of Scotland'.[504] Eduardo Majeroni played Robert, Earl of Essex. Melbourne-born Flora Anstead[505] appeared in the role of Queen Elizabeth for the first time. Giulia Majeroni did not appear in this play, but appeared in the after-piece vaudeville *Nephews and Nieces*, displaying her versatility.[506]

As though inspired by the 'serious' or 'high art' repertoire of the Majeronis. Rose chose as her next play the new version, by W. G. Wills, of the historical drama *Jane Shore*, about the mistress of Edward IV. This play had its first London production only six months before. (The early eighteenth-century

---

501 *Era*, 29 April 1877.
502 *Era*, 20 May 1877, p. 4.
503 *Argus*, 5 April 1877.
504 ibid.
505 Born to the pioneer Liardet family at Frankston in 1844. She took the stage-name of Flora Anstead (Liardet) d.1901. She was married to William Dodge theatrical agent.
506 *Argus*, 5 April 1877.

playwright Nicholas Rowe had written a tragedy based on this subject). In Wills's play the flawed 'heroine', of the popular 'fallen woman' type, was a reformed character who bestowed charity to the poor and resisted the demands of the villain Gloster [sic] (a Richard III character) to speak against the young princes in the tower. Gloster sentences her to starvation – until a kindly baker takes pity on her. The tragic ending shows Jane horrified at the death of her child and dying with her forgiving husband. Advertisements stated that Lewis had the sole rights in Australia and New Zealand.[507] Having lost three children, two brothers and her mother while in India, it is likely that Rose was able to express some of her own grief in such plays.

Nevertheless, after three weeks of heavy melodrama or quasi tragedy, Rose returned to pantomime as Feramuz in *Lalla Rookh* and Prince Precious in *The Orange Tree and the Bumble Bee*. During June an odd production of *The Octoroon* was performed, with Rose as Zoë and Hans Phillips as George Peyton.[508] Lewis had engaged the then touring Georgia Minstrels to provide 'authentic' Southern atmosphere. Unlike most minstrel companies who performed in 'blackface' make-up, these were real African-Americans who, as it were, performed in a genre that had been created to parody African-American slaves.[509]

In June–July, Rose turned from the tragic Zoë to a new 'heavy' role as an adventuress in a translation of the French play *Cora, L'Article 48*. Henry E. Walton was her leading man. This was followed by a revival of *Blue Beard* with a 'Baby Ballet' and some performances of *The Shaughraun* with Walton, who specialised in Irish comedy. Meanwhile, the Lewis's eleven-year-old son George, who had been schooled at Stacy's South Yarra College, started his secondary education at Wesley College, a nearby school for the well-to-do on St Kilda Road.[510] Young George was their first-born and now only remaining child.

The noted but ageing Shakespearian actor William Creswick arrived in Melbourne unexpectedly in July 1877. Creswick was 64 and accompanied by his actor son Charles and daughter-in-law actress Helen Ashton. Creswick was having difficulty in finding a theatre. He was seen to be past his prime and his style was of the 'old school' of declamatory acting.[511] The management at the Theatre Royal and the Prince of Wales Opera House claimed they were

---

507 *Argus*, 7 April 1877.
508 Hans was the son of Alfred and Elizabeth Phillips, London actors who had arrived in Melbourne in 1855.
509 *Argus*, 11 June 1877; *Lorgnette*, 22 June 1877.
510 Wesley College Archives. Information from Andrew Lemon.
511 'Howard Vernon's Life', *Advertiser*, 5 May 1923.

booked up and had no room for the old actor. Seeing a chance to promote his own business, Lewis stepped in and offered Creswick the Academy of Music. Perhaps the Lewises were glad to end a season by an inadequate actor named Charles Dillon Junior which had not been a success.[512]

Creswick played more than 90 performances to packed houses before leaving for Sydney in early December.[513] For all his 'old' style, people flocked to see him in Shakespeare and the earlier nineteenth century repertoire by Lord Lytton and Sheridan Knowles.[514] With Helen Ashton and Flora Anstead taking most of the leading female roles, Rose played with Creswick only in secondary roles and *The Jealous Wife* and *Katherine and Petruchio* a popular adaptation of *The Taming of the Shrew*.[515] Neild, Creswick's most enthusiastic fan in Melbourne, estimated that up to 5000 people had attended the two benefits before the actor's departure for Sydney. This was a little far-fetched given that the capacity of the theatre was 1200, but it indicates very crowded houses.

After Creswick's departure, Rose ended the year in one of her favorite roles, Peg Woffington in *Masks and Faces*, and as Crusoe in a new pantomime/burlesque, *Robinson Crusoe*, written for Lydia Thompson by H. B Farnie. Like another panto on this subject produced in 1879, the text was full of racist jokes and 'nigger' minstrel references. Willie Edouin, dressed in black body suit and black face make-up, had starred as Friday with Thompson in London and New York and as he had with *Blue Beard* he had arranged that the Lewises were given sole rights to its production in Australia and New Zealand.[516] The Lewises were also sent the costume designs as shown by a comparison of photographs of Lydia Thompson, now in the Harvard Theatre Collection, and an illustration of Rose as Crusoe in the *Australasian Sketcher* of 19 January 1878. Both are dressed in simulated goat skin and wear white satin boots. One review notes that: 'Mrs. Lewis plays Robinson Crusoe in a charming costume to represent goat's hair' and states that 'she enacts the character with all the ability she has displayed in burlesque on former occasions'.[517] The even more verbose Dr Neild, after a long paragraph pointing out that the pantomime was not much like Defoe's novel, excitedly, and probably sexually aroused, describes Rose's performance and costume:

---

512 See *Argus* reviews (possibly by James Smith) 12 August to 27 September 1877 where Dillon was described as 'sapless, saporless and lifeless'.
513 *Australasian*, 15 December 1877, p. 754.
514 'Creswick's 'triumph', *Era*, 24 March 1878.
515 *Argus*, 10 December 1877.
516 *Argus*, 24 December 1877.
517 *Argus*, 25 December 1877.

CHAPTER ELEVEN

Rose as Crusoe – in a similar costume to Lydia's (see p. 147) – in the Melbourne production. *Australasian Sketcher*, 19 January 1878.
Newspaper Collection, State Library of Victoria

> I have never seen Mrs. Lewis to greater advantage than in this part ... There is a freshness, a sparkle, an ease, a dash, and a vivacity, which renders everything she does acceptable. And her dress is the perfection of pretty roughness. You do not stay to inquire if Robinson Crusoe wore such elegant white boots ... and as to the white snowy softness of his coat and cap, you know quite well that some goats have long silky fleeces and that it is from fleeces of this kind that Mrs. Lewis selected the material for her dress. It has a cool, soft soothing daintily comfortable look, which puts you in the pleasantest possible frame of mind.

Neild also liked Fred Thorne as Friday and the children's ballet trained by Mrs Lewis.[518] Like most burlesques and pantomimes there were localised 'hits' at politicians and current affairs. From a review of the same production in Geelong in 1880 we find excerpts from the localised playscript where

---

518 *Australasian*, 29 December 1877, p. 819.

there are 'hits' at the colony's politicians: in a jingle Crusoe takes the illiterate Friday through the letters of the alphabet, each letter representing a candidate in the forthcoming February 1880 election. For example:

> A is for Andrews; *who'll* back him to win?
> B stands for Berry; we must put *him* in[519] [and so on]

The latter line refers to the stormy Victorian premier, Graham Berry, member for Geelong.

The year 1878 opened with the continued success of *Robinson Crusoe*. But after a seven-week season of fun Rose was back in melodrama in *Jane Shore* and *Clouds*.[520] The latter, by Frank Marsden, an American, was a work in the 'society' drama genre: where a deserted wife disguises herself as a servant in the home of her husband's family and reveals both his duplicity and that of his 'fiancée'. It could be called a comedy-drama as there was a happy ending and it contained some comic characters as well as a suffering heroine. Neild found it 'a good play' but 'had no claim to originality'. He liked Rose's emotional but natural acting. 'In this character of the injured woman Mrs Lewis was seen at her best. Her earnestness was bold, her passion unexaggerated, her tenderness real, her pathos unartificial.' He goes on to give an idea of the quality of Rose's voice in the scene where she denounces the 'villainess'.

> Mrs. Lewis has a power of voice which when she likes, she can make to act on the listener like the sound of silver trumpet. And this is without loudness. To be candid with her she does not always use her voice with this result; but she so used it on this occasion ... During the whole of this scene the audience listened with that sort of attention which bespeaks a strong thrall. It was tension of interest that now and then – but not too often – happens, and which when it does happen, is long remembered.[521]

Australia's first production of Wagner's *Lohengrin* had been performed at the Prince of Wales Opera House during August and September 1877. An ambitious venture by William Saurin Lyster, it had starred German soprano Antoinetta Link as Elsa and Italian tenor Pietro Paladini in the title role.[522] Tasmanian-born playwright Garnet Walch could not resist attempting a

---

519   *Geelong Advertiser*, 16 January 1880.
520   *Era*, 21 April 1878.
521   *Australasian*, 23 February 1878, p. 242.
522   Harold Love, *The Golden Age of Australian Opera*, Currency Press, Sydney, 1981, p. 251.

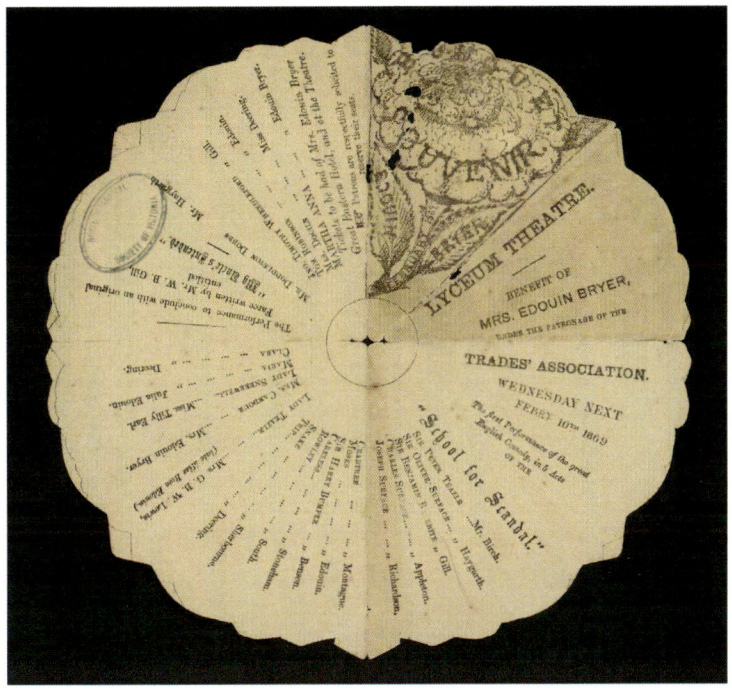

Above: Programme for *The School for Scandal*. Calcutta, February 1869. Accession no. 30328 1020 19527, Theatre Programme Collection, State Library of Victoria

Left: A somewhat over-dressed J. B. Howe, who played dual roles in *The Corsican Brothers* prior to joining the Lewis Company in India, c.1871. Emma Nelson's Family Album. Private Collection

Austin Shanghai, Calcutta 1873.
Possibly Lewis's 'Mongolian Tom Thumb' of the 1860s, now a young man.
Emma Nelson's Family Album.
Private Collection

W. G. Carey, Rose's new leading man in India, 1870s.
Ward Family Collection, Mitchell Library, State Library of NSW

Top: The Jumna Bridge, an important rail-link for the Lewises' Indian tours, c.1874.
Emma Nelson's Family Album. Private Collection

Bottom: The Williamsons in *Struck Oil*, *Australasian Sketcher*, 8 August 1874. Note the vignettes with contemporary portraits of the couple.
Newspaper Collection, State Library of Victoria

A serious looking Julia Edouin and her fiancé, William Forbes Grahame, c.1874.
Emma Nelson's Family Album. Private Collection

Emma Nelson and her friend Caroline May. Calcutta, c.1874.
Emma Nelson's Family Album. Private Collection

Carte-de-visite of Lydia Thompson (with her 'hairy' dress and white satin boots) as Crusoe, and Willie Edouin (with false nose and black body stocking) as Friday, c.1876. Harvard Theatre Collection, Houghton Library, Harvard University

This wood-cut is one of the few images of Rose from the period of her time at the Academy of Music. *Australasian Sketcher*, 16 February 1878.
Private Collection

Julia Edouin in America, cabinet photograph c.1881.
Harvard Theatre Collection, Houghton Library, Harvard University

Title page from Rose's 1892–93 scrapbook.
Private Collection

Aarons opulence: the Grand Salon promenade in the Academy of Music, 1880s.
Private collection

Rose Lewis in London, 1892. Photograph by Alfred Ellis.
Guy Little Collection, Victoria and Albert Museum Archives

Rose in action as Pompadour.
Gordon Ireland Photograph Album (Australian Actors and Actresses p. 4b), c.1895. MS 6135,
Australian Manuscripts Collection, State Library of Victoria

Above: Rose as Hamlet in 1895.
John Riley Scrapbook. Private Collection

Right: Rose as Hamlet, as she appeared in the *Bulletin*, 8 June 1895.
Newspaper Collection, State Library of Victoria

Willie Edouin caricatured by L. J. Binns in his most popular part – as the grotesque 'Heathen Chinee' in *Blue Beard*, 1890s.
Private Collection

Left: Frances Grahame – Julia Edouin's daughter, and Rose's niece and daughter-in-law.
Melbourne *Punch*, 21 July 1898.
Newspaper Collection, State Library of Victoria

Below: Portrait of George Lewis in the Melbourne *Tatler*, 21 May 1898, p. 18.
Newspaper Collection, State Library of Victoria

Above left: The cover of *Souvenir of Mrs. G. B. W. Lewis' Professional Jubilee Testimonial Benefit, Theatre Royal October 3rd 1902*, which contrasts Rose as a child with the grim Rose of 1902. (Lillie E. Davis was Emma Nelson's daughter).
Theatre Programme Collection, State Library of Victoria

Below left: G. B. W. in 1905. This portrait was published in his obituary in the Melbourne *Leader*, 21 July 1906.
Newspaper Collection, State Library of Victoria

Below: Rose in her final role – Mrs Putter in the comedy *Paddy the Next Best Thing*, in *Play Pictorial*, no.221, p. 30, 1920.
British Library

Mrs. Bingle Mrs. Putter
(MISS CHRISTINE JENSON). (MISS ROSE EDOUIN)

PADDY: "Never mind, Mrs. Bingle, if the sun has caught your nose a bit. Here's the wonderful tonic I'm mixing for you, Mrs. Putter."

The Lewis Grave in the Melbourne General Cemetery. Its child-like angel was a monument to Victoria May, chosen by Rose and G. B. W. on their return to Melbourne in 1876.
Photograph by the author.

burlesque of this serious story: in true burlesque style he replaces the magical swan with a goose, which then becomes a representation of the supreme court judge Sir Redmond Barry! And who better than Rose to play the mysterious knight? Neild was much entertained by the show:

> I suppose Mr. Walch intended the audience should laugh ... That is what burlesques are made for. It is full of bustle and change and variety and glitter and pretty women. Mrs. Lewis is quite at home as the champion knight ... On Saturday night there were a good many local allusions ... mostly pointed at the ministry. On Monday ... most of them were cut out – I suppose because they pointed at the ministry.[523]

Years later a writer in Melbourne *Punch* remembered Rose 'made up to appear like Paladini' and she and Fred Thorne causing screams of laughter with their version of the duel ... Harry Daniels invested Ortrud with a very broad humor, while Elsa, played by Jessie Grey, sang a lot of songs not by Wagner'.[524] After appearing in *The Colleen Bawn* with amateurs on St Patrick's Day 1878,[525] Rose appeared in a season of plays including Robertson's new comedy *Progress* about which Melbourne *Punch* commented that 'Mr. Lewis has made a hit at his pretty theatre ... Mrs. Lewis "carries" off the acting with her admirable taste in dress and acting', 'The exquisitely carved furniture' the Lewises had brought from India was used on the set.[526]

Since the opening of the Academy of Music, Lewis and Aarons had several disputes over the running of the front of house regarding which of them had control of the various entrances of the building and who could issue complimentary tickets.[527] Suspecting that Aarons was not happy with him as lessee and was likely to break their contract, in June 1878 Lewis acquired the lease of the Prince of Wales Opera House, and for a few months he was lessee of both theatres with Rose as 'Directress' of each.

After two years back in Melbourne, there were signs that Lewis was accepted into the theatre community. For example, Melbourne *Punch* of 10 September was referring to him as 'G. B. W.' and calling him 'Mr. Alphabetical Lewis'. On the other hand he was perhaps making enemies. In several letters to the *Argus* editor, he argued against George Coppin's monopoly of the copyright of many plays. Lewis objected to paying fees to Coppin, especially

---

523 *Australasian*, 16 March 1878, p. 211.
524 Melbourne *Punch*, 1 October 1925.
525 *Argus*, 19 March 1878.
526 Melbourne *Punch*, 28 March 1878, p. 127.
527 *Argus*, 11 December 1876; 1 June–21 December 1877.

when he (Lewis) was producing the plays for charity performances.[528] The Lewises had rehearsed the Boucicault play *Janet Pride* but, as Coppin had control of the copyright, another play had to be substituted.[529]

Lewis's fears about Aarons proved correct: after several advertisements proclaiming that Lewis had no claim on the Academy of Music, Aarons took sole possession of the 'pretty little theatre'.[530] Unfortunately the houses at the Academy had not been consistently 'crowded'. In his later insolvency proceedings in 1879 and 1880, Aarons cited 'poor houses' for his inability to make a profit from his huge investment in the theatre.[531] He, of course, blamed the Lewises for this. However, the causes of the Academy failure more likely go back to Neild's lines spoken by Rose at the opening in 1876: 'Another theatre, and wherefore pray?/When we are told that two will hardly pay./Another theatre – the scheme's absurd,/Two do not fill; then why erect a third?'. Among other factors were Rose's inability to draw the large audiences she had experienced in India and, apart from the Majeronis and Creswick, the lower standard of the other companies engaged when Rose was not appearing. It should be remembered that the seating capacity of the Academy of Music was smaller than the other Melbourne theatres: only 1200 as opposed to the 3000 of the Theatre Royal and the Opera House, and 1600 of the Princess's (Lewis's old Amphitheatre) and therefore box-office receipts were lower. Unfortunately for Aarons, his management proved no better than that of the Lewises; eventually the theatre had to be sold at a creditors' auction in 1879.[532]

When the actor J. L. Hall returned from a visit to England, Rose supported him in Boucicault melodramas and H. J. Byron comedies.[533] She disappears from the bills in June and others take over, such as the West Indian actor Morton Tavares and his wife in *London Assurance*, *The School for Scandal*, *The Two Roses* and *Richelieu*.

In September 1878, the indefatigable Mr Creswick returned from seasons in Adelaide and Sydney. Again he was grateful to Lewis for providing a theatre, this time the Opera House. Also, perhaps, the Lewises were grateful for such a drawcard for their new venture at the Opera House. Creswick

---

528   13 March 1878. Letters to the Editor re argument about Coppin's Dramatic Society fees, see *Argus*, 13, 14, 15, 18, 21, 23 March 1878. Lewis gives his address as Shanghai Villa.
529   *Era*, 21 April 1878.
530   *Australasian*, 23 November 1878, p. 658.
531   See advertisements in *Herald*, *Argus*, 1879, 1880.
532   *Argus*, 7 May 1879.
533   *Era*, 25 August 1878.

CHAPTER ELEVEN

continued with the production of Shakespeare and repertory comedies. This time he added *Macbeth* to his performances with tragedienne Adelaide Bowring as Lady Macbeth.[534]

Rose, now 'Directress' of just the Opera House, was pregnant with her sixth child so was not performing on its stage. But, as ever, she was active training children, including her nephew Master George Bryer and ten-year-old Mary Weir, for the next Christmas pantomime *Pluto*, starring Fred Thorne and Miss Beatrice, an English burlesque artiste.[535] The critics liked the panto, particularly the 'baby Harlequinade' played by children between the ages of six and fourteen. The Australian correspondent for the *Era* regretted that 'Mrs. Lewis herself is not in the cast as her burlesque representations are always much admired'.[536] The *Argus* review of 25 December expressed concern for the 'baby Harlequinade' which included 'Baby Flora [Graupner], aged six who sang 'Fireworks on the brain' with perfect self possession:

> It is difficult to repress a wish that some kind fairy would appear and "put them in their little beds" but it is consoling to read in the advertisement that this troupe of performers is taught in kindness, and they one and all take delight in what they do …

It is not surprising that after the intensive work preparing and directing the pantomime, Rose was delivered of a still-born baby in mid-January 1879.[537] This must have been a terrible blow. She was almost 35 and after at least six pregnancies she had only one surviving child. Infant mortality was widespread in the nineteenth century so perhaps it was not the tragedy that it might be today. One of her exemplars, Fanny Cathcart (Mrs Robert Heir) had lost all her babies within weeks of their births.[538] However, Rose may have regretted some of her stressful theatrical activity in the months leading up to the birth.

Nevertheless, one month later, the resilient Rose reappeared on stage as Lady Marsden in the 1875 melodrama *All for Her* by Merivale and Simpson with Wybert Reeve, an English actor-manager touring Australia as her leading man. Rose was thought especially good in emotional scenes. She

---

534 *Australasian*, 14 September 1878, pp. 338–339.
535 *Era*, 9 March 1879.
536 *Era*, 9 March 1879, p. 7.
537 Melbourne General Cemetery Records, 17 January 1879.
538 See Janette Gordon-Clark, 'The Progress of the Stars: Actresses and their Repertoires in Australia from the 1850s to the 1890s', Ph.D. Thesis, Department of English, Monash University, 2000, p. 290.

was 'received with a perfect shower of bouquets' on her reappearance on the stage.[539]

By March George's lease of the Opera House was terminated when William Saurin Lyster's Opera Company returned for a season. At her benefit, Rose gave what had become her usual speech mentioning her birth in 1844 and her first performance as a dancer at Marylebone Theatre in 1851. She also thanked her 'friends behind the curtain' as well as the public for their kindness.[540]

After only two-and-a-half years in Bourke Street theatres, the Lewises were without a theatre, so they decided to 'take to the road' again. They went to Sydney. Rose Lewis had not yet performed in Sydney, capital of the colony of New South Wales. The young Edouin Troupe's only venture into NSW was just over the border to Albury in April 1859. For the first time in their 'partnership' George, now 61, was not the manager of a theatre or circus company. He was, of course, Rose's manager. It is likely that he arranged for Rose and Fred Thorne to play under the management of actor Edmund Holloway with Holloway's stock company at the Royal Victoria Theatre in Pitt Street, Sydney's largest theatre. It was often redecorated until its destruction by fire in 1880.[541]

Rose's 'first appearance' in Sydney was in *Jane Shore* on 10 May 1879. The critic of the *Sydney Morning Herald* spoke of her thrilling the audience:

> In the scene where she implores her husband to tell her of her child, she played with intense passion, and expressed the impulses of maternity very feelingly. The groan too, with which she swoons when she hears that her child is dead seems to burst from a heart overcharged with misery.[542]

As usual she won fine praise in burlesque, this time as Selim in *Blue Beard*. The young Bland Holt, later to be an important actor-manager in Australia, took the role of Corporal Zong Zong, or 'Heathen Chinee'.[543] Rose ended the season in *The Jealous Wife* and *Aladdin*.

The *Sydney Morning Herald* of 9 June 1879 commented on Rose's Sydney season:

---

539 *Argus*, 17 February 1879.
540 *Argus*, 3 March 1879.
541 Ross Thorne, 'Royal Victoria Theatre' in Philip Parsons, ed., *Companion to Australian Theatre*, Currency Press, Sydney 1995, p. 512.
542 *Sydney Morning Herald*, 13 May 1879.
543 *Sydney Morning Herald*, 5 June 1879.

CHAPTER ELEVEN

> Mrs. G. B. Lewis made her last appearance at the Victoria Theatre on Saturday night … This lady has been popular since she appeared here as Jane Shore, and few actresses who have visited Sydney have deserved a higher meed of praise. The application of her intellect to study … have been the means of developing her into an actress who is bold and effective in drama; who gives not only clever but scholarly readings of her parts and who is more than pleasing in light comedy. Indeed when she places on one side the conventionalisms of drama and reveals herself in the guise of a comedienne, she is absolutely charming.

The Lewises spent the remainder of 1879 and early 1880 at home and in short seasons in Adelaide and Victorian country cities. Rose had not visited Adelaide since 1862 when she played at the Victoria Theatre with Greville's company. At the time of Rose's visit in August 1879, the recently rebuilt Adelaide Theatre Royal in Hindley Street was managed by James Allison. His stock company included two people, Carry George and her husband Robert Lawrence, from the Lewises' 1872 Indian season.

Rose featured her well-worn roles as Jane Shore, Mrs Oakly in *The Jealous Wife* and the title role in *Aladdin*, as well as Stella Gordon in *Clouds*, Selim in *Blue Beard* and Cora in the play of the same name.[544]

Returned to Melbourne by 26 September, Rose found a sheaf of legal papers to deal with. More than six years after her mother's death in Calcutta, Rose signed the probate papers for Sarah Bryer's estate. This was valued at £105.[545] These legal matters probably involved some contact with her father. As John Edwin Bryer he signed the consent affidavit of his wife's estate, mentioning his 'eldest daughter Rose'. Often listed as J. E. Jones, he was living with Isabella Jane Wing and their three children Blanche, Edwin and Herbert.[546]

Still without a theatre in Melbourne, at the end of the year the Lewises took their production of the *Robinson Crusoe* pantomime to Ballarat and Geelong. By now a reliable railway system had greatly improved travel to these cities.[547] Coastal shipping was another way of touring between the

---

544 *South Australian Register*, 8, 9, 11, 12, 14, 18, 19, 21, 23, 25, 26, 27 August 1879.
545 PROV, VPRS29/P, Unit 226, Item 637, 26 September. Probate on Rose's mother's estate. Lists beneficiaries: 'Her husband John Edwin Bryer, her sons John (since deceased) and William of the United States of America and her daughter Julia Graham of Calcutta, India – and myself – next of kin her survivors and no others.
546 Melbourne Directories, Sands & McDougall 1871–1875, John E. Jones Livery Stables, 1 Napier Street, Fitzroy.
547 Victorian Railways History website, 4 April 2009.

colonies. They opened at the Theatre Royal, Ballarat, on 25 December.[548] By the end of January they had also enjoyed a successful season at the Geelong Mechanics' Institute, where Rose starred as Robinson Crusoe and Jane Shore.[549]

By early 1880 Melbourne theatre gossip must have been rife with rumours of Aarons's financial troubles at the Academy of Music. Here was a chance for the Lewises to return to their former theatre.

---

548 *Ballarat Advertiser*, 25 December 1879.
549 *Geelong Advertiser*, 16 January, 22 January 1880; *Australasian*, 24 January 1880, p. 115.

Chapter twelve

THE LEWISES AT THE BIJOU THEATRE, 1880–1885

The year 1880 promised to be a prosperous one for Melbourne. An International Exhibition was to be opened at a great building nearing completion in Carlton just outside the city.[550] As well as attracting business and trade entrepreneurs there was sure to be large numbers of visitors from the countryside and the other colonies. Therefore greater audiences at entertainments could be expected.

Lewis's rival, the bankrupt Joseph Aarons, was now managing the Academy of Music for the lessee James O'Meara, who, as theatre historian Veronica Kelly surmises, was most likely Aarons's 'front-man'. The owner was Thomas Cooper MLA who had bought the building at the auction in July 1879. There might have been some arrangement between the three to keep Aarons at the Academy,[551] though the theatre was still losing money under his management. Matters came to a head when Aarons tried to stage a version of W. S. Gilbert and Gilbert A'Beckett's *The Happy Land*, localised by Melbourne writer Marcus Clarke where various politicians, including the premier of the colony, Graham Berry, were ridiculed. Production of the play was banned by political censorship.[552] Aarons's four-year association with the Academy was at an end.[553] The Lewises would have remembered their trouble with a version of the same political satire during the 1874 Calcutta season when the Viceroy walked out in protest.

---

550 The Royal Exhibition Building still exists and is on the World Heritage List.
551 Veronica Kelly, 'The banning of Marcus Clarke's *Happy Land*: Stage Press and Parliament', *Australasian Drama Studies*, Vol. 2, No. 1, October 1983, p. 108.
552 For details of this production see Kelly op. cit.
553 Aarons died of hepatic congestion haemorrhage (a condition related to heart and liver disease) at the age of 53 in 1886. Death Certificate. His estate was valued at £2,450. VPRS 7591, File Number 34/254; VPRS 28 P2 link.

THE SUPPRESSED PLAY: THE DRESS REHEARSAL

Cover of the *Australian Sketcher*, 31 January 1880, showing the three 'mortal' politicians and the classically costumed 'Fairies' of *The Happy Land*. (Some Melbourne buildings can be seen in the background, including the new Exhibition Building). Newspaper Collection, State Library of Victoria

O'Meara's lease lapsed in March 1880, and the Lewises' patience and persistence were finally rewarded. G. B. W. Lewis was granted a licence for what he now called[554] 'Lewis's Bijou Theatre'. His first star was his old friend William Creswick who had played under his management at the Academy and the Opera House. Now nearly 70, Creswick had toured in New South Wales, Tasmania and South Australia and was returning to England. This would be his last season in Australia. Rose took several leading and supporting roles opposite Creswick, parts that had been played by Helen

---

554 Chief Secretary's Inward Registered Correspondence: PROV, VRPS 3991/P, Unit 1136.

CHAPTER TWELVE

Ashton and others in the two previous Creswick seasons. Rose's interpretation of most of these roles and her 'nicely modulated and expressive voice'[555] were praised by critics, in particular, Dr Neild.

The good doctor often used his weekly columns in the *Australasian* to expound his theories on theatre, be it Shakespeare or popular burlesque. Though he never returned to England after arriving in Melbourne in 1852, Neild obviously kept up with the current London theatre newspapers for developments in modern drama. Nevertheless he loved the 'old school' of actors of the declamatory method that had been current when he first attended theatre in the England of his youth in the 1840s. He therefore was delighted with Creswick's style of performance, seeing the old actor as a great educator for the colonies.[556]

One of the first successes of the season was G. W. Lovell's 1840s emotional play, *Love's Sacrifice*, about an apparent crime by a father, Matthew Elmore, and his daughter's love and sacrifice. All ends happily after a melodramatic revelation by another character, and the villain's evil designs are thwarted. It was Rose's first appearance in the role of Elmore's daughter, Margaret, and she had only a short time to learn it. After dealing with Creswick's performance, Neild moved on to that of Rose:

> Considering that this is the first time Mrs. Lewis has played the part of Margaret Elmore her success is the more notable. From this time she may add it to her best essays. Bright, emotional, powerful, yet clear, self-contained, and never uncertain, she declared the character in every situation with an unerring exactness, and whenever a strong emphasis was required, she uttered it, but always with an entire freedom from excess ...[557]

But it was her Fool in *King Lear* that caught Neild's highest accolade: 'It would be difficult to apportion to this representation an excess of praise'. Furthermore, Neild saw signs that she had studied the part well:

> The wit, wisdom, and the satire being expressed as if the speaker uttered it unconsciously ... as if she were thinking aloud ... her Fool delivers his sententious truths in the manner of half asides, as if he were singing to please himself ... At the same time Mrs. Lewis preserves a certain colouring of sadness, which, as we know, is always the concomitant of

---

555 *Argus*, 18 March 1880.
556 *Australasian*, 24 April 1880, p. 530.
557 *Australasian*, 20 March 1880, p. 370.

philosophic humour ... Lear's Fool, then, must take its place among Mrs. Lewis's prominent successes.'[558]

Rose's Portia in *Julius Caesar* was another part which Neild thought was 'at all points, what the classically charged mind understands by a fair, bright Roman matron'.[559] He also liked her Mrs Oakly in *The Jealous Wife*. Neild admired the historical accuracy of her characterisation: 'One might reasonably ask her if she had met Dr. Johnson lately at Mrs. Thrale's or of the zest of her jealous 'business', 'although her paroxysmal passion reaches almost to explosion point, it is never pushed beyond the limits of expressiveness'. He concludes with praise for her very wide range.[560] Other roles opposite Creswick included Lady Allworth in Massinger's seventeenth century comedy beloved by tragedians, *A New Way to Pay Old Debts*, and Emma, Tell's wife in Sheridan Knowles's *William Tell*.[561] She also played the Queen (Gertrude) in Creswick's *Hamlet* and was Katherine in *Katherine and Petruchio*, David Garrick's shorter version of *The Taming of the Shrew* on the last night of Creswick's season.[562]

Gilbert and Sullivan's successful opera *HMS Pinafore* had played to crowded houses in Sydney and Melbourne since December 1879, with the Williamsons starring in the roles of Captain Corcoran and Josephine. Juvenile versions of the opera had been playing in England and USA with many children's touring companies. Having obtained permission from J. C. Williamson (sole copyright owner in Australia and New Zealand) to produce her version of the Gilbert and Sullivan opera, Rose prepared her child pupils for a juvenile version of *HMS Pinafore*. This opened on 24 April 1880.[563] After the profit and excitement of the Creswick seasons, this 'Lilliputian' production was to be the most successful and longest-running show staged by the Lewises. It ran from April to July. The first production was to have had their son George, aged 14, performing but, 'Owing to the illness of Master Lewis, who was to have appeared as Captain Corcoran, the part had

---

558 *Australasian*, 10 April 1880, p. 466.
559 *Australasian*, 17 April 1880, p. 498.
560 *Australasian*, 10 April 1880, p. 466.
561 See *Argus*, 17, 29, 30 March, 7–9, 12, 16, 21, 22 April 1880.
562 Creswick was presented with 'a massive silver claret jug, two goblets and a salver with the inscription: 'Presented to William Creswick, Esq., by his friends and admirers at the Bijou Theatre, Melbourne, Victoria, Australia 22 April 1880.' (*Argus*, 23 April 1880). Sadly, this gift had to be sold by Creswick's destitute widow in 1888 (*Lorgnette*, February 1889).
563 *Argus*, 21, 25 April 1880. Williamson was plagued by 'pirate' productions of *Pinafore*, and remembering how the Lewises had helped him in Calcutta, most likely gave Rose special permission.

CHAPTER TWELVE

Some *Australasian Sketcher* illustrations of the juvenile *HMS Pinafore*, 8 May 1880. These sketches of Rose's son George as Captain Corcoran are, apart from a photograph of the boy as an infant, the only known images of her only surviving child.
Newspaper Collection, State Library of Victoria

to be studied, both words and music, by Mrs. Lewis, who towered above her diminutive pupils like Gulliver among the Lilliputians.' The *Argus* critic was particularly struck by Flora Graupner aged eleven as Josephine:

> Mrs. Lewis has found another Rose Edouin in little Flora ... Exceedingly pretty and with a look of rare intelligence with her large expressive eyes, this diminutive beauty sang the music ... with the utmost accuracy, walked about the stage like a prima donna of twenty years' standing ... and took the audience by storm.'[564]

Neild, now writing without his nom de plume or any signature, as usual praised Mrs Lewis for her intelligence and 'remarkable aptitude for developing the natural talents of children'. He went on to consider that 'for some weeks past, she has been playing difficult parts in support of Mr Creswick, some of them for the first time in her life, one cannot but be impressed with the extraordinary physical power she must possess to enable her to go through the actual work required in the several duties of acting, managing and specially training'.[565] Young George finally made his debut in the role in June. On the sixtieth night, on 2 July, there was a double cast: Rose as Captain Corcoran in Act I and 'Master George Lewis' as Captain Corcoran in Act II. On the last night, J. C. Williamson gave a generous address where he praised Rose and her juveniles for their talent and enterprise.[566]

By the conclusion of *HMS Pinafore*, the Lewises must have known that novelist and playwright Marcus Clarke had fallen on hard times and ill health. In order to help they generously offered some employment to his

---

564 *Argus*, 26 April 1880.
565 *Australasian*, 1 May 1880, p. 562.
566 *Australasian*, 10 July 1880.

actress wife. Before her marriage in 1869, Marian Dunn had been popular on the stage of Melbourne's Theatre Royal. Now billed as Mrs Marcus Clarke she starred in seven plays, between 3 and 24 July at the Bijou, including a comedy, *Daughter of Eve*, written by her husband. She opened in *Child of the Regiment* (a popular version of Donizetti's opera *La Fille du Regiment*). Dr Neild noted that although Mrs Clarke 'is a very charming actress' and possessing a refined manner, twelve years of retirement had adversely affected her singing voice and her come-back was not an overall success.[567] Nevertheless, at perhaps £1.15.0 per week, a star's three week salary would have helped the Clarke household in its poverty. At the end of this season Marian Clarke shared the bill with Rose in the comedy *My Wife's Daughter*.[568] The Lewises' generosity and probable friendship with the Clarkes was to be shown just over a year later when on the death of Marcus Clarke theirs was the first company to hold a theatrical benefit towards the fund in aid of the now destitute Marian and her six young children.[569] That G. B. W. should appear at the dedication of the Marcus Clarke Memorial at Melbourne General Cemetery in 1898 is evidence of a continuing friendship between the Lewises and Marian Clarke who by then had been appointed Victorian Registrar of Births, Marriage and Deaths.

Meantime Rose must have had word that her sister Julia, now a widow, had left India for America with her young daughter Frances May Grahame, and had gone to Boston USA to tour with their brother Willie Edouin's Sparks Company.[570] Her husband, William Grahame, had died in Darjeeling.[571] It is likely that Julia was already ill with tuberculosis as she did not become a regular performer in Willie's company.[572]

In August 1880, the Lewises decided to take the juvenile *HMS Pinafore* company to Sydney. They booked the old Queen's Theatre in York Street 'by special arrangement with Mr J. C. Williamson' and boarded the coastal steamer *Barrabool* for Sydney on 19 August with a large complement of child performers.[573] The company was mainly well received in this capital city. The *Sydney Morning Herald* critic praised the children's performances especially 'little Flora Graupner' and 'Mrs. Lewis' for 'the manner in which

---

567 ibid.
568 *Australasian*, 24 July 1880.
569 *Argus*, 6 August 1881. By 1882 the fund had reached £1000.
570 *Lorgnette*, 3 July 1880; *Melbourne Bulletin*, 19 November 1880, p. 2.
571 India Office, British Library: Ecclesiastical Records, Darjeeling, 28 May 1879: William Forbes Grahame, Zamindar's Agent, aged 41. Cause of Death: Ulceration of the bowels.
572 See *New York Clipper*, 14 March 1891 for report of Julia's death.
573 http://mariners.records.nsw.gov.au/1880/08073bar.htm.

CHAPTER TWELVE

she has trained them'.[574] A short paragraph in a New Zealand weekly reported that:

> The Juvenile "Pinafore" Company is drawing immense houses in Sydney. The attendance during the week ended August 29th was over 8000, the largest ever seen at the Queen's Theatre.[575]

The 'Music and Drama' critic in the *Sydney Mail*, however, notes that while the 'juveniles have caught the public taste' he cannot 'sympathise with the idea':

> Apart from the objections which must present themselves ... as to the employment of a company of children in a theatrical performance at night, it is to me entirely out of place and at variance with the ideas of the composers. Dr Johnson's comment the dancing dogs would force itself upon my memory: "One cannot expect them to do it well: the wonder is that they do it at all." ... The orchestra at times is very bad, and one is forced to the conclusion that Messrs. Gilbert and Sullivan's joint work appeals so vividly to popular taste that any representation finds favour.[576]

Returned to Melbourne by 27 September, it is likely that the Lewis management of the Bijou was experiencing financial difficulties so, in late October they took the opportunity to cash in on both the International Exhibition and the Melbourne Cup race week. They knew inter-colonial and country visitors would swell the box office takings with a return of the juvenile *HMS Pinafore*.[577]

The next week melodrama was back with Rose as Lady Inez in *Shadows*, and interestingly, as Janet's mother in the old Boucicault melodrama *Janet Pride*.[578] As in India, one of her problems seems to have been the lack of a strong leading man in the company.

At the 22 December performance Rose, as Lady Teazle, brought some unlooked-for drama in this polite comedy when she fainted.[579] Was she pregnant again? Or just over-tired with preparing 104 of her pupils for the chorus of the pantomime? The *Argus* report said that her problem was a type of 'hysteria' brought on by overwork. Yet within a few days she was performing again, this time as Goody Two Shoes in the panto of the same

---

574 *Sydney Morning Herald*, 23 August 1880.
575 *Otago Witness*, 11 September 1880.
576 *Sydney Mail*, 4 September 1880.
577 *Argus*, 1 November 1880.
578 *Argus*, 15, 29 November 1880.
579 *Argus*, 22 December 1880.

name. Fred Thorne was her co-star.⁵⁸⁰ The panto continued, as usual, into the New Year.

In early February, the Lewises took their juvenile *HMS Pinafore* company to Adelaide for a three-week season. Most of the performers who had appeared in Sydney travelled to the South Australian capital together with members of the 'efficient Orchestra' from the Bijou Theatre, Melbourne' conducted by James Ure.⁵⁸¹ One critic concentrated on the opera itself with its 'pleasant fun', and 'sparkling music', before acknowledging that 'the children acquitted themselves remarkably well'.⁵⁸²

Rose's repertoire for the rest of 1881 consisted of comedies such as *Uncle*, *The School for Scandal* and *Masks and Faces* and melodramas such as *A Sister's Penance*, *The Wonder*, *The Hidden Hand*, and *Liz*, 'a powerful Lancashire drama'. *Liz* was an unusual vehicle for Rose. Based on a Frances Hodgson Burnett 1877 novel, the story was set around a coal mine and Rose had to speak in a strong North of England dialect. She perhaps too old for the part of plucky young girl Liz but the *Argus* critic described her performance as 'a very capable piece of acting'.⁵⁸³ Similarly, when she again played Mdlle Marco in *The Marble Heart* the *Argus* reviewer complained that she 'does not look the part'.⁵⁸⁴ Perhaps her age (37) and possibly being overweight became a problem when she assumed femme fatale roles.

* * *

By early August 1881, Melbourne and its theatre world were in mourning for writer Marcus Clarke. The Lewises, possibly thinking of his destitute widow and six small children, were the first theatre managers to hold a special benefit for the family on 6 August.⁵⁸⁵

During the year Rose was teaching stage skills to children and rehearsing them for her production of the *Juvenile Tambour Major* based on the French opera bouffe *La Fille du Tambour Major* which played from 24 September to 3 November.⁵⁸⁶ The *Argus* critic was unenthusiastic about the production.

580 *Australasian*, 1 January 1881; *Lorgnette*, 8 January 1881.
581 *South Australian Register*, 4 March 1881.
582 *South Australian Register*, 16 February 1881.
583 *Argus*, 4 April 1881.
584 *Argus*, 22 August 1881.
585 *Argus*, 5 August 1881. 'Benefit for the widow and orphans of the late Mr. Marcus Clarke'.
586 *Argus*, 26 September 1881. This was to be the first version of the Offenbach work. Nellie Stewart starred in the first full production at the Princess's in 1882.

CHAPTER TWELVE

> It must be conceded that … Offenbach's music is not well adapted for childish voices … a child's voice is thin and weak, and is unavoidably shrill when it has to be strained to fill a large building; while as there can be no baritones or basses in the choruses there can be very little light and shade, a reasonable amount of unison, and scant harmony.

Nevertheless the audience loved it. Again there was great appeal in children playing adult parts. Even if they could not sing all the music, Rose had drilled them well. 'The ensemble of the groupings was a particular feature, almost if not equal to that on the Opera House stage'.[587] The cast included 13-year-old Flora Graupner, 15-year-old Mary Weir and 13-year-old Chrissy Peachey (real name Metzger), all of whom went on to some success on the adult stage. 'Little' Chrissy Peachey who became Christine Peachey, had success as a young adult and married actor and playwright George Darrell[588] before her early death at 24; Graupner had a reasonably successful stage career in Australia and England, before becoming psychologically disturbed;[589] Weir joined the ballet of J. C. Williamson productions and retired from the stage in 1899 when she became the second Mrs J. C. Williamson.

In November the Lewises produced 'a comedy-drama' *Her Evil Star*, by local playwright Garnet Walch.[590] Although we lack the play script Walch published a prose version of the story (with fewer characters) in 1883. This gives some idea of the action and dialogue (rather in the way Wilkie Collins published a short novel of his play *The Frozen North*, written in collaboration with Charles Dickens). The plot was similar to many melodramas: ill-treated wife thinks husband dead – he returns to menace her. In *Her Evil Star*, the setting is a pastoral property in Victoria's Western District near the coast. The evil husband is shipwrecked near the homestead and rescued by farm workers. Who should he find staying with the squatter but his wife and young daughter?[591] The wife, played by Rose, loves the squatter's son and attempts to poison the villain, but her better nature and a vision of her child praying stops her. After a sensational scene when the evil husband falls to his death down a cliff, all is resolved happily. Walch's play was not a

---

587 *Herald*, 26 September 1881.
588 Melbourne *Punch*, 14 August 1890, p. 100.
589 Frank Van Straten, *Florence Young: and the Golden Years of Australian Theatre*, Beleura House and Garden, Mornington, Victoria, 2009, p. 46.
590 *Argus*, 7 November 1881; *Australasian*, 12 November 1881, p. 627.
591 Veronica Kelly suggests that the *Loch Ard* wreck near Portland in 1878 inspired Walch to locate the action in the Western District. See Veronica Kelly, 'Early Australian High Comedy to 1890: Performing the Colonial Bourgeois Self', in *Southerly*, Autumn 2004, Vol. 64, pp. 66–67.

success with patrons and was withdrawn after only a week. The Melbourne *Herald* of 12 December 1881 commented that the Lewises had been good supporters of Australian plays and that it was a pity that the public had not come to the drama in greater numbers. Indeed, the Lewises had produced plays and burlesques by local writers: *Pluto* by George Fawcett; *Gulliver*, *Lohengrin* and *Her Evil Star* by Garnet Walch; and *Daughter of Eve* by Marcus Clarke.

The remainder of the year was occupied with various melodramas, followed by Rose as Lady Gay Spanker in *London Assurance* with Wybert Reeve.[592] Rose did not appear in the Bijou Christmas pantomime, *Gulliver, or Harlequin King Liliput*, written by Garnet Walch. Her old colleague Carry Nelson, another former child star from the 1850s era did so instead. By now Nelson was a successful burlesque and pantomime actress in the British provinces. The Lewises engaged her for the role of Gulliver. The *Argus* reviewer commented that Nelson had 'left the colony a bright clever girl full of promise … She returns with that promise more than fulfilled'.[593] Appropriately Rose's pupils formed the ballet of Lilliputians.[594]

At this time Pollard's Lilliputian Opera Company, a possible rival for Bijou patrons, opened at Hudson's Theatre the small hall in Bourke Street. They presented the French comic opera *Les Cloches de Corneville*. The Pollards were a 'family' company, mostly inspired by the international success of the juvenile *HMS Pinafore* and that of the Lewis production. Historian Peter Downes suggests that the Pollards were also inspired by the Lewis company's juvenile productions.[595]

In January 1882, the theatre gossip page of *Melbourne Bulletin*[596] noted that 'Mr. Lewis has let the Bijou for three weeks to the Montague Turner opera company'. The next snippet stated that Lewis was planning to go to 'England if he can sell his houses in St Kilda Road', and indeed these properties were advertised to be auctioned toward the end of January.[597] Perhaps his business was in trouble and Lewis wanted to travel to England to engage better talent. However, at the same time, the English tragedian John Burdett Howe, Rose's leading man in the 1871 Calcutta season, arrived

---

592 *Argus*, 19 December 1881.
593 Carry was the daughter of musician Sydney Nelson, who toured Victoria and Tasmania with his son and daughters. The girls later became successful burlesque actresses in London. *Era*, 4 February 1899.
594 *Argus*, 27 Dec 1881.
595 See Peter Downs, *The Pollards: A Family and its Child and Adult Opera Companies in New Zealand and Australia*, Steel Roberts, Wellington, NZ, 2002, pp. 16, note, p. 200.
596 *Melbourne Bulletin*, 27 January 1882.
597 *Argus*, 21 January 1882.

CHAPTER TWELVE

in Melbourne for another tour of the Australian colonies. Only one of the Lewis properties, Shanghai Villa, and land was sold so they decided to stay in Melbourne to host Howe at their theatre, moving to another of Lewis's properties.

Howe acted under the Lewises' management for a six-week season. This time Rose played mainly second leads. Howe was accompanied by his actress wife Julia Hayward, who played leading parts such as Desdemona and Ophelia while Rose took the roles of Emilia and Queen Gertrude. It is likely that Rose realised that at 38 she needed to take older roles as a transition to what we now call 'character' roles. As seen in one of her speeches in India, she was fairly clear-eyed about her earlier transition from child performer to adult roles. In the drama *The Chain*, with Julia Hayward as the pathetic heroine, Rose played a Russian adventuress. According to the *Argus* reviewer she 'elevated the part … into a prominence which it would not otherwise have received in the hands of an inferior actress'.[598] Like many tragedians, Howe also specialised in 'Oirish' parts such as Myles-Na-Copaleen in *The Colleen Bawn*. In this season, Rose only 'pleased' in *Shamus na Leena*, taking a secondary part of Lady Mary Maguire (critics found her 'unexceptional as the buxom widow').[599] Her Emilia in *Othello* however was liked, and her Gertrude was 'satisfactory'.[600] The old play *Black Eyed Susan* proved a success for both Rose and Burdett Howe.[601]

In June Jonathan Dewhurst, another touring English provincial tragedian, arrived back in Melbourne after touring to New South Wales and Tasmania. He had commenced his tour at the Melbourne Theatre Royal but was now looking for a theatre.[602] G. B. W. was happy to oblige him. With Dewhurst, Rose played in the 1833 Sheridan Knowles tragedy *The Wife: a Tale of Mantua*. The *Argus* review of 12 June found her 'not well suited to Mariana', a young girl, yet liked her 'intensity of feeling in some scenes'. In the *Merchant of Venice*, with Dewhurst as Shylock, Rose made 'an admirable Portia', with 'good elocutionary effects' in the trial scene.[603] This was followed by the perennial *Katherine and Petruchio* and *Much Ado About Nothing*.[604]

---

598 *Argus*, 30 January 1882.
599 *Argus*, 13 February 1882.
600 *Argus*, 21 February 1882; *Argus*, 25 February 1882, 13 March 1882.
601 *Argus*, 13 March 1882.
602 See Philip and Susan Taylor, *Jonathan Dewhurst: The Lancashire Tragedian*, The Book Guild, Sussex, 2001.
603 *Argus*, 19 June 1882.
604 *Argus*, 23 June 1882.

CIRCUS AND STAGE

After two-and-a-half years at the Bijou, it was clear that business at the little theatre was not doing at all well. Writing in the *Era*, Neild blamed the Shakespeare season for the lack of patrons: 'The Bijou Theatre is closed. The ill-advised Shakespeare season was a dismal failure. The works of our immortal bard were not suited to the theatre or the company … Mr. Lewis thought discretion the better part of valour [and] he closed the theatre.'[605] Perhaps Rose was glad of a break but, as usual, she seemed to need some theatrical activity: she directed the ballet of the Theatre Royal Christmas pantomime *Jack and the Beanstalk* for Williamson, Garner and Musgrove.

The 'rest between engagements' also enabled Rose to concentrate on her school for juvenile performers. After the sale of Shanghai Villa in April 1882 the Lewises had moved into 1 Georges Terrace further south on St Kilda Road.[606] This 'palatial residence' of three stories had a school room attached where Rose could teach. It was later described as a 'miniature theatre' so pupils had a real experience of the exits and entrances.[607] Lewis later had an iron shed attached to the back of the house to store old Bijou scenery and costumes. Real estate advertisements provide detail of the size and positions of the rooms while furniture auction advertisements describe the decoration. Judging by a later sale catalogue of the furnishings, the house was decorated in cluttered high Victorian style with imported Indian and Chinese furniture, pier-glass mirrors and ornaments such as curios from their Asian travels: ivory carvings, jade ornaments, Pekin cloisonné and other enamel work, as well as numerous oil paintings. Each house and garden in the terrace was 24 feet wide and a 'noble depth' of 330 feet. The Lewises kept two mares, a buggy and a milch cow in stables at the back of the property.[608] Years later

---

605 *Era*, 16 September 1882, p. 14.
606 Rate Books; Sands & McDougall Melbourne Street Directories. Street numbering had not yet been adopted for St Kilda Road. The site of Georges Terrace is now occupied by Chevron Apartments.
607 *Today*, 13 September 1894, p. 10.
608 The dining room, 17.6 feet by 17.00 feet, covered by a bordered Brussels carpet was furnished with a carved black walnut suite upholstered in tapestry, a 'telescope' dining table and Italian Walnut Chiffonier, this room opened through folding doors into a breakfast room, 16.6 x 15 feet next to the pantry, kitchen (which had a gas stove) and laundry. Upstairs a 23 x 17.6 drawing room opened on to a spacious balcony with a view of Port Phillip Bay and St Kilda Park (now the Albert Ground). A large pier glass mirror over the fireplace reflected the elaborately carved Indian ebony suite, tables and bookcase, a Schwechten upright grand piano and lacquered Japanese cabinets. Everywhere there were oil paintings and curios from their Asian travels: ivory carvings, jade ornaments, Pekin cloisonné and other enamel work. Also on this floor were three bedrooms containing half-tester and French bedsteads with a large 3-door mahogany wardrobe and an elaborately carved Canton bedroom suite in the main bedroom. There

CHAPTER TWELVE

it was commented that in building these large terrace houses in the 1870s, Lewis was 40 years ahead of his time.[609]

Throughout the year, G. B. W. Lewis was able to sub-lease the Bijou to various companies, including Fred Marshall's comedy company, the Montague Manners Opera Company and the Rosa Towers Company.[610] The Majeronis and actor manager Wybert Reeve, now in charge of the Theatre Royal Adelaide, took the theatre for a season of comedies. None of these ventures were very successful.[611]

The Lewises' son George, aged 17, was now calling himself George Encyl Lewis (most likely to differentiate himself from his father).[612] He had left Wesley College and started his architecture articles with William Salway, architect and neighbour of the Lewises on St Kilda Road.[613]

In August 1883, Rose took Hudson's Theatre for a day to introduce her pupils at a public performance. Perhaps she was already thinking of forming a company with her students, now that the Lewis stock company had dispersed. Nevertheless, a pantomime troupe was got together and Rose ended the year at the Bijou as Ganim in the pantomime *Forty Thieves* with J. L. Hall. During the season, on 29 January 1884, Rose turned 40. For the next two months she played comedy with Hall and Jessie Grey, first in *Our Girls*[614] and then as Winifred in *Our Loves*.[615] Also with Hall she played the dual roles of Mildred and Alice in the old 1869 melodrama by H. J. Byron *Blow for Blow*.[616] Considered by critics to be 'unsuited' to the part of the consumptive sister, Rose finished the season in early March as the 'flirtatious' Mrs Parminter Blake in the 1880 Arthur Wing Pinero farce *Imprudence*.[617] By the end of the month Lewis found a new sub-lessee in the American singer Emelie Melville's English Opera Company. As well

---

was one bathroom on the first floor and another three bedrooms and two bathrooms on the floor above, probably servant's quarters. This description is based on auction advertisements in *Argus*, 12 October 1876, 26 January 1882 and 16 January 1892.
609 *Otago Witness*, 'Notes by Pasquin', 3 March 1892.
610 *Argus*, 31 March 1883.
611 'News from Australia', *Era*, 23 June, 7 July, 11 August, 18 August, 1 September, 6 October, 29 December 1883.
612 The origin of the name 'Encyl' has not yet been traced. Perhaps it was a school nickname: a shortening of the word 'encyclopaedia' indicating that young George was something of a 'know-all'. George Lewis junior was to use this middle name for the rest of his life.
613 Miles Lewis, Architectural Index, University of Melbourne, Dept of Architecture and Building [microform], State Library of Victoria.
614 *Argus*, 7 February 1884.
615 *Argus*, 11 February 1884.
616 *Argus*, 25 February 1884.
617 *Argus*, 1 March 1884.

as works such as *The Bohemian Girl* and *Maritana*, Melville also produced *Il Trovatore* in English.[618] When the firm Williamson, Garnet and Musgrove needed to move the very popular cross-dressing comedian John F. Sheridan and his plays *The Widow O'Brien* and *Fun on the Bristol* to another theatre they were able to take the Bijou for a time.[619]

Rose continued teaching her young pupils and, no doubt inspired by her brother Willie's Sparks Company in America,[620] decided to take a company of young performers to New Zealand. Although at first thought to be a 'juvenile' company, it included at least ten adults. The *Leader*, quoting the *Otago Witness*, remarked that Rose was making a 'somewhat novel experiment of commingling of adults and juveniles.'[621] They were to be on tour in New Zealand until 31 January 1885.

According to the *Leader* report, the Lewis Sparks Company consisted of 'H. A. Douglas, Mr. St Lawrence, Mrs. Lewis, Mrs. J. P. Hydes, & co.' also 'Misses M. Weir, P. Young, M. Pullen, C. Peachey, Marie Brooks, Alice Brooks, "Little Florrie Russell", Messrs. E. D. Haygarth, W. Forbes, H. Hoyte, C. Thomson, and Caesar'. The Lewises and some of their troupe left Melbourne for the Bluff, New Zealand on the steam ship *Te Anau*.[622] The Sparks Company opened at the Princess Theatre Dunedin on 14 October, with Rose as Peg Woffington in *Masks and Faces*.[623] Prices were 4/-, 2/6 and 1/-. Other plays in the repertoire included *Blue Beard*, *Clouds*, *The Jealous Wife*, *Aladdin*, *Jane Shore*, *Leah the Forsaken*, *Cora*, *Not True*, *Our Widow* and *Love's Sacrifice*.

The theatre critic of the Dunedin weekly, the *Otago Witness*, was ambivalent about the company. Suspecting that *Masks and Faces* had been chosen to 'conceal the company's weakness' he applauded the choice of the old play which 'lifts the curtain of the past' and for the strength of Rose's performance. However the reviewer was unhappy with the other actresses who 'do not invite much notice', especially in the comedy-drama *Clouds*. The critic went on to state that he thought that Rose's talents were wasted on the play: 'This piece shows in nearly every line the magic touch of the amateur playwright … As for the remaining ladies they appeared to have tasted freely of what Edwin Forrest called the ether and opium of dramatic art – elocution lessons'. This

---

618 Allison Gyger, *Opera for the Antipodes*, Currency Press, Sydney, 1990, p. 13; *Argus*, 13 September 1884. Melville enjoyed a six month season at the Bijou.
619 *Argus*, 13 September 1894.
620 Willie Edouin was touring the USA with his Sparks Company.
621 *Leader*, 25 October 1884, p. 26.
622 *Argus*, 11 October 1884, 'Shipping Intelligence' *Te Anau*.
623 *Leader*, 11 October 1884; *Dunedin Herald*, 16 October 1884.

perhaps gives us a view of the limitations of what Rose was trying to achieve in both in her school and in the Sparks Company. Later reviews of the New Zealand season show that in *Masks and Faces* Chrissie Peachy [sic] at fifteen was playing actress Kitty Clive, the sophisticated rival of Peg Woffington, and Mary Weir at fourteen was playing the young wife, Mrs Vane.[624] Perhaps Rose was reliving her childhood, remembering how her parents had taught her stage skills. Or, was she happy to be the only experienced performer so that her own undoubted talents would stand out even more?

The Pollards, now enjoying some success and touring New Zealand, followed the Sparks Company into Dunedin with their production of *Les Cloches de Corneville* opening on 1 November. The rather hard-to-please reviewer of 'Notes by Pasquin' continued his criticism of child performers: 'What degree of artistic merit could children possibly attain? Obviously not a high one. The success ... of Mrs. Lewis's troupe of juvenile "Pinaforists" in Australia a few years ago was owing not to any excellence in the representation of the opera, but to the spectacle of children, who were expected to do so little, doing so much'.[625]

The *Dunedin Herald* was more encouraging in its review of *Blue Beard*, where Rose 'threw much life and vigour into her acting' and Christine Peachey had 'sprightly grace'.[626] The *Otago Witness* reviewer liked only Rose as Selim:

> She was arch, graceful, vivacious – everything she should have been. There is a swift, subtle intelligence about her gestures and facial expressions that is noticeable in everything she does, from the "legitimate to pantomime'

This review includes a rare description of her singing voice, with the lower notes 'still good'.[627]

Soon the company was travelling up the South Island to Timaru for a two night stand.[628] They would have boarded a coastal steamer for these journeys, as New Zealand railways were still largely undeveloped.[629] They opened in

---

624 'Notes by Pasquin', *Otago Witness*, 25 October 1884 in its theatre column. Nevertheless this critic saw Christine Peachey as Kitty Clive, Mary Weir as Mrs Vane. Rose 'at home in the part'; *Lyttelton Times*, 1 November 1884, 3 November 1884. Prices: 4/-, 2/6, 6d.
625 *Otago Witness*, 8 November 1885.
626 *Dunedin Herald*, 24 October 1884.
627 *Otago Witness*, 1 November 1884.
628 *Timaru Herald*, 30 October 1884; they then proceeded to Ashburton.
629 See Adrienne Simpson, 'Putting entertainment on the map: the New Zealand touring circuits in 1874', in *Australasian Drama Studies*, No. 26, April, 1995.

Christchurch on 1 November and performed until 20 November. By this time *Jane Shore* and *Leah the Forsaken* were added to their schedule. Leaving Christchurch, the company steamed to Wellington where they performed until 12 December. After some performances in Napier, they arrived in Auckland on 26 December 1885. Like many other critics, the Auckland *Observer* was struck by Rose's versatility at being able to perform on Tuesday as the burlesque hero Selim in *Blue Beard* and on Wednesday play the tragic heroine Jane Shore, remarking that 'It is easy going from the sublime to the ridiculous, but from the ridiculous to the sublime is not an easy matter'. Of her performance in *Jane Shore* the critic praised (possibly with tongue in cheek):

> the emotional acting of Mrs. Lewis in the fourth act made everyone feel so utterly miserable that it requires a wonderful amount of control to prevent one from shedding tears.[630]

The company played at Abbott's Opera House until 29 January, before embarking on the *Te Anau* for Australia.

Because of its novelty, the Lewis's tour was probably successful, but it had been extremely strenuous. After it they decided to retire. Their lease of the Bijou was about to expire. Rose gave her last Bijou performance during Lewis's lease on 2 March 1885. The following day,[631] after almost five years as lessee and directress, the Lewises left the Bijou. Their time at the theatre had been a mixed success. There had been the popularity of the *HMS Pinafore* seasons and tours, and Rose's pantomime performances, together with some of her melodramatic starring roles, had shown her versatility. The last Creswick season at the Bijou with Rose supporting the old tragedian had also been successful. But, as was often the case, apart from the consumptive Edwin Adams, Creswick and Howe, Rose had been ill-served by the acting quality of her leading men. The Lewis stock company varied in quality: although Hans Phillips and George Richard Ireland were competent performers, others had failed to draw audiences from the Royal, the Opera House and the Princess's. Nevertheless, Rose could now 'retire' to St Kilda Road and continue teaching. With investments and rent from other property, their finances seemed secure with investments and rent from the other three houses in the terrace.

---

630   Auckland *Observer*, 10 January 1885.
631   *Australasian*, 7 March 1885, p. 458.

Chapter thirteen

RETIREMENT AND BACK TO ENGLAND, 1885–1893

The retirement of theatrical people can cause problems for the biographer who lacks an archive of their personal papers. However, some references to the Lewises in newspapers give some idea of their movements and life. For the next seven years the Lewises 'retired' to St Kilda Road. Their son George Encyl continued his architectural studies with William Salway and in December 1885 won an Institute of Architects prize of ten guineas for the design of small library or museum.[632] Yet, as events were to show, young George's interests and talents were musical rather than architectural. Rose continued her teaching of young theatrical hopefuls and there are 'snippets' of news that old George retained his interest in circus by using his vacant land next to Georges Terrace as a circus ring.[633] At the end of his lease of the Bijou, G. B. W. moved dray-loads of scenery and costumes from the theatre to a purpose-built storeroom attached to his home.[634] This indicates that he still had hopes to manage further theatrical ventures.

Meanwhile the Lewises would have read of the success of Rose's brother, Willie Edouin, who had returned from America to London where he was manager of the Royalty Theatre. He was starring there with his wife, Alice Atherton, in various farces and comedies such as *Blackberries* and *Turned Up*.[635] The couple had three children: two daughters, Daisy and May, soon to go on the stage; and a son Lionel.

By 1887 there may have been some financial trouble to disturb the Lewises' retirement. George still owned a great deal of real estate, both the houses he had built and vacant land in South Yarra and on St Kilda Road, but most

---

632 *Argus*, 5 December 1885.
633 Undated *Bulletin* clipping, c.1890.
634 *Brisbane Courier*, 14 December 1888.
635 Programme cast lists at Mander and Mitchenson archives, London.

were mortgaged.[636] A 'snippet' in the *Otago Witness* of 22 April 1887 states that 'Mrs. G. B. Lewis is selling her wardrobe and books, &co., preparatory, it is supposed, to her retirement from the profession'. It is not known if this sale was carried out. Yet, by the late 1880s, G. B. W. was on the board of at least two booming companies: the Land Credit Bank of Australasia Limited and Daniel White carriage builders.[637] A highlight in Rose's theatre life during this interim period came in September, when she was persuaded by Guilia Majeroni to play Queen Elizabeth in one performance of *Marie Stuart*.[638]

The year 1888 was celebrated as the centenary of European settlement of Australia and was an important one for the colony of Victoria. Opening in August, an international trade exhibition was to be held in the still splendid Exhibition Building. As at the time of the 1880 exhibition, the Melbourne theatre world looked forward to an influx of visitors to city theatres. Now no longer performing on stage, Rose no doubt looked forward to an exciting time of attendance at theatre and concerts. But the year was to be a trying one for the Lewises. First, her sister-in-law Tilly Earl, widow of her brother John Edouin, died at the age of 46.[639] Then, later in the year, her perhaps still estranged father John Edwin Jones Bryer died on 20 November at the age of 79. He had married his common-law-wife, Isabella Jane Wing, 49, three days earlier.[640] It is not known if there had been any reunion between Rose and her father or if Lewises attended the funeral.

Life at Georges Terrace continued with Rose teaching her stage pupils, G. B. W. exercising his horses on his vacant land on the corner of St Kilda Road and Commercial Roads (perhaps he was imagining his equestrian circus days), and their son pursuing his architectural and musical interests. At this time Rose had only one servant, Frances Perry, 23, from a farm at Caralulup near the Talbot area north of Melbourne. Fanny, as she was known, would have cooked and cleaned for the family. She was later described as a 'quiet, respectable girl' keeping company with a young letter carrier from Williamstown. Rose noticed that after returning from a visit to her late father's farm Fanny had shown signs of depression and had wanted to leave Rose's service feeling unworthy of her wages. A neighbour noticed

---

636 Land Victoria (Formerly Lands Department) Certificates of Titles for Lewis's St Kilda Road properties.
637 *Argus*, 1 November 1888; *Argus*, 1 October 1890.
638 'Notes by Pasquin', *Otago Witness*, October 1888.
639 *Lorgnette*, 20 February 1888.
640 Marriage and Death Certificates; Death Notice in *Argus*; funeral notice 24 November 1888.

CHAPTER THIRTEEN

her in the garden waving her arms about in a strange way at this time. In late October the Lewises attended the theatre but were not alarmed when Fanny failed to let them in. When they found her bed un-slept-in next morning they assumed that she had gone home to the farm. Lewises informed the police of her disappearance. But the girl was not located. The Lewises hired another servant and life went on as usual.[641]

Then on Friday 30 November the quiet of the Lewises' home turned to horror and 'incomprehensible mystery' when, investigating the source of a strong stench seeming to come from the scenery shed, G. B. W. and his son decided that the smell (possibly a dead cat) was coming from the top of a pile of 'flats'. George climbed to the top and exclaimed. 'Oh God, there's a dead man up here' then "Oh it's Fanny!'". Her decomposed body was lying in a 'nest' of old theatre costumes on top of a stack of 'flats' 15 feet above the ground.[642] It appeared that Fanny, reportedly in a depressed state over a family property dispute, had hidden in the scenery shed and starved herself to death![643] She had been missing for five weeks. The extreme heat during that time and her position high up near the iron roof perhaps accounted for the advanced decomposition of her body. However, it is probable that she died only a week or two before her body was found. By midday, Georges Terrace and the houses of Fanny's friends around Melbourne were invaded by reporters questioning the Lewises and others about the servant and the strange circumstances of her life and death. Rose immediately concluded that the girl had committed suicide, and she told of Fanny's depression and worries about some land near Talbot she and her sister owned.[644]

An inquest was held at the Morgue on 4 December before a jury, with coroner Dr Richard Youl in charge. As well as giving details of the deceased's stomach and bowel contents, the two medical practitioners Doctors Moore and Maudsley, who performed the post mortem, stressed that their examinations had found that Fanny Perry was a 'virgin'. This evidence would have quashed suspicions that Fanny might have been pregnant and that her depression was caused by this fear. The doctors declared that there was no sign of violence on the body and agreed with the government analyst Dr Blackett that there was no presence of poison in the body. Dr Blackett also found that two bottles discovered near the body did not contain any toxic substance.

---

641 This section is based on newspaper reports and inquest evidence.
642 *Argus*, 1 December 1888.
643 PROV, VPRS 24/P, Unit 538, Item 1515. There are discrepancies between the Inquest Papers and the newspaper reports – eg. in the latter the word 'virgin' is replaced with 'respectable' and 'menstruating' is not mentioned.
644 *Herald*, 30 November 1888; *Argus*, 1 December 1888.

Fanny Perry's sister Martha told how they were joint owners of 30 acres of land of their late father's farm. Martha Perry also deposed that their mother, who was epileptic, had remarried and how Fanny was at odds with her step-father who was working the farm. Martha was afraid that their mother would have no home if the land was sold and the money divided. Nevertheless, Martha did not believe that her sister was unduly depressed about this matter.

The Lewis family gave evidence at the inquest. George Lewis, 23, described how he had climbed up on the scenery and found the body. G. B. W.'s deposition described how the family had attended the theatre on the night before Fanny's disappearance, and how they were not worried when she did not open the door on their return. When next morning they found her bed unslept-in, but all her effects still in the room, G. B. W. reported her 'being missing to the police'. Lewis also mentioned finding 'soiled linen' in Fanny's room which indicated to him that she had been menstruating at the time of her disappearance. (This was taken up by some newspaper theorists, influenced by current psychological theory, as a cause of depressive hysteria which could have led to her suicide.)

Not all the witnesses at the inquest believed that Fanny was excessively depressed at the time of her disappearance. Yet Rose, now spending more time at home, perhaps knew her servant better than others. She described how Fanny had wept and seemed obsessed by her wish to sell her late father's farm and 'go away from everybody'. Fanny also expressed her anger against her stepfather: 'my stepfather has driven me to this; I want my money'.

The coroner declared that Fanny Perry had not been murdered, that the body was too decomposed to state the cause of death and ordered the jury to declare the open finding 'found dead', and close the inquest. It was left to newspapers, seizing on the sensation of the case, to ask how Fanny had climbed more than four metres to the top of a stack of theatre 'flats', settled herself on some old theatrical costumes and waited for death by starvation. They also asked whether Fanny or someone else had been coming and going from the shed during the first part of her disappearance as a copy of the *Argus* dated 15 November had been found near the body. This raised the question of why the Lewises had not noticed anything strange except for a moan coming from the shed two weeks before. They thought it must have been a cat. None of these queries was answered.

The final official word is in a memo dated 7 December 1888 to the chief commissioner of police, Hussey Malone Chomley, where he was informed

CHAPTER THIRTEEN

that further investigations had added nothing to the case; 'There seems little doubt that the girl voluntarily killed herself by starvation'. The author of the memo also expressed disapproval of the press – he regretted 'that a leading daily journal should have circulated false and mischievous rumours regarding the deceased and persons with whom she was associated.' It is likely that Fanny's relatively low social status as 'a servant-girl' contributed to the closing of the case and the seeming unwillingness by the police to fathom the mystery.

For two weeks after the inquest the press continued a campaign to solve the mystery. Indeed, *Melbourne Punch* likened the 'St Kilda mystery' to the local best seller novel by Fergus Hume *The Mystery of a Hansom Cab*.[645] An editorial in the Melbourne *Daily Telegraph* cited Edgar Allan Poe's *Murders of the Rue Morgue* and likened the 'St Kilda Road mystery'[646] to the works of the French crime-novelists Du Boisgobey and Gaboriau. Under the heading 'A Hypothetical Elucidation', a writer signing himself 'Reflective' suggested that Fanny might have spent some time wandering around the city staying in hotels and lodging houses, then, some time later, disoriented and confused, she returned to the Lewis house at night, and that she crept into the shed for shelter. 'Reflective' also postulated that that Fanny might have had an epileptic seizure in her 'bed' near the iron roof in the very hot shed and been unable to call for help.[647]

The papers continued to criticise the police for removing evidence before the scene had been examined by detectives and the Coroner for not calling for a prolonged investigation. For example, the *Brisbane Courier* of 14 December cited the Perry case in part of an editorial about police incompetence in criminal proceedings. They did not look for clues carefully enough.[648] All the newspapers pointed out that there had not been insufficient followup of the inconsistencies in the evidence. By early 1889, however, press speculation about the mystery had virtually disappeared.[649]

There is no indication that the police regarded the three Lewises as being 'persons of interest' or being implicated in any crime.[650] Some of the newspapers implied criticism of the Lewises for not enquiring further and

---

645 Melbourne *Punch*, 6 December 1888, p. 505.
646 Melbourne *Daily Telegraph*, 4 December 1888.
647 *Herald*, 5 December 1888.
648 See *Argus*, 5 December 1888; *Brisbane Courier*, 14 December 1888.
649 The recent digitisation of Australian newspapers by the National Library of Australia has expedited historians' ability to search the press.
650 Police records and inquest papers.

of Rose for jumping to the conclusion that Fanny's starvation was related to her depression.[651]

What must have been a subject of scandalised gossip does not seem to have affected the Lewises' social standing. For example, G. B. W. and his son were invited to the governor's levee the following year,[652] and Rose continued her theatre school.[653] We have no evidence of the effect on the Lewises of the ghastly death of their servant. Like much of the Lewis story we cannot know their inner feelings. Rose's evidence at the inquest speaks of her sympathy for the 'girl' when she retold the problem about the property. Rose showed some sensitivity in trying to find the reasons for the servant's distress and certainly painted a picture of a very disturbed young woman (Rose's evidence at the inquest reads rather like a play text).

The Lewises continued their connection with the theatre world, Rose teaching theatre skills to children and sometimes producing or appearing in special performances. Even G. B. W. appeared on the stage as an extra at the Theatre Royal on 23 March 1889, when there were matinee performances at both the Theatre Royal and the new Princess's. These were to benefit the great Melbourne scenic artist John Hennings, whose sight had been impaired after an illness. At the Theatre Royal, as well as actors such as Rose and her sister-in-law Elizabeth Edouin Bryer, G. B. W. played a member of the jury in a scene from *Pickwick Papers*. He was accompanied by theatrical identities Dr J. E. Neild, Dr L. L. Smith and scenic artist George Gordon. Rose appeared in the Trial Scene from *The Merchant of Venice* at the Princess's.[654]

G. B. W. was by now regarded as something of a theatrical patriarch. At a luncheon in August for the visiting actor Charles Warner, he was invited to talk on his early experiences in Melbourne.[655] Unfortunately no detailed report of this meeting has yet been found.

The Lewises would have been affected by the destruction by fire on 22 April of their old theatre, the Bijou, where they had enjoyed mixed success after their return from India. This 'pretty little' theatre had been, for some time, the Melbourne headquarters of the successful Brough and Boucicault Comedy Company.[656] The Bourke Street façade of the building by Reed and

---

651 *Age*, 3 December 1888.
652 *Argus*, 5 December 1889.
653 *Argus*, November 1889.
654 *Argus*, 21 March 1889; *Lorgnette* (review), 30 March 1889; *Leader*, 30 March 1889.
655 *Evening Standard*, 15 August; *Table Talk*, 16 August 1889.
656 *Age*, 23 April 1889.

CHAPTER THIRTEEN

Barnes was undamaged, but it was nearly a year before a new theatre opened to new designs by George R. Johnson.[657]

On 19 November 1889, nearly a year after the horror of their servant's death, the Lewises held a ball celebrating their silver wedding anniversary. The function was reported in great detail in the society pages of the weekly *Table Talk*. It was a splendid occasion with 120 guests.[658] As noted earlier, they made an impressive pair. The garden was 'illuminated by hundreds of Chinese lanterns'. The ball was held in the large upstairs drawing-room from where guests could take the air on the balcony to admire a view of Port Phillip Bay. A pier-glass mirror over the fireplace reflected the guests in the sumptuous room with its Oriental décor, thick Brussels carpet and upright grand piano.[659]

Actor-manager Henry Harwood, an old colleague of G. B. W.'s from the circus days proposed the toast.[660] *Table Talk* reported on the guests and listed some of their gifts. These included silver articles such as cruets, entrée dishes, knives and forks and serviette rings. Numerous telegrams were read. The Lewis's wealthy neighbours, such as the Hentys, the Mowbrays and the Salways, were not listed among the guests; but Mrs Henry Westley (Alice Wiseman), wife of G. B. W.'s solicitor, and Rose's sister-in-law Lizzie Bryer were there, as was a 'Miss Sayers' (probably Alice, the fiancée of Rose's nephew William Bryer).[661]

Rose rounded off the year with a special performance by her pupils of the old melodrama *Love's Sacrifice* at the Temperance Hall in Russell Street.[662] An interesting family event took place at Geelong on 17 January 1890 when William Edwin Bryer, son of Rose's late brother Charles, married Alice E. Sayers of Geelong. Evidence that there was some family contact between John Edwin Jones Bryer, Rose's father, and his second family is shown by the fact that Blanche Bryer, his daughter by Isabella Wing, was one of the

---

657 Philip Parsons, ed., *Companion to Australian Theatre*, Currency Press, Sydney, 1995, p. 87.
658 *Table Talk*, 22 November 1889, p. 16.
659 Information gleaned from *Argus* auction advertisements.
660 Harwood had toured with Lewis's circus as a rider.
661 The guests named in the *Table Talk* article give a cross-section of the Lewises' friends. Apart from the Harwoods and Mrs Emery Gould they don't seem to be particularly theatrical. The list includes Mr and Mrs Henry Burrows, Mrs E. Gould (possibly the singing teacher Mrs Emery Gould), Miss O'Shanassy, Mrs J. W. Smith, the Misses Maud and Florry Smith, Mr and Mrs J. L. Young, Mrs and the Misses H. K. Bennett, Mr Pilley, Mr Church, Mr and Mrs Harwood, Mr and Mrs Bradshaw, Mr and Miss Conor-O'Brien, Messrs W. E. Wilson and Mendell, the Misses Ellis, Nichols, Annear and Sayers.
662 *Lorgnette*, 20 December 1889.

bridesmaids. Further, William's cousin and Rose's son George Encyl Lewis was best man.[663] Rose did not attend.

In March 1890, Dr J. E. Neild, now aged nearly 67, severed his connection with the *Australasian* newspaper and its theatre criticism.[664] It was said that the irascible Neild refused to alter his inflated admiration for the American actress Cora Brown-Potter. This was at odds with the opinion of the *Argus* theatre critic James Smith. (The weekly *Australasian* was published by the daily *Argus*.) Two theatrical benefit matinees were held at the Princess's on 19 and 26 July to express the theatrical profession's appreciation of Neild. These events netted more than £700. Rose and one of her pupils, Rudolf Leonard Truebridge, played the scene from *Henry VI* with Rose as the fierce Queen Margaret where she mocks the King.[665]

Rose and her pupils continued to be mentioned in the press. An article on the actress Christine Darrell describes her as 'a pupil of Mrs. G. B. W. Lewis for a considerable time, and from that experienced artiste she received her early training in acting, dancing &c'.[666] Also in September the young actress Eugenie Duggan made her debut as Juliet. Rose had coached her in the role. 'This young lady has been under the tuition of Mrs. G. B. W. Lewis for some time past, and she gave a well-studied interpretation of Juliet.'[667] Duggan, sister of actor and playwright Edmund Duggan, and from 1898 wife of theatre manager William Anderson, was a successful leading lady on the Australian stage for the next two decades.[668]

In March 1891, Rose received the news that her sister Julia Edouin, Mrs W. F. Grahame, had died in Philadelphia aged 42 from tuberculosis. Julia had not performed on the stage for several years and had been living in a boarding house with her young daughter, Frances May Grahame.[669] This young woman eventually joined her aunt Rose in England in 1892.

Meanwhile, in June, the great French actress Sarah Bernhardt was touring Australia. In Melbourne she played her large repertoire in French at the Princess's. The Lewises most likely attended – and Rose might have had sad thoughts of ambitions unfulfilled.

---

663 *Table Talk*, 17 January 1890, p. 16.
664 Harold Love, *James Edward Neild: Victorian Virtuoso*, Melbourne University Press, 1989, p. 307.
665 *Argus*, 28 July 1890; *Bulletin*, 30 August 1906.
666 *Melbourne Punch*, 14 August 1890.
667 *Argus*, 13 September 1890.
668 See Margaret Williams, 'William Anderson', *Australian Dictionary of Biography*, Vol. 7, pp. 63–64.
669 *Lorgnette*, April; *Table Talk*, 24 April; Melbourne *Punch*, 14 May; *New York Clipper*, 14 March 1891; U.S. Death Certificate.

CHAPTER THIRTEEN

By 1891, Melbourne was on the brink of financial disaster. The 1880s Land Boom had led to unbridled investment by banks and individuals and G. B. W. Lewis had been something of a pioneer land boomer as far back as 1865 when, on his return from Asia, he used much of the money he had made as a circus and drama entrepreneur to buy land in South Yarra and along the St Kilda Road. He had also added value to these ventures by building houses on some of the blocks of land. As we have seen, he built Shanghai Villa, his dwelling for a few years, in 1865 and had Georges Terrace and Victoria House built by 1873. Financing the expense of mounting tours to India might have come from the various mortgages on these properties.[670] During the Lewises' absences in India Shanghai Villa was let and eventually sold.[671] When they moved to No. 1 Georges Terrace there would have been rent from the other three houses in the terrace. After one of their successful tours to China, G. B. W. auctioned much of the furniture bought on the tour. This income, together with profits from his theatre ventures, would have made the couple quite wealthy. However, in 1891 the Lewises lost nearly all their money with the failure of the banks[672] and G. B. W.'s remaining properties had been heavily mortgaged and were sold.[673] The Lewises must have had some money left, for, in late 1891 they decided to sail to England taking young George with them. Perhaps seeing Bernhardt had made Rose eager to make an attempt, after 35 years, to appear again in London theatre. Her son, despite having qualifications as an ARIVA architect with rooms at 237 Collins Street, had musical ambitions and hoped to study in London.[674]

In late January 1892, G. B. W. made a codicil to his will making Rose the sole executrix.[675] Their financial difficulties are indicated in a report that Rose sold her theatrical library to Cole's book store in Melbourne. This included prompt-books from Calcutta, Bombay, Melbourne and the Cremorne Pantheon Theatre, reflecting her career in the 1850s, 1860s and

---

670 Land Victoria (Formerly Lands Department), Certificates of Titles for Lewis properties; MMBW Map of City of Melbourne, Parish of Melbourne North.
671 See Miles Lewis – Melbourne Mansions Database on line University of Melbourne, www.fmpro.abp.unimelb.edu.au/fmi/iwp/cgi?-db=mmdb.
672 No record of Lewis's bankruptcy has so far been found. He may have made a secret composition with his creditors or signed his property over to his wife. She was declared insolvent in 1897, see next chapter.
673 See Rate Books after 1892. All the houses G. B. W. built had been demolished by the 1950s.
674 *Sands & McDougall Melbourne Street Directory 1892*. George Encyl Lewis was to have several terms at the Royal Academy of Music in 1892–1893.
675 Dated 25 January 1892, PROV, VPRS 226, Item 99/245.

1870s.[676] They seemed desperate to get to London and put the contents of their house up for sale – the stress of the last few days before leaving must have been intense, seeing all their possessions being sold.

Rose was given a benefit at the Bijou Theatre on the afternoon of Saturday 23 January, two days before leaving Melbourne. She was supported by performers from most of Melbourne theatres. The Brough company played scenes from *Antony and Cleopatra* and Rose played Mrs Oakly in *The Jealous Wife*, one of her favourite comedy roles.[677] The benefit was not a financial success – the Sydney *Bulletin* of 6 February reported that 'there was an erroneous idea abroad that the Lewises were going "home" with a pile and didn't receive more than hundred or two'.[678] The family sailed to England on the *Oruba*, arriving at Plymouth on 1 March.[679]

Australians in London were a source of press interest in Australia and the weekly *British Australasian* of 4 March 1892 reported that they were staying at 22–24 Montague Street, Bloomsbury. Soon George Encyl, aged 26, was studying at the Royal Academy of Music, Tenterden Street, London. He had been recommended by the Australian actor-manager W. J. Holloway, who was then playing Kent and understudy to Henry Irving's King Lear at the Lyceum.[680] Young George passed his entrance exam on 13 May. His principal study was Harmony and Composition, with Violin as second study. He was paying £11 guineas per quarter for this tuition.[681]

Rose's ambition to act in London during her stay was fulfilled at a matinee performance at the Strand Theatre, managed at the time by her brother Willie Edouin. On 26 July 1892, she played Mrs Oakly in *The Jealous Wife* with Herbert Flemming as Mr Oakly.[682] The recently discovered scrapbook 'Newspaper Criticisms of Mrs GBW Lewis (Miss Rose Edouin) dating from Tuesday 26th July 1892 – her re-appearance in London' contains no fewer than 38 reviews of this single performance. Decorated with flourishes and careful hand printing and writing often seen on architectural plans, it was probably compiled by her son George Encyl Lewis. It indicates how vitally important Rose's *rentrée* to London was to her family and her career.

---

676 Sydney *Bulletin*, 27 February; 12 March 1892. No trace of these memorabilia has yet been found.
677 *Argus*, 23 January 1892; *Argus*, 25 January 1892; *Bohemia*, 21 January 1892.
678 I am indebted to Elisabeth Kumm for this reference.
679 *European Mail*, 4 March 1892, p. 33.
680 David Holloway, *Playing the Empire*, George G. Harrup, London 1979, p. 62. Rose attended the performance when he took over the role from the ill Irving.
681 Royal Academy of Music Entrance Register 1874–1896, pp. 393–94.
682 *Freeman's Journal*, 27 July; *The Times*, 30 July; *Era*, 30 July; *Theatre*, August 1892.

CHAPTER THIRTEEN

They had gambled everything on the hope of her success on the stages of her youth.

After questioning the revival of such an old play as the *Jealous Wife*, many of the critics went on to compliment Rose on her portrayal of Mrs Oakly in the 'old comedy'. Others condescendingly praised her, after so many years in Australia, for being 'now an actress of first-rate ability, without a touch of the exaggerated methods which have come to be associated with players hailing from the Antipodes.'[683] He thought it a pity that the performance came so late in the season for other theatre managers to access her talents. Some of these reviews acknowledged the Lewises' experience in Melbourne and Calcutta theatre.

Although she could not, at first, find parts in the West End, Rose's time in England was spent profitably in provincial theatre. Now nearly 50, she was able to play character and 'old woman' roles. In August, she travelled with Willie Edouin's Company on a tour of the provinces to Bristol where, billed as 'Miss Rosie Lewis', she played the comedy role of Letty Lightfoot in the farce *Master and Man* at the Prince's Theatre.[684] By October, she was playing the same role in Leeds at the Theatre Royal.[685] November found her back in London in an afternoon recital with her son at the Strand Theatre. Rose would have delivered various Shakespearian speeches and recited poetry, while George Encyl played the piano and bow zither.[686] The latter instrument was mildly popular in the second half of the nineteenth century, having been invented in central Europe in the 1860s.

Not doing too well in the theatre, Rose had hopes of opening a theatre school and advertised in the theatre weekly *Era* in November 1892 and March 1893. 'Mrs. G. B. W. Lewis (Miss Rose Edouin) at liberty. Pupils received. 24 Montague Street, Bloomsbury'. But this came to nothing.[687] By March 1895, George Encyl had left the RAM and was living in Chiswick, possibly taking private music lessons. Rose meanwhile was touring with her

---

683 *The Figaro*, 6 August 1892, clipping in 'Newspaper Criticisms of Mrs GBW Lewis (Miss Rose Edouin) dating from Tuesday 26th July 1892 - her re-appearance in London', p. 3. As well as containing clippings of reviews of her time in London there are many loose cuttings from earlier performances in Melbourne and Sydney and some from her later time back in Melbourne and final return to England. These seem to be from other scrapbooks. The last few pages are in Rose's handwriting listing her roles in 1900–1903. I am indebted to actress Gemma Reeves of Dublin who gave me this scrapbook in 2012.
684 *Bristol Evening News*, 9 August 1892.
685 *Era*, 29 October 1892.
686 *Era*, 26 November 1892.
687 *European Mail*, 20 January 1893, p. 25. A brief article expressed Rose's hopes.

brother Willie around the southern counties as Agatha Honeycutt in the farce *Modern Wives*. They played at theatres such as those in Hastings, The Gaiety, The Eastbourne and The Portsmouth.[688] Rose and Willie were back at the Strand in London by July for 26 performances of *The Sleepwalker* in which Rose played Gwendolyn Blister.[689] This was followed in October by a month's season at the same theatre of *The Lady Killer*, with Rose playing the comic character of Mrs Robjohn, supporting her brother and sister-in-law, Willie Edouin and Alice Atherton.[690]

During this period, Rose's niece Frances May Grahame joined them in England from America. In October 1892, Rose was reported as expressing her decision to remain in England to act and to become 'a teacher of dramatic elocution'.[691] However, as she regretfully told an interviewer in 1893, her husband, now aged 75, and her niece could not face another London winter after that of 1892/1893, so they had decided that they should return to Australia via South Africa. The *European Mail* of 29 November 1893 interviewed G. B. W. and Rose in an article titled rather exaggeratedly comparing Lewis to a West End impresario, 'The Antipodean Augustus Harris'. G. B. W. said he hoped to talk over 'old-times' with the Cape Colony governor, Sir Henry Loch, whom he had met when the latter was Governor of Victoria. With their son George Encyl and Rose's niece, the couple left London on *Lismore Castle* for a tour of South Africa, arriving at Cape Town on 21 December. In an interview by the *Cape Argus*, Rose was described as a 'dramatic reciter. Her principal achievements, she tells us have been in India, China and the Australian colonies where she was well known and highly popular.' Rose also mentioned her recent 'critical' success in London, intimating that they would have stayed but for family illness.[692] They were to stay in South Africa for one month. During this time Rose and her son and niece gave 'Dramatic and Musical Recitals' at Cape Town's Mutual Hall and around the suburbs.[693] A review of their Claremont performance stated, 'These recitals, which are of an artistic and refined character, have received the highest press opinions. The programme is compiled from the works of Shakespeare, Dickens, Tennyson and others'. One of Rose's specialties was

---

688 *Era*, 20 May 1893; *Era*, 27 May 1893; *Era*, 1 July 1893.
689 *The Times*, 27 July; *European Mail*, 2 August 1892.
690 J. P. Wearing, *The London Stage, 1890–1891: A Calendar of Plays and Players*, Scarecrow Press, Metuchen, N. J., 1976, Vol. 1; *Australasian*, 18 November 1892.
691 Melbourne *Punch*, 22 September 1892, p. 180.
692 *Cape Argus*, 21 December 1893. The reporter thought that Rose's 'invalid sister' had caused them to seek the warmth of the Cape, when in fact the invalid was her niece Frances Grahame.
693 *Cape Argus*, 26 December 1893; *Lorgnette*, February 1894.

CHAPTER THIRTEEN

a recitation of Tennyson's 'Rizpah' in costume and Clement Scott's 'The Midnight Charge'. The critic went on to comment on the bow zither (played by George Encyl Lewis) as a 'rather uncommon little instrument, which in the hands of an artist is extremely sweet and expressive'.[694] It seems, however, that their time in the Cape Colony was not the success they had hoped for. They returned to Melbourne by the *Australasian*. Apart from the press records of Rose's performance, it is difficult to get an impression of the Lewises' renewed experience of their birthplace. Of course they went to theatre. In various press interviews on her return to Australia she gives brief opinions of seeing the acting styles of West End stars such as Ellen Terry, Olga Nethersole and Charles Wyndham,[695] and of her interview with Henry Irving. To her intense disappointment and frustration, when Rose applied to Irving for the role of the Queen in W. G. Wills's *Becket* the age-old problem of 'type casting' reared its head. The great actor did not engage her, saying that he had no roles for her as she specialised in comedy.[696] After their decision to return to Australia with an eye for future productions, they bought rights to some plays and also some costumes of the 1888 romantic drama *The Pompadour*.[697] It was perhaps at this time that Rose, dressed and made up as Madame Pompadour, was photographed by Alfred Ellis the famous photographer of theatricals. A cabinet portrait of Rose, by Ellis, survives in the Victoria and Albert Museum archives in London. It has been skilfully altered to make her look younger and slimmer. All this expense must have consumed much of the profit Rose had made during her return to the English stage.

---

694 *Cape Argus*, 29 December 1893.
695 See chapter fourteen.
696 'Mrs. G. B. W. Lewis', *Table Talk*, 31 August 1894, p. 8.
697 See chapter fourteen. By this time many Australian theatre managers, including J. C. Williamson and Bland Holt often paid large sums to West End entrepreneurs such as Augustus Harris to import scenery and costumes from a previous London season.

Chapter fourteen

RETURN TO AUSTRALIA AND 'POVERTY', 1894–1907

The Lewises must have dreaded their return to Australia. Rose had been moderately successful in the English provinces and had enjoyed some critical mention in London. But they now had no home in Melbourne. For the next thirteen years, G. B. W. and Rose Lewis spent their time between semi-retirement and occasional inter-colonial tours and performances, with Rose still teaching. First, hoping to gather funds for a season of full theatre productions, and together with George Encyl and Frances Grahame, they went to Hobart for three weeks of performances at the Town Hall and the new Hobart Exhibition Building.[698] The performances by Rose with the support of her son and niece were a far cry from those of the Bourke Street theatres or London's West End. These were intimate recitals of poetry and scenes from Shakespeare, rather like the performances Rose gave with her pupils in the 1880s and the recitals in Cape Town. By this time G. B. W. was a shadowy presence as manager, with his son advertised as 'Hon. Manager' of the little troupe. One of the items George Encyl played on his bowed zither at an afternoon performance at the Town Hall was the Stephen Foster song 'The Old Folks at Home'.[699] Rose seems to have hoped that Hobart would be a good place to open her theatre school. An advertisement in the Hobart *Mercury* of 1 March announced Mrs Lewis's 'Academy of Elocution' at Highfield Hall, Murray Street (possibly where the family was staying). It is not known if any pupils applied. The Lewis troupe performed at an evening performance at the new Hobart Exhibition Building.[700]

By the middle of the year it was clear that this venture with Rose and her son and niece was not going to be a success. The Lewises and Frances

---

698   *Mercury*, 23, 27, 28 February 1894.
699   *Mercury*, 27 February 1894.
700   *Mercury*, 7, 8 March 1894.

CHAPTER FOURTEEN

returned to Melbourne in July.[701] George Encyl Lewis, now nearly 30, realised that his musical ambitions had not much future in Australia. At the end of June it was announced that he was going to England to work with G. H. Snazelle, a popular vocalist who had toured to Australia in the 1890s.[702] After arriving in London, George Encyl was soon advertised as accompanist to Snazelle. He was reported as painting 'charming scenery' for the entertainer as well as playing the bow zither and other instruments supporting Snazelle at the Egyptian Hall in Regent Street.[703] George Encyl later secured a position as conductor in the actor-manager Ben Greet's Shakespeare season at the Richmond Theatre Royal, Surrey.[704]

The 'society' weekly *Table Talk*, of 31 August 1894, interviewed Rose about her ambition to establish a dramatic college and her plans to return to London in 1895. Yet the Lewises' funds were too low for this. The next month Rose was interviewed by the weekly *Today* about her return to Melbourne and her dramatic school. She spoke nostalgically of the entertainments she had given at her home in St Kilda Road 'where a miniature theatre was created and pupils had a real experience of the exits and entrances'. She also spoke at a meeting of the Shakespeare Society. The weekly *Today* commented that 'She is a capable impromptu speaker and gave several anecdotes of her early professional life including her first meeting with Samuel Phelps'.[705]

Going on tour was often a way of staying in the theatrical world. In December 1894 and January 1895 the Lewises took a company to Ballarat and Bendigo. While in London the Lewises had secured the Australian rights to a play by W. G. Wills,[706] *La Pompadour* (written in conjunction with Sydney Grundy), and *Like No Other Love* by popular actor playwright Mark Melford.[707] *The Pompadour*, as it was titled in London, starred Herbert Beerbohm Tree as Narcisse, Pompadour's grotesque and mentally disturbed husband, and Maud Holt (Mrs Tree) in the title role. The drama played for more than 100 nights at Tree's Haymarket Theatre in 1888. It was not a critical success. Most of the reviews were unfavourable, pointing out its excessive

---

701 PROV, VPRS Inward Passenger List of *Wakatipu*, arrived Melbourne from Hobart 25 July 1894.
702 *Australasian*, 30 June 1894, p. 1127.
703 *Era*, 6 June 1894; 7 July 1894; *Lorgnette*, August 1894.
704 *Era*, 26 January 1895.
705 *Today*, 13 September 1894, p. 10.
706 Wills, who died in 1891, had enjoyed some success as a playwright for Henry Irving's London Lyceum Theatre.
707 *Table Talk*, 31 August 1894, p. 8. Mark Melford (1851–1914), *Like No Other Love* was not produced in England until 1905, see Richard Clarence, *The Stage Cyclopaedia: A Bibliography of Plays*, Burt Franklin, New York, 1909, p. 250.

length, poor dialogue and historically inaccurate plot.[708] Being a Herbert Tree production, however, it provided a lavish spectacle of representations of Louis XV's Versailles and hence was popular enough with audiences. One wonders why Rose, now with vastly reduced resources in Australia, chose to produce this 'romantic drama' and spectacle. She had acquired some of the original costumes[709] so perhaps thought these would be enough to satisfy colonial audiences. Rose continued playing highly emotional 'fallen women' such as Jane Shore, Lady Isabel and Madame Pompadour. As well as Pompadour and Jane Shore she starred as Vane Liddiard in *Like No Other Love* at the Ballarat Academy of Music.[710] The Lewis's were using this provincial tour as a kind of 'off Broadway try out' before taking the plays to Adelaide, Launceston and Melbourne. Their company included Frederick Charles Appleton, one of Rose's leading men in India, and his wife actress Jenny Bryce, Hans Phillips, Clement Wakefield and Leonard Rudolf Truebridge, a thirty-year-old actor who had been one of her pupils in the 1880s.[711] The company opened at the Ballarat Academy of Music with *Jane Shore*. Rose was greeted by a crowded house, and the review stressed her 'wonderful histrionic talent'.[712]

Like No Other Love was one of the plays for which Rose had acquired the rights in London. Described as an 'emotional drama', this play contained a mystery with Rose playing one of two half-sisters, her niece Frances playing the other. For good measure there was a drunken husband and a detective character. This play was well received in Ballarat and Bendigo but for some reason does not seem to have been played elsewhere.

More importantly she produced *Hamlet*, playing the title role herself, with a local amateur actor W. L. Paine as Laertes and her own 'strong company'.[713] A female playing Hamlet was not new: the famous Mrs Siddons had played it in the English provinces from about 1745[714] and Rose would have seen performances of *Hamlet* with Louisa Cleveland in the title role in 1867.[715]

---

708 *Illustrated London News*, 7 April 1888.
709 *Argus*, May 1895.
710 *Ballarat Courier*, 27, 28, 31 December 1894, 3, 4 January 1895.
711 Born in Maldon in 1864, Truebridge seems to have left the theatre c.1900 and moved to Sydney where he died in 1943, see *Sydney Morning Herald*, 18 May 1943.
712 *Ballarat Courier*, 27 December 1894.
713 *Ballarat Courier*, 4 January 1895.
714 Celestine Woo, 'Sarah Siddons as Hamlet: three decades, absent breeches, and rife critical confusion' in *ANQ*, Vol. 20, No. 1/Winter 2007; see also Tony Howard, *Women as Hamlet: Performance and Interpretation in Theatre, Film and Fiction*. Cambridge University Press, Cambridge, UK, 2007, p. 39.
715 Gordon-Clarke op. cit., p. 294.

CHAPTER FOURTEEN

More recently, in 1882, the American actress Louise Pomeroy had played Hamlet with some grudging success at the Theatre Royal, Melbourne. Noting that Pomeroy was 'not letter-perfect', the critic pronounced that 'Female Hamlets are provoking absurdities'.[716] Rose seems to have had a genuine interest in Shakespeare scholarship perhaps going back to her time as a child with Phelps at Sadler's Wells and her remarkable Puck. Also, for example, her Fool to Creswick's King Lear was thought exceptional by Dr Neild, her interpretation indicating close study of that role.[717] One gets the impression that Rose, after playing the recently written roles of Madame Pompadour and Jane Shore had not prepared herself sufficiently for the role of Hamlet. The *Ballarat Courier*'s reviewer, repeating the opinion of Pomeroy's critic, was not very impressed by Rose's performance:

> It cannot be said that her assumption of the character of the melancholy Prince of Denmark was an unqualified success and she was by no means letter perfect, her memory failing her on several occasions.[718]

After this one performance of *Hamlet*, the Lewis company travelled to the Princess Theatre in Bendigo, where they played a similar repertoire.[719] After some remarks on the doubtful desirability of a woman playing 'gloomy Dane', the *Bendigo Advertiser*'s critic gave quite a detailed review of Rose as Hamlet, also noting that she was not text perfect, but: 'in the interview with the Queen, in the graveyard, and in the final scene she was most powerful'. Although the critic thought Rose 'looked the part, much better than was expected … Her good voice, clear enunciation and excellent modulation, made her very effective in most scenes, but there was at times evidence that she was not perfect in the text.'

The same critic wondered why Rose's Hamlet 'was made to keep his cloak on during the play'. Perhaps Rose, like Mrs Siddons and others, draped her cloak for modesty. A failure to memorise the text of Hamlet was described in many of her subsequent performances.[720] Did she have 'a mental block'? Or were these reviews, like that of Louise Pomeroy, quibbles against the very idea of a female Hamlet? The company returned to Melbourne after a week. A short season was all that they could expect in the provincial cities of Victoria.

---

716 *Argus*, 21 August 1882.
717 See chapter ten.
718 *Ballarat Courier*, 5 January 1895.
719 *Bendigo Advertiser*, 7, 8, 10, 12, 14 January 1895.
720 *Bendigo Advertiser*, 12 January 1895.

A stage event also in the family was a benefit for Rose's sister-in-law Lizzie, (Mrs Edouin Bryer) at the Melbourne Opera House in Bourke Street.[721] Meanwhile the Lewises were living in rented accommodation in Albert Road, Albert Park.[722]

By March 1895 they had secured a booking at the Adelaide Theatre Royal. Before leaving for Adelaide they enjoyed a 'sojourn' in Launceston.[723] There they played their current repertoire of 'romantic dramas' and added the tear jerker *East Lynne*, with Rose playing the so-called dual role of Lady Isabel and this character's disguise as Miss Vine. Rose twice performed as Hamlet. Unlike the carping criticism of the Ballarat and Bendigo performances an Adelaide critic pronounced Rose's Hamlet 'word perfect'.[724] For her small role in *Jane Shore*, Frances Grahame was described as 'a clever little lady'.[725] The company returned to Melbourne by the coastal steamer *Coogee* on 30 March and thence to Launceston.[726] The weekly *The Tasmanian*, of 6 April 1895, summed up the season in Launceston thus:

> I am sorry that Mrs. Lewis had not, financially speaking, a successful season in Launceston. The downstairs business was fairly satisfactory, but the usual patrons of the dress circle kept religiously away … [Mrs. Lewis] had risked considerable expense in bringing nearly twenty people over to Tasmania.

The article goes on to mention that the larger companies of J. C. Williamson and Brough and Boucicault had also experienced disappointing seasons.

Rose now had six weeks to prepare for a short season at the Melbourne Bijou from 4 May, opening in the title role in *La Pompadour*. A brief article about this play in the *Weekly Times*, 4 May, was accompanied by a woodcut portrait of Rose as Pompadour. The image was based on the Alfred Ellis photograph of Rose.[727] The *Age* critic questioned the wisdom of putting on this play 'for a limited season of six nights, considering the cost of mounting and presenting' a production involving all the opulence of the age of Louis Quinze. He admits that the scenery was 'sumptuous enough, that the costumes were 'there in all their gorgeousness' but 'the

---

721 *Argus*, 23 January 1895; *Truth*, 15 September 1906, p. 2.
722 Melbourne *Punch*, 22 November 1894, p. 32. Short paragraph giving the address of Rose's school as Buffalo, Albert Street, Albert Park.
723 *The Tasmanian*, 2 March 1895.
724 *South Australian Register*, 9 March 1895.
725 *Launceston Examiner*, 25 March 1895; 27 March; 28 March 1895; 30 March 1995.
726 *Launceston Examiner*, 1 April 1895.
727 This is the only image of Rose during her visit to London that I have found. The photograph shows signs of being 'airbrushed'. She looks slimmer and her jaw finer.

cast was scarcely strong enough to carry them off to advantage'. While admitting that Rose was a 'finished actress' the reviewer found her unsuited to the role which called for traces of vulgarity beyond her powers. He was scathing at Truebridge as Pompadour's mad husband, summing up the young actor's performance with the words, 'Mr. Truebridge is *not* a second Beerbohm Tree'.[728]

Rose's Melbourne debut as Hamlet was on 10 May. Ophelia was played by Frances Grahame.[729] The *Table Talk* review was the most favourable and descriptive of her appearance. Could the critic be Dr Neild?:

> Mrs. Lewis looked the part well, and, as might be expected from the artist she is, sacrificed her own bright and pretty face to her idea of what Hamlet's face should be. By not darkening the eyes in the conventional way, by keeping the skin sallow, and by the suggestion of a moustache, the face was made to represent that of a thinker …

The review went on to praise her 'fine voice' imparting the old 'Shakespearian swing to the speeches' but also using the 'modern colloquial style'. Other reviewers continued the criticism that her memory sometimes failed her. A facetious paragraph in the *Bulletin*, above a Talma photograph of Rose as Hamlet, first discussed her appearance: 'The recent reappearance of Mrs. G. B. W. Lewis as Hamlet, at Melb. Bijou who hadn't previously seen the old-time favorite since her return from Hingland.' First the paragraph comments on her figure as having:

> disposed of much solid flesh of late years and although the figure of her Hamlet doesn't suggest a nervous disease, it compares favourably with the outlines of several male tragedians in the same capacity. Absurdly high heeled shoes and a superfluity of false hair on her head and face were the chief objections to this lady Hamlet.

Turning to her performance the writer praised the way she spoke her words but also noticed that 'her memory proved "fluffy"'. The article ended in derision by blaming her shoes for her memory lapses, 'They must have been giving the estimable artist a bad time'.[730] Her insistence on playing Hamlet had, in some circles, made her a figure of ridicule. Yet there is evidence that she had studied and treasured the role. As if to justify her taking the role she issued a circular, 'Why has Mrs. Lewis studied *Hamlet?*' with the programme

---

728   *Age*, 6 May 1895.
729   *Table Talk*, 17 May 1895, p. 7; *Leader*, 18 May 1895, p. 22.
730   Sydney *Bulletin*, 8 June 1895.

MRS G. B. W. LEWIS.

An engraved version of the Ellis portrait (see p. 151), published in the Melbourne *Weekly Times*, June 1895.
Newspaper Collection, State Library of Victoria.

on the first night of the Melbourne performance. The answer according to the circular was that she was performing the role 'as an elocutionary study'.[731] Her 'Notes on Hamlet' was bequeathed to a friend in her will.[732]

Like the 'try-out' seasons at the end of 1894 and beginning of 1895, this short Bijou season did not go well and it was to be the last time Rose appeared as star in a full scale production in Melbourne. She perhaps realised that her attempts at stardom in melodrama and Shakespeare were futile. Now aged 51, she opted for the more modest goals of small-scale presentations, teaching and taking 'old woman' parts in place of emotional heroines.

Over the next few years 'Mrs. G. B. W. Lewis' is noted in the theatrical pages of the Melbourne press as giving several recitals with her pupils led by Frances Grahame and Truebridge. One such occasion was a 'Winter Afternoon Dramatic Recital' at the Old Court studio in Collins Street on 29 June 1895.[733] Another, on 12 October, was at the little Gaiety theatre in the Bijou building.[734] On 29 February 1896, Rose gave dramatic costume recitals with Frances May Grahame and company at the Alfred Hall, St Kilda. Items included 'The Midnight Charge' by Cyril Scott and an Irish comedy 'Leap Year'. She charged one shilling for these shows.[735] Rose proved to be a popular lecturer with women's groups. On 4 June, she gave a lecture at the Austral Salon on her life in the theatre, also performing excerpts from the plays *The Hunchback* and *Romeo and Juliet* – with Rose as the Nurse and Frances Grahame as Juliet. The Lewises' old friend Dr Neild proposed the vote of thanks. The lecture was repeated ten days later.[736] Later in the year Frances obtained her first role outside the Lewis Troupe in Australian professional theatre when she was engaged by Bland Holt at the Theatre Royal. When there was a change in the casting during his production of Vane Sutton's *For England*, Frances took over the role of the 'betrayed girl' at very short notice.[737] Her performance was well received.

The Lewises' financial troubles came to a head in July 1897, when, the *Argus* of 14 July reported the 'Insolvency of Mrs. G. B. W. Lewis … Rose

---

731 *Leader*, 18 May 1895, p. 22. The circular has not been located.
732 British Probate records: Principle Registry of the Family Division, High Holborn, London, WC 1 V 6NP, Rose Lewis died 24 August 1925 will, signed 29 May 1924.
733 Melbourne *Sun*, 5 July 1895, p. 11.
734 Melbourne *Sun*, 26 October 1995, p. 19.
735 Melbourne *Punch*, 27 February 1896.
736 *Table Talk*, 12 June 1896, pp. 6–7. The Austral Salon was an important part of Melbourne's cultural life. Founded in 1890 by women writers with interests in art and music it continued well into the twentieth century. See Juliet Peers, *More Than Just Gumtrees*, MSWPS, Melbourne, 1993, pp. 6–7.
737 Melbourne *Punch*, 14 January 1897, p. 28.

Lewis of Albert Road South Melbourne, teacher, wife of G. B. W. Lewis'. Causes listed were the 'closing of the financial institutions in which the insolvent's means were invested; and inability to continue payment on calls therein.' Her liabilities were £491/2/6 while her assets were 10/-. Most of her valueless shares were in the Standard Bank of Australia and the Land Mortgage Bank of Victoria. She also had shares in carriage builders on St Kilda Road and an iron foundry in South Melbourne.

Over the years Rose had been billed as tragedienne, comedienne and dramatic actress. Now at the end of 1897 she was billed as 'Mrs. G. B. W. Lewis (the popular elocutionist)' in a 'one off' Christmas Night 'Popular Entertainment' at the Theatre Royal. The programme included items by local performers such as violinist Alberto Zelman junior (son of the Lewises' orchestra leader in Calcutta), singer Maggie Stirling and organist and accompanist W. G. Turner, together with a series of 'New Living Tableaux' called *Placida, the Christian Martyr*. The *Age* review of 28 December 1898 highlighted Rose's recital of the poem 'The Leper' as one of the 'brightest features of the programme', referring to Rose as 'an old Melbourne favorite who was received with a great manifestation of pleasure'. For all this sentiment about an old favourite, the number of Rose's stage engagements was diminishing.

Rose and G. B. W. would have been pleased with the steady progress of their son's career in England. George Encyl Lewis had found some success in provincial and metropolitan theatre. He was touring as orchestra director of *The Gay Parisienne*, which had started in July at the Great Grimsby Theatre Royal, and was followed by two weeks at the London Gaiety Theatre, a season at the nearby Croydon Theatre Royal, then on to Folkestone by September.[738] By 1898 George Encyl, now 33, was conducting at the London Strand Theatre, at the time managed by his uncle Willie Edouin.

The late 1890s was a quiet period for Rose. Like many times before, her stage career seemed at a standstill, but there was always teaching. She was listed in the 1898 Melbourne Street Directory as an elocution teacher at 333 Albert Road, South Melbourne. This was also their residence and that of her niece. Frances Grahame's professional acting career was improved by an engagement with the London actor Charles Cartwright touring under the aegis of Harry Rickards's Comedy and Dramatic Company. At the Theatre Royal Melbourne, she was given small parts in the Henry Arthur Jones' play *The Middleman*, and the comedy *The Squire of Dames*, an adaptation of

---

738 *Era*, 18 July, 8 August, 12 September 1896.

CHAPTER FOURTEEN

a Dumas *fils* play, where she played the small part of a schoolgirl.[739] Frances toured with the company to Perth. Her performance in *The Squire of Dames* was noted for the way she 'allowed none of the humour of the part to remain hidden'.[740]

Towards the end of 1898, Rose was approached by Harry Rickards's management to play the 'old woman' role of Mrs. Phoebe Brindle in *The Dovecote*, starring the popular Australian-born soubrette Pattie Browne at Sydney's Theatre Royal.[741] A *Sydney Morning Herald* article on Rose highlighted the parallel between the play where she spoke lines about being happily married for 34 years and the fact that she and her husband had been themselves married for 34 years.[742] In November there was an article noting both G. B.W.' s 80th birthday and their 34 years of marriage.[743] In spite of Rose's success in *The Dovecote* she had to wait until the following August for a similar role, when she played an American army wife Mrs General Varney in American drama *Secret Service* at Her Majesty's in Sydney.[744] In Melbourne, in September, Rose was interviewed by *Table Talk* and indicated her pride in her son's progress in England. She may also have been pleased by her brother Willie's success creating the role Tweedlepunch in *Florodora* at Lyric Theatre in London. A Melbourne weekly reported that Willie was earning £150 per week.[745]

Meanwhile, in October 1899, Frances Grahame was acting with 'Williamson and Musgrove's Famous Dramatic Company' in Brisbane, Queensland. *Table Talk* carried a short article on Frances Grahame, 'niece of Mrs. G. B. W. Lewis and Mr. Willie Edouin … just returned to Melbourne after tour of Queensland'. She had played Dacia in Wilson Barrett's hit play *The Sign of the Cross*, and other small roles in *The Royal Divorce* and *The Three Musketeers*.[746] Sometime after this tour Frances sailed to England to try her luck, no doubt hoping for support from her cousins. George Encyl Lewis had been musical director at the Liverpool Prince of Wales theatre with May Edouin's Company.[747]

---

739 *Argus*, 11 July 1898. This was one of Rickards's touring companies and included his daughter Noni playing small parts.
740 *West Australian*, 20 August 1898.
741 *Sydney Morning Herald*, 18, 24 October 1898.
742 *Sydney Morning Herald*, 29 October 1898.
743 *Table Talk*, 11 November 1898, p. 3.
744 *Sydney Morning Herald*, 26 August 1899.
745 Melbourne *Sun*, 16 November 1899, p. 11.
746 *Brisbane Courier*, 21 October 1899.
747 *Era*, 15 September 1900.

CIRCUS AND STAGE

Rose, returned to Melbourne and busy with her school, was perhaps despairing of getting parts but was still a theatrical personality who could comment on stage matters. In June 1900, under the heading 'The Art of Acting: Old Methods and New Views of a Reactionary', Rose's opinions were published in the Melbourne *Argus*:

> The new school of actors declare that they represent the school of natural acting, but I maintain that it is the school of pronounced idiosyncrasies and extravagance of characterisation ... The old school of acting has been called exaggerated, but everything the great actors of the past did had an object in it, and in that sense exaggeration is necessary. It is a matter of common knowledge that the expression of emotion must be emphasised in order to appear natural on stage.

She goes on to criticise various well-known actors such Charles Wyndham, Olga Nethersole, and even her great contemporary Ellen Terry! These actors, she thought, were too full of mannerisms, spoke too softly and had the habit of turning their backs to the audience.[748] Perhaps she remembered her statement while learning her craft 'that the difficulty was not to act, but to act less'.[749]

By September, however, Rose was given the role of Madame Vinard, the sympathetic land-lady, in J. C. Williamson's revival of the popular play *Trilby* starring the Americans Edith Crane and Tyrone Power at Her Majesty's, Exhibition Street. Rose was 'warmly greeted on her appearance'.[750] By late 1900, the Lewises would have heard that their son, now aged 35, had married his cousin Frances May Grahame 25 at St Pancras Registry Office, London on 15 October 1900.[751] There is no record of Rose's opinion of the match except that she does not seem to have leaked the news to the Melbourne press as she might have done if she had approved of it. By this time, it must have been apparent that Frances was ill with consumption. Like her mother Julia, after the onset of her illness Frances was not getting roles in theatre. On 5 November 1900, Rose produced one performance of her adaptation of the drama *The Wreck of the Inverness* at the Gaiety Theatre in Melbourne. The Melbourne *Sun* of 9 November 1900 thought the stage management good but the plot implausible.

---

748 *Argus*, 20 June 1900.
749 See chapter five.
750 *Argus*, 1 September 1900.
751 Marriage Certificate, London, 1900, 1b 288.

CHAPTER FOURTEEN

The new century did not find Rose very happy about her career. In yet another *Table Talk* interview, in April 1901, 'Mrs. G. B. Lewis At Home' is described as having:

> a complexion like a girl's, plentiful brown hair, and beautiful little teeth … as she chats, her full-toned voice, with its distinct enunciation, proves perfectly fascinating and one longs to hear it upon the stage.

Rose goes on to mention their losses and that she would like to act again – 'if anyone asked'. She proudly talked of her son working his way up in London, but not his marriage to her niece.[752]

One notices that after 1895 most of Rose's stage roles occur late in each year. It is possible that this was deliberate so that she could concentrate on her Academy of Elocution during the school year. On 5 October 1901, *Trilby*, starring Edith Crane and Tyrone Power, was revived at the Princess's. Rose again played Madame Vinard. The *Argus* reviewer commented 'Mrs. G. B. W. Lewis's interpretation of Madame Vinard is excellently done, and recalled the many triumphs of that lady in years past'. One week later, for George Musgrove, Rose played Mrs Camilla De Peyster in the David Belasco comedy-drama *The Charity Ball* at the Princess's supporting Crane and Power. 'Rose's 'delightful crispness' in the comedy plot was singled out among the smaller parts.[753]

In March 1902, the Lewises received the news that Frances May Grahame Lewis had died aged 26 in Islington, London.[754] It seemed that the Bryer 'family disease' tuberculosis had struck again. Rose, 58, had no roles until 30 August 1902, when she played Mrs Carbury in the comedy *The Lady From Ostend* at the Bijou.

In September, many in the Melbourne theatre community proposed a testimonial benefit for Rose.[755] This took place on 3 October with Rose's pupils and others performing. Rose herself played Peg Woffington in Charles Reade's *Masks and Faces*.[756] Reviews spoke of the 'crowded house' and that it was 'chiefly a social gathering'. Madame Nellie Melba, then in Melbourne to see her father and give some concerts, was in the audience.[757] A souvenir

---

752 *Table Talk*, 11 April 1901, p. 25.
753 *Argus*, 12 October 1901.
754 Death Certificate, b 218 d., also inscribed on the Lewis grave in the Melbourne General Cemetery.
755 *The Stage*, London, 25 September 1902.
756 *Argus*, 3 October 1902; *Age*, 4 October 1902, p. 15; *Australasian*, 11 October 1902, p. 856.
757 *Adelaide Advertiser*, 9 October 1902. The paper tells us that Melba had paid for her own reserved box for Rose's Testimonial.

programme was produced for the occasion and distributed throughout the house. This contains an extraordinary story of Rose's early life, mainly dealing with her father's desertion of her mother and brothers and sisters in 1850. The cover has two photographs of Rose: one as a wide-eyed child of about eleven, the other as an older woman with a tragic expression (see p. 156). Perhaps this expression was assumed for a tragic role or possibly she chose the photograph to indicate to the public a sad and unfulfilled life.

The last part of 1902 saw Rose playing in comedy at the Bijou under the management of English actor-manager Charles Hawtrey, first as Aunt Martha in *A Message from Mars* and then as Madame Moppert in *In the Soup*. The young Gregan McMahon, later to be an important actor-manager in Australia, played Mons. Moppert.[758]

In England, George Encyl had adapted the Edouin's old entertainment from the 1850s, *Frolics in France*, as a musical. He would have sent the score to Rose during the year. The Melbourne *Sun* of 29 October reported that a rehearsal of the 'new musical comedy by Mr. George Encyl Lewis' would take place next afternoon at the Bijou.[759]

Rose's career seemed to be improving by January 1903, when she was engaged by Nellie Stewart, then starring at the Princess's, to play the role of Nathalie, Zaza's maid, in David Belasco's version of the French play *Zaza*. From a salary register in the George Musgrove archives we find that Rose was earning £10 per week. The star of course, earned £100 per week.[760] Although Rose was playing a servant, she made the role an important sympathetic and supporting one.[761] Nellie Stewart toured this play successfully to Sydney[762] where Rose received a special mention in the *Sydney Morning Herald* review for her Nathalie, where she was praised for her 'wonderful animation and comic humor. No one reading the few poor lines would believe that talent could do so much with them. It was a tour de force'.[763] Nellie Stewart did not

---

758 *Punch*, 13 November 1902, p. 702. *In the Soup* lasted until 22 December.
759 *Sun*, 29 October 1902, p. 9; brief report, *Sun*, 5 November, p. 9. No review has been found.
760 George Musgrove Records 1896–1905. MS 12450 Series ii., Financial Records, salary records, F box 3304/4, Comedy and Dramas Season 30 January–25 February 1903, Australian Manuscript Collection, State Library of Victoria.
761 *Herald* 16 January 1903; *Punch*, 29 January 1903; *Australasian*, 31 January 1903, p. 259; *Leader*, 31 January 1903.
762 Nellie Stewart, *My Life's Story*, John Sands Ltd. Sydney 1923, p. 146.
763 *Sydney Morning Herald*, 16 March 1903. Towards the end of the *Zaza* season the *Bulletin* of 21 March 1903, p. 30, rather maliciously reported an anecdote of Rose having trouble with a howling dog at one of her recitals in Gippsland venues.

CHAPTER FOURTEEN

take *Zaza* on her tour of New Zealand[764] and Rose returned to Melbourne and her teaching. Around this time, on the back fly leaf of her scrapbook, she wrote a list of 'My Latest Successes 1901 – 2 – 3'. These included Mrs de Pester in *The Charity Ball*, Madame Vinard in *Trilby*, the Countess in *Daughter of the Regiment* and the Nurse in *Romeo and Juliet*.[765] These were all 'old woman' roles indicating that perhaps at last she was reconciled to this type of part rather than as a heroine in heavy melodrama. Her part in George Musgrove's production at the Princess Theatre of *The Daughter of the Regiment* required Rose to sing in a comic trio.[766] This last page of what seems to be her only surviving manuscript is about the nearest we can come to Rose's 'inner life'.

For the next few years the Lewises were rarely mentioned in press reports. Rose's 'Academy of Elocution' continued its listing in the street directory and must have been the main source of income for the couple. Perhaps George Encyl, successful as a provincial theatre director in England, sent them some funds from time to time.

In an effort to re-invigorate her career Rose formed 'the Edouin Musical Farce Company' of sixteen 'English and Australian artists' (including her nephew George Bryer) opening in Ballarat on Boxing Day 1904 and in Bendigo on 9 January 1905. Top of the bill was the perennial *A Trip to Paris* in George Encyl's musical version, this time acknowledging Cooper's authorship. Rose's played her usual parts which 'moved the audience to roars of laughter'.[767] But it seems that the enterprise did not succeed. Later in the year the theatrical community must have been aware of the comparative poverty of the Lewises. Led by their old colleague J. C. Williamson, a meeting was held on 1 June 1905 to plan a benefit for G. B. W. Lewis. Williamson was the main speaker and the visiting English actor Roy Redgrave recited.[768] There were sympathetic comments about the Lewises losing their fortune in the land boom but they had kept a 'stiff upper lip'.[769] The matinee benefit was held on 8 June at Her Majesty's Theatre in Exhibition Street. The American actress Minnie Tittell Brune played Napoleon's tragic

---

764 Nellie Stewart seems to have regretted taking the 'fast' role of Zaza with its 'Zaza Kiss'. See *Otago Times*, 29 April 1903, p. 61, and 11 February 1903, p. 14.
765 These are the only words in her handwriting in the Lewis Scrapbook.
766 *Argus*, 15 August 1903. This was only performance of the opera by Donizetti as Musgrove and the musical director, Gustave Slapoffski and his soprano wife were involved in a court case.
767 *Bendigo Advertiser*, 4, 10 January 1905.
768 *Table Talk*, 1 June 1905. Redgrave was the father of actor Michael Redgrave.
769 *Australasian*, 21 July 1905.

young son in the first act of *L'Aiglon*, and Rose produced part of George Encyl's version of the Edouins' old play *Frolics in France* with Rose as Aunt Theodosia. *Table Talk* declared her 'Both clever and funny'. The takings were the good sum of £330.[770]

Rose was to wait until July 1906 for another suitable role on the professional stage, that of Lady Elizabeth Wynnegate, the hero's mother in *The Squaw Man* at Her Majesty's. This play was in the then popular 'wild west' genre. The melodrama was about a member of the British aristocracy unjustly exiled to America and dubbed a 'squaw man' when he formed a relationship with an Indian girl and fathered a son. When he inherits the title the Indian girl (like Belasco's *Madame Butterfly*) conveniently kills herself, allowing him to marry the white aristocratic heroine and return home with his son.[771] Such plays, where sentimental racism was part of the story, were regarded as trivial by the critics but were very popular among audiences. Rose's performance was described as being in her 'invariably able manner'.[772]

Just as Rose was succeeding in this character role, G. B. W. Lewis developed cystitis and was admitted to the nearby Alfred Hospital.[773] He survived the operation 'for an internal complaint' but died of complications two days later, on 18 July 1906. He was 87.[774] Obituaries praised his 'exemplarily and respectable' character and concentrated mainly on his career as a theatre proprietor. Also mentioned was his tallness and commanding manner.[775] Reminiscences written in the 1930s depicted G. B. W. as 'magnificent' even in old age, making the most of his height and keeping order 'front of house'.[776] However, writing in the 1920s, singer/actor Howard Vernon remembered a penny pinching authoritarian Lewis:

> Circus men were always hard to deal with – at least I thought so when I was a boy. The whip was always ready for a hesitating youngster when practising a flip-flap or handspring.

---

770 *Australasian*, 10 June 1905, p. 1345.
771 Belasco's play opened in New York in 1900 and was the basis for the Puccini opera of 1907.
772 *Argus*, 5 July 1906.
773 The hospital was near the Lewises' former house in Georges Terrace.
774 Lewis's Death Certificate lists senile decay and cystitis as the causes of death.
775 Obituaries: *Herald*, 18 July 1906; *Age, Argus, Daily Telegraph* 19 July 1906; *Australasian*, 21 July 1906, p. 146; *Weekly Times*, 21 July 1906, p. 19; *Leader*, 22 July 1906, p. 36; *Bulletin*, 26 July 1906, p. 11; 2 August 1906, p. 11; 2 August 1906. 'Mr G. B. Lewis died in Melbourne last week at age of 90. He married a sister of Mr Willie Edouin the well-known comedian', *British Australasian*, by cable, p. 16.
776 'Melodious Memories', *Age*, 2 July and 9 July 1938.

CHAPTER FOURTEEN

Remembering G. B. W. as lessee of the Bijou, Vernon recalled:

> He [Lewis] could never understand why an actor demanded a living wage, having been reared in the lap of "just enough". He would look – on treasury day – at the gentlemen who received a tenner a week as if he were a scorpion ready to sting his vitals.[777]

Although his achievements were largely forgotten by the time of his death, Lewis should be acknowledged for his many entertainment enterprises. Like Coppin he was a good performer and like Coppin he built and was proprietor of several theatres. Unlike Coppin, Lewis took theatre and circus to Asia, where he introduced mid-century Western popular entertainment ranging from horse dramas and pantomime to Boucicault and Shakespeare. Here he was, on a small scale, an 'agent of empire' making money while his various ventures strengthened colonial ties in India and Australia. Most subsequent references to Lewis mentioned the £30 000 he had supposedly arrived with at the end of 1853 and his great losses in the Depression of the 1890. Rose signed George Benjamin William Lewis's probate papers in early August. His estate was valued at £189.[778]

Rose soon returned to the cast of *The Squaw Man*. The weekly *Truth* of 11 August reported that 'Mrs. G. B. W. Lewis … will shortly sell off her goods and chattels and will travel with the "Squaw Man" company'. As well as a Victorian provincial tour, the company had seasons in Adelaide and Sydney and finished in New Zealand in March 1907. Within four months of the end of this tour Rose was in London.

With closest relatives, her son George Encyl, and her brother Willie Edouin, having chosen to work in the northern hemisphere Rose decided to return to London to live and work, an ambition that the health of her husband and niece had thwarted. Her son and brother could offer some support and possibly some stage roles. Family bereavements continued when Rose's sister-in-law Elizabeth Edouin Bryer died aged 65 on 12 July 1907.[779] 'Lizzie' (Naylor) was the mother of Rose's actress niece Lillie May Bryer, and nephews, actors George and William Bryer. The latter was manager for the Brough Flemming Company. However, Lizzie Bryer was the last family member of Rose's generation in Australia.

---

777 *Advertiser*, 4 May 1923. As a child Vernon might have answered one of Lewis's wanted advertisements for boys to train for the circus.
778 Probate Records 8 August 1906, PROV VPRS 7591/P2, Unit 392, File 99/245.
779 Mrs Edouin Bryer was buried at Melbourne General Cemetery in the Lewis grave.

Chapter fifteen

ROSE HOME IN ENGLAND

A saddened but still vigorous Rose, now 63, arrived in London in July 1907.[780] Initially, she may have stayed with her brother Willie Edouin at his flat at 19 Bedford Mansions, Bloomsbury, or moved on to 'theatrical digs' such as 112 Netherwood Road, West Kensington, an apartment house.[781]

During the thirteen years since her last visit, the London theatre scene had changed, perhaps even more than during her previous absence between 1857 and 1892. Henry Irving had died and actor-manager Sir Herbert Beerbohm Tree was at the height of his popular powers at His Majesty's Theatre, with his spectacular productions of Shakespeare, the classic repertoire and more recent works. Rose would have approved of Tree's part in founding the Academy of Dramatic Art in 1904, although by the time she arrived he had largely lost interest in the project.[782] Frank Benson was another important actor-manager with his Shakespearian presentations at the Stratford-upon-Avon Memorial Theatre and at London's Shaftesbury Theatre. As well, there was Ben Greet's touring company taking productions of Shakespeare to the countryside.[783] Rose's late career was to be involved with these managers, who respected her work playing 'old women' in Shakespeare and other dramas.

By this time also the modern drama of Ibsen, Wilde, Shaw and Pinero and others had created a more naturalistic theatre. Rose had expressed a disapproval of the early stirrings this new type of acting when interviewed by *Table Talk* on her return from England in 1894. Also, given her age, there were fewer 'old woman' parts in these plays, although she might have made a good Miss Prism. Nevertheless, despite the rise of more 'intellectual' drama, the West End and the provinces retained a menu of popular dramas, so, apart from Elizabethan roles, Rose kept to the more 'crowd pleasing'

---

780   *Era*, 26 July 1907.
781   This address was given as Rose's former home in her Will and Death Certificate.
782   Hesketh Pearson, *The Last Actor-Managers*, Methuen, London, 1950, p. 16.
783   'Sir Frank Benson' and 'Sir Ben Greet', *Oxford Dictionary of National Biography*, London, 2004, http://www.oxforddnb.com.ezproxy.lib.monash.edu.au/view/article/33548.

comedies produced by Robert Courtneidge and others, where she could still make people laugh.

Rose reverted to the stage name of 'Rose Edouin' or, occasionally, 'Mrs. Rose Edouin Lewis'. On her arrival she was described in the *Era* and the *British Australasian* as an actress returning from Australia and a 'fine grand dame and "character" actress'.[784] And indeed, for the next thirteen years Rose took many such 'old woman' or 'character' roles on the West End and provincial stages. Her first role, however, was as 'Aunt Theodosia's chum' in her own play *A Spree in Paris* – based on *Frolics in France* for which George Encyl Lewis had written music. Rose had presented a studio performance of the musical at the Melbourne Bijou in 1902.[785]

With the help of the Lord Chamberlain's files at the British Library, an interesting story about this play emerges. These records have been kept since the time of Charles II, when all plays performed in London had to be licensed by the Lord Chamberlain. Rose had applied for a licence in September 1907, but had been refused because she had not named a theatre. Her letter expresses her frustration at the paradoxical situation: 'I cannot name a theatre until I obtain a licence but cannot get a licence until I name a theatre'.[786] By mentioning a theatre in Seacombe, near Liverpool, a licence was granted but *A Spree in Paris* opened first at the Theatre Royal, Belfast on 25 November, 1907.[787] A comparison of the licensed texts of Rose Edouin's *A Spree in Paris and What Happened* (1907) and the F. Fox Cooper play *Frolics in France*, commissioned more than fifty years before in 1856, shows that there are many similarities. Both plays feature an engaged baronet who goes to Paris 'for fun' while his fiancée follows him in disguise and plays several roles to confuse him and 'teach him a lesson'. Cooper's version was in the nineteenth-century genre of such plays as *The Spoiled Child* and others where the actress displayed her versatility by taking several parts. *Frolics in France* had been a great success in Melbourne and the goldfields in the late 1850s and a good vehicle for the already versatile 13-year-old Rose as the fiancée Lady Clarinda. The 1907 play *A Spree in Paris* was, of course, somewhat different. It was a musical, adapted by Rose and for adults, with a score written by her son. Instead of one actress playing all the disguises,

---

784 *British Australasian*, 12 September 1907, p. 16; *Table Talk*, 17 October 1907.
785 *Sun*, 29 October 1902, p. 9; brief report, *Sun*, 5 November 1902, p. 9.
786 Her application letter dated 23 October 1907 in *A Trip to Paris, A Musical Comedy* in Lord Chamberlain's Records (Card Index) No. 60 licence issued 18 November 1907; *Frolics in France*, ADD MS 52, 962Z, British Library MSS.
787 Eric Irvin, *Gentleman George*, University of Queensland Press, St Lucia, Queensland, 1980, p. 150; *The Stage*, 30 November 1907.

Rose divided them between three actresses: the fiancée Lady Clara, her aunt Theodosia and the latter's 'Chum' played by Rose. However, much of the dialogue and situations were the same: for example in the 1856 version Lady Clarinda pretends to be Mademoiselle Taglioni Vestris Twirlington; in the 1907 play Lady Clara assumes the role of a French dancer of the same name and so on. In both works, the dialogue for this part is written in an odd pseudo-French accent that must have been penned by F. F. Cooper. For example: 'And I vill sing and I vill dance ... I smile at dem and say to dem – bonjour'.[788] The *Era* critic declared it 'a slight production' lasting barely two hours;[789] within ten days Rose and George Encyl had moved the play together with most of the cast to Merseyside. The play opened at the Irving Theatre in Seacombe just across the river from Liverpool where it was more favourably received.[790] It is not known what Rose did next. Sometimes it is difficult to trace provincial actors particularly when they are, like Rose, playing small and secondary roles. But it is likely that Rose got some parts in the Liverpool area.

By April 1908, both Rose and George were in London at the funeral of Rose's brother Willie Edouin who had died, of cerebral disease and idiopathic Eryrisiples[791], at his London home aged 62.[792] Willie had been the most successful member of the Edouin family. He left Australia in 1865 at the age of 19 with William Birch, a showman with a moving panorama.[793] After travelling around the North Pacific, including visits to Shanghai and Yokohama, the pair arrived in San Francisco. Here Willie perfected his comedic abilities, appearing at the Metropolitan Theatre with the Howson Troupe from Australia. In a performance of the extravaganza *The Sheep's Foot* he was termed 'a capital clown'.[794] By mid-1867 we find him on the East Coast of America in New York.[795] By November 1870 he had won a place in the Lydia Thompson company at Wood's Museum. The year 1871 saw him joined by his brother John and wife Tilly Earl performing at Wallack's Theatre in New York with Lydia Thompson. For the next three years together with Willie's American wife Alice Atherton née Hogan the

---

788 Lord Chamberlain's Office. *A Trip to Paris*, op. cit., p. 33.
789 Eric Irvin, op. cit, p. 150; *Era*, 30 November 1907; *The Stage*, 30 November 1907.
790 *The Stage*, 5 December 1907.
791 Death Certificate, William Frederick Bryer.
792 *The Times*, 15 April, 17 April 1908; London *Daily Telegraph*, 15 April 1908 mentions his early days and criticises his mannerisms; US cutting dated 14 April, New York Public Library.
793 PROV, VPRS 948, Outward Passenger List for *Golden Hind*.
794 San Francisco *Daily Morning Call*, 5 February 1867.
795 *Era*, 23 June 1867.

CHAPTER FIFTEEN

four toured America with the Thompson troupe. Their progress was often reported in the Melbourne weekly *Australasian*.[796]

Willie returned to London with Lydia at the end of 1874, and in April 1875 created his most notable role, that of the Heathen Chinee in H. B. Farnie's burlesque *Blue Beard*.[797] After a tour around Britain,[798] Willie and Alice went back to America with Lydia Thompson's company with Willie as Friday and Alice as Queen Ylang-Ylang in Thompson's production of H. B. Farnie's *Robinson Crusoe* at Wallack's.[799] By November 1879, the couple had left the company and were in San Francisco with Rice's Surprise Company at New Standard Theatre.[800] In 1882, they were on tour with Willie's own Spark's Company to Boston. They are next noted in Buffalo, on 16 November 1882, with his Sparks Company in *Dreams*. Next, they appear in San Francisco, on 18 May 1884, at the Opera House in *A Bunch of Keys*.[801] The Edouins returned to England in 1884, appearing at the Brighton Theatre Royal with Lionel Brough in *The Babes* on 1 September 1884.[802]

By 1887, the Melbourne *Table Talk*, of 29 April, noted that Willie was manager of the Royalty Theatre, London. Among Willie's performances in December 1887 were the double-bills *Blackberries* and *Turned Up* and *The Coming Clown and Modern Wives*.[803] Now quite well-to-do, Willie is listed in *Kelly's Post Office Directory London 1888* as living at 25 Acacia Road, St John's Wood.[804] The Edouins' only son Lionel died in 1888 aged eight.[805]

Willie was lessee, manager and director of the Strand Theatre from 1891 to January 1895. In 1898, towards the end of his life, he secured another important comedy role – as Tweedlepunch in *Florodora* at the Lyric Theatre where he was reported to be earning £150 per week.[806] His wife Alice Atherton, who had been performing in New York, died suddenly in 1898, and from that time Edouin's health and career declined. He died on 14 April 1908 at his home at 19 Bedford Mansions, survived by two actress daughters

---

796 *Australasian*, 27 February 1872, p 531; *Australasian*, 18 May 1872, p. 627; *Australasian*, 25 February 1874. p 275; *Australasian*, 13 June 1874, p. 756.
797 *Australasian*, 5 June 1875, p. 723.
798 Programme Playbill, V&A Theatre and Performance Archives.
799 *The Stage*, 12 September 1877
800 *Lorgnette*, 30 January 1879; *Lorgnette*, 17 April 1879.
801 Playbill, New York Public Library.
802 Playbill in the Mander and Mitchenson Collection, Briston University.
803 Programme cast-list Mander and Mitchenson Collection, Bristol University.
804 There is a photograph of this house marked 'Uncle Willie's house' in the picture collection of the State Library of Victoria. The building is still there in St John's Wood, London.
805 *Lorgnette*, 12 January 1889, p. 3; *Table Talk*, 18 January 1889, p. 12.
806 Programme Playbill Mander and Mitchenson Collection, Bristol University.

Daisy Bryer (sometimes called Daisy Atherton) and May Edouin. Like the obituaries of many older performers, there were some mistakes in his. Some gave his age as being greater than it was and most gave incorrect details of the Edouin family's time in Australia.[807]

Meanwhile, George Encyl Lewis had a good position at the Adelphi Theatre in the Strand where he conducted 32 performances of *The College Widow*, an American comedy.[808] In July, mother and son were performing south of the Thames at the Camberwell Palace. Evidently Rose had adapted part of *A Spree in Paris* where a character endlessly quoted Shakespeare as *A Shakespearian Lunatic*.[809] Soon, however, Rose was travelling in *The Dairymaids* provincial tour in the 'old woman' part of Penelope Pychase, first at the Blackpool Grand Theatre and then in the same role at Cork Opera House in Ireland.[810] In April 1909, still at the Adelphi in the West End, Rose was playing the character roles Madame Baron in *The Devil* and Mrs Cogbill in *Come Michaelmas*. George Encyl Lewis was musical director.[811] The Sydney *Bulletin*, of 3 March 1910, reported that Rose was playing in Berlin as the Nurse in *Romeo and Juliet*. According to a Broken Hill newspaper, Juliet was played by American Fay Davis and Romeo by her English partner Gerald Lawrence. The couple later appeared in silent films. Lawrence is described as having studied with Rose, perhaps when she taught elocution in London possibly at Ben Greet's school.[812]

Rose next appears in theatre news in 1913, a year which was to be notable one for her. Tree, of His Majesty's Theatre, engaged her for several roles. Early in the year she had appeared at the North London Kilburn Empire, when she played her own dramatic sketch called *Queen Mary of England*.[813]

Herbert Beerbohm Tree had been the foremost actor-manager in London since the 1890s. He was noted for his exceptional character acting, and his sumptuous and realistic staging of plays ranging from Shakespeare to Shaw before huge audiences.[814] He had run the opulent His Majesty's Theatre in

---

807 *The Times*, 15 April, 17 April; London *Daily Telegraph*, 15 April 1908 mentions his early days and criticises his mannerisms; US cuttings 14 April 1908, New York Public Library.
808 J. P. Wearing, *The London Stage, 1900–1910: A Calendar of Plays and Players*. Scarecrow Press, Metuchen, N.J., 1981, Vol. 2.
809 *The Stage*, 9 July 1908.
810 *The Stage*, 6 August 1908; *The Stage*, 20 August 1908.
811 *The Times*, 27 April 1909; programme cast-list V&A Theatre and Performance Archives.
812 *Barrier Miner*, 4 February 1910; *Era*, 4 December 1909; loose clipping in the Lewis scrapbook, 'Newspaper Criticisms of Mrs G. B. W. Lewis (Miss Rose Edouin) dating from Tuesday 26th July 1892 – her re-appearance in London'.
813 *The Stage*, 6 February 1913.
814 B.A. Kachur, 'Sir Herbert Beerbohm Tree', *Oxford Dictionary of National Biography Online*, www.oxforddnb.com.ezproxy.slv.vic.gov.au/view/article/36549. Tree's dates:

the Haymarket since its opening in 1897. Tree engaged the 69-year-old Rose to play Mrs Candour in *The School for Scandal* where her performance was described as 'quaint and comic'.[815]

Meanwhile, Tree was planning a complicated production of Richard Strauss's opera *Ariadne auf Naxos* to be sung in German but with an interpolation of Molière's *Le Bourgeois Gentilhomme* in English translation. Tree commissioned the successful novelist and playwright W. Somerset Maugham to translate the play as the *Perfect Gentleman*. Tree took the role of Monsieur Jourdain and Rose played Madame Jourdain. The young Thomas Beecham conducted the opera.[816] So, the elderly Rose played a small but important role opposite the famous Sir Herbert. The audience included 'several members of the Royal Family, five crowned heads of Europe … the Prime Minister and Mrs. Asquith … Mr. and Mrs. Bernard Shaw and Mr. Saint Saens.'[817] However, this production of Strauss's 1912 Stuttgart version was not a success. It was a mishmash of a translated Molière play and von Hofmannsthal's and Strauss's opera sung in German. Maugham's rendering was in straightforward English, but the critics did not like Tree, extravagantly costumed, playing Monsieur Jourdain with a cockney accent. Nor did they like the deletion of some important characters.[818] As the down-to-earth Madame Jourdain, Rose had lines such as 'You're crazy, father, with all your whims; and it's come upon you since you began to mix yourself up with grand people! (starts darning)'.[819] During an argument with her husband, Madame Jourdain exits with the words, 'I don't care! I'm defending my rights, and all the women will be on my side'. (Could Maugham be echoing the current suffragette movement?)

By the end of June 1913 Tree had returned to his annual Shakespeare Festival productions. Rose was engaged for the role of the Nurse in *Romeo and Juliet* with 63-year-old Tree as Mercutio, Phyllis Neilson-Terry as Juliet and Philip Merivale as Romeo. Rose must have been pleased with the opinion of J. T. Grein, dramatic critic for the *Sunday Times* who stated:

1852–1917.
815 *The Times*, 14 April 1913; *Era*, 19 April 1913.
816 *The Times*, 28 May 1913; cutting from V&A Theatre and Performance Archives [Galley proof for an article in *Theatre Notebook*, 1972].
817 *Evening Standard*, 28 May 1913.
818 Christian P. Gruber, 'Somerset Maugham's Perfect Gentleman 1912–1913', in *Theatre Notebook*, Vol. XXVI, 1972, pp. 151–158. See also *The Stage*, 29 May 1913, p. 22.
819 Applications to the Lord Chamberlain for Theatre Licences. *The Perfect Gentleman* an adaptation by Mr Somerset Maugham of *Le Bourgeois Gentilhomme*, British Library, LCP No. 1685, p. 40.

There was one other impersonation that calls for special comment; it was the Nurse of Miss Rose Edouin, low comedy if you like, but comedy as Shakespeare must have intended it – a dear old soul, with an eye to the main chance and the inclinations of a good-natured go-between. Not since the days of the famous Mrs. Stirling have we enjoyed a nurse so natural and so humorous.[820]

The *Era* critic also approved of her characterisation: 'One of the successes of the production is the Nurse of Miss Rose Edouin who gives a really fresh reading of that character'.[821]

For the next seven years, between the ages of 69 and 76, Rose continued in character roles. In 1914, she starred as Mistress Gursey in the Elizabethan play by Henry Porter *The Two Angry Women of Abingdon*.[822] By the end of the year World War I had begun, and the Shakespearian actor-manager Sir Frank Benson chose *Henry V* as an appropriately patriotic play for a season at the Shaftesbury Theatre, London. Rose made a hit in this play in the small part of the Hostess. *The Times* critic praised the way she expressed 'true feeling' in her description of Falstaff's death.[823] Benson was noted for his annual Summer Shakespeare Festival at the Memorial Theatre at Stratford-upon-Avon. In 1916, he cast Rose as Mistress Quickly in *The Merry Wives of Windsor*,[824] and as the Old Widow in *All's Well that Ends Well*.[825]

Since her encounter with 'modern' theatre in London in the early1890s after nearly 40 years in the colonies, Rose had, at various times, expressed her disapproval of the new 'naturalistic' theatre.[826] We get a young actor's view of an old fashioned and dogmatic Rose during this season through the memoirs of Reginald Denham (later to be a successful stage and film director). With her nineteenth-century attitudes to elocution, acting style and her voice like a 'silver-trumpet', she was remembered by Denham as 'an incomparable old harridan of the old school'.[827] By this time Rose could

---

820 Reprinted in the Wellington New Zealand *Evening Post*, 6 September 1913. An influential figure in British theatre circles, Dutch-born Jacob Thomas Grein was theatre critic on many London papers between 1894 and 1935. See Michael Orme, *J. T. Grein*, John Murray, London, 1936, p. 165. Like Rose, Fanny Stirling (1815–1895), was successful in 'old woman' roles in her later career.
821 *Era*, 5 July 1913.
822 *The Times*, 22 April 1914.
823 *The Times*, 28 December 1914.
824 Programme cast list, 27 April 1916, V&A Theatre and Performance Archives.
825 *The Stage*, 4 May 1916.
826 See chapter fourteen.
827 Reginald Denham, *Stars in My Hair*, Crown Publishers Inc., New York, 1958, p. 66.

CHAPTER FIFTEEN

afford to have such attitudes. She was an 'old woman' on stage and in real life and had regular work around London until she was in her late seventies.

Rose's non-Shakespearian roles included a revival her part of Penelope Pyechase in *The Dairymaids*, this time at the Aldwych.[828] She toured as Mrs Budd in *The Light Blues*[829] and as Rambha in *The Toy Cart* at the Stage Society.[830] Rose, no doubt assuming a Bronx accent, toured as Mrs Potash in the popular American comedy *Potash and Perlmutter* based on New York Jewish stories by Montague Glass.

Meanwhile, in January George Encyl was musical director at the Welsh town of Mountain Ash (Aberpennar)[831] and *The Stage* of 11 January mentioned that he had composed 'some of the music' for the pantomime *Cinderella* at the Exeter Theatre Royal. But it seems that while Rose was touring, in ever robust manner in 1918 as Mrs Semple in *Daddy-Long-Legs*, her son's health was failing. The ultimate maternal sorrow of a child dying before its parent occurred on 1 December 1918 when George Encyl Lewis aged 53, died from oesophageal cancer at the Royal Manchester Infirmary. Rose, now nearly 75, had lost all her children. Yet she was not without a close relative for comfort. Her niece May (Edouin) Edwards, daughter of Willie Edouin, seems to have taken over and informed the authorities of her cousin's death.[832]

Typically, within seven months the resilient Rose was back in London as Mrs Enderwick in *The Bantam V.C.* at St Martin's Theatre with the young Australian Dorothy Brunton playing the juvenile lead.[833]

The comedy *Paddy, the Next Best Thing* at the Savoy, in which Rose was to play her last stage role, was not a critical success. The starring role of the Irish girl Paddy was taken by the American Peggy O'Neil, who according to *The Times* review, failed with her 'Irish' accent. Rose played the small part of Mrs Putter (one of the patients at the pharmacy where Paddy worked).[834]

Rose seems to have spent the next four years at her lodgings at 112 Netherwood Road West Kensington, a few doors from her niece May and her actor husband Fred Edwards.[835] In her later years Rose kept in touch with the Australian press, often at Christmas sending best wishes to the

---

828 *The Times*, 24 May 1915.
829 J. P. Wearing, *The London Stage, 1910–1919: A Calendar of Plays and Players*, Vol. 1 Scarecrow Press, Metuchen, N.J., 1982.
830 *The Times*, 3 July 1917.
831 *The Stage*, 4 January 1917.
832 Death Certificate. May Edouin was born in the 1870s and died in 1944.
833 *The Times*, 19 June, 14 July, 24 July 1919.
834 *The Stage*, 26 February 1920.
835 Information in George Encyl Lewis's Death Certificate 1906.

Argus or her photograph in the role of Mrs Potash to Melbourne *Punch*.[836] At the same time, the press often reported on her career in London.[837] It is possible that Rose was still teaching, although she was suffering from heart trouble. Ill health may have been the reason for her moving to the spa town of Harrogate, Yorkshire, for by May 1924, when she signed her will, she was living at 141 Kings Road, Harrogate. Also living in Harrogate with a young daughter was her friend Alice Edith Carrick, now a widow. As a child Alice Edith Browne had toured with Rose's companies in Australia some time in the 1890s.[838] It was at Alice Carrick's house, 4 Butler Road, that Rose died of 'valvular heart disease' on 24 August 1925, aged 81.[839] Her estate was valued at the rather small sum of £61-15-2.[840] The executors were Alice Carrick in England, and Rose's nephew William Bryer in Australia. For such a small estate Rose left very detailed instructions about the distribution of her few remaining possessions, including some jewellery, to various friends. These goods and chattels can be read as a reflection of her life. For example, her time as a child performer and her continued interest in preparing children for the stage is perhaps reflected in the bequest of her piano to Alice Carrick's young daughter Elsie Louise; yet with the practical proviso that the piano should be sold to defray expenses if the Carricks needed to return to Australia, or, if not, for the 'money [to] be banked for Elsie Louise Carrick'. Remembering her time in India, Rose left her Indian embroidery and carved picture frames to her 'dear friend' Mrs Aitcherley of Surrey. Thinking of her later stage career, she bequeathed to Miss Camile Ronalds 'my "Hamlet" Study Book' together with 'one pair of carved frames' and the "Nurse and Juliet" photograph. One wonders if after the distribution of a few legacies of £5.0.0 there was much left of the residue which was bequeathed to her Australian niece, actress Lilly May Bryer daughter of her brother Edwin Charles.

---

836 Melbourne *Punch*, 21 February 1918, p. 40.
837 She might have had contacts at the Australian weeklies, *Bulletin*, *Table Talk* and Melbourne *Punch*.
838 *Daily Telegraph*, (London) 25 August 1925. Information on Alice Edith Browne born 1886, from Graeme Haigh, Genealogical Services, Sydney.
839 Obituaries. *The Times*, 25 August 1925; *Argus*; *Age*, 26 August; *Bulletin*, Melbourne *Punch*, 3 September 1925, p. 18; 10 September 1925, p. 18; 1 October 1925, p. 18; *Australasian*, 3 September 1925, p. 255.
840 In her Will, written on 29 May 1924, Rose her stated addresses were 'formerly of 112 Netherwood Road, Kensington Park, but residing at 4 Butler Road, Harrogate'. Executrix Alice Edith Carrick. Australian Executor, William Bryer. UK Probate granted 10 September 1925. British Probate records: Principal Registry of the Family Division, High Holborn, London, WC 1 V 6NP, Rose Lewis died 24 August 1925, will, signed 29 May 1924.

CHAPTER FIFTEEN

The final clauses of the will are devoted to Rose's wish for an interment in 'as simple manner as possible' and a strong wish to be cremated. Her directions show an enduring love for G. B. W. and a possibility that she would be returned to Australia:

> If I should die in Australia I still desire to be cremated but I direct that my ashes be placed in my late husband's grave in the Melbourne Cemetery and my memorial cut on the clean slab of the monument on the before mentioned grave.[841]

Rose was cremated at Harrogate on 27 August 1925.[842] Someone, probably her nephew William Bryer, added her name to G. B. W's grave stone.

Extensive obituaries were published in Australia and England appreciating her long career. Most emphasised her versatility. Her death prompted some theatre people to send letters to the *Bulletin*'s 'Poverty Point' theatrical memories column. One of the correspondents, 'D.E', enumerated her various roles and summed up her career with the words:

> In her girlhood she must have played before grey-whiskered warriors who had fought at Trafalgar and Waterloo: in her old age she delighted Diggers from Australia and Maoriland … veterans of Lone Pine and Mont St Quentin.[843]

It is perhaps significant that for several years after her death the *Argus* 'In Memoriam' notices carried an advertisement from Josephine Samuell, one of her elocution pupils.[844] Each notice carried words such as 'ever grateful pupil' and described Rose as 'A great actress, a wonderful teacher, and a generous friend' and 'inserted by one of her many loving and grateful pupils'.[845]

From the mid-1850s to the first quarter of the twentieth century Rose Edouin's acting talent was acknowledged in most reviews. One can speculate that if she and her family had stayed in London, Rose might have, given her talent, enjoyed great success on the London stage as an adult. Or, if she had not gone to Asia and married George Lewis but stayed in Melbourne, would

---

841 The G. B.W. Lewis monument is quite impressive. The main pedestal is topped by a statue of a winged angel in the form of a child dressed in classical style. Rose's name is present on the flat slab below G. B. W.'s name. The pedestal commemorates the deaths of the Lewis children including George Encyl Lewis and his wife Frances May in London.
842 *Argus*, 24 August 1928.
843 *Bulletin*, 3 September 1925, p. 37.
844 *Argus*, 24 August 1925, 1926, 1927, 1928, 1929 and 1932. Josephine Samuell (1866–1962) had appeared in one of Rose's pupil concerts at the Theatre Royal in 1891.
845 *Argus*, 24 August 1929.

she have become a local star? Or what might have been her fame if she had gone to America with her brother Willie? Her actual career had, however, several high points. Foremost of these was her time in India. For nine years from 1867 to 1876 she was an undisputed star. During those years she had few rivals and press views of her performances were generally favourable, their main criticism being that she was too versatile. As 'Directress' and wife of the proprietor of the Calcutta theatre she was able to choose any role. The high hopes she must have had for their return to Melbourne and the Academy of Music were to some extent fulfilled in her success in pantomime/burlesque, her classical roles supporting Creswick and in her juvenile *HMS Pinafore* company. By the 1880s she had found that teaching was another of her talents. Having learned stage craft from an early age she was keen to pass on her knowledge to children. Also, having lost most of her own children, teaching was a way of retaining contact with young people. Perhaps she saw talented children like Mary Weir and Flora Graupner as surrogates for her two lost daughters.

The slow decline of her stage career was to be expected. The energetic, mature actress of the 1870s and 1880s found that, by the 1890s, the weight of years was preventing her from performing convincingly in the roles she wanted – of young, emotional and appealing, if also fallen, heroines. Her last attempts at such roles were as Jane Shore and Madame Pompadour. It is not surprising that she favoured what we see now as inferior plays by Wills and Grundy. She had, after all, grown up in the London theatre of the 1850s where spectacle and melodrama were popular. Also these roles were strong women's parts. Despite her audacity in attempting Hamlet she remained rather old fashioned. If her sojourn in 1890s London did not convert her to the new drama of Ibsen, Pinero, Wilde and Shaw her love and study of the English language and of Shakespeare remained. The transition into 'character' and 'old woman' roles, together with her continued energy, extended her career into her 77th year. All this, despite many sadnesses, made her life, on and off the stage, a valiant and fulfilling one.

The Lewises, now largely forgotten, made their mark on the entertainment world of Britain, India, China, Australia and New Zealand. While many other unsung entertainers have tried similar feats, the sheer scale, energy and prolonged effort of Rose Edouin and George Lewis marks them as exceptional and worthy of remembrance.

BIBLIOGRAPHY

Published works

Allen, Shirley S, *Samuel Phelps and Sadler's Wells*, Wesleyan University Press, Middletown, Connecticut, 1971.

Allston Brown, T., *History of the American Stage*, Dick & Fitzgerald, New York, 1870.

Arnold, David, *Science, Technology and Medicine in Colonial India*, Cambridge University Press, Cambridge, 2000.

Bagot, Alec, *Coppin the Great*, Melbourne University Press, Melbourne, 1965.

Banerji, Nilanjana. 'Edouin, Willie', *Oxford Dictionary National Biography Online*.

Bezić, Nada, 'Ilma De Murska', in *Grove Music Online. Oxford Music Online*. http://www.oxfordmusiconline.com.ezproxy.lib.monash.edu.au/subscriber/article/grove/music/07815.

Blanchard, E, L., *Harlequin and the Forty Thieves*, with local annotations by Mr Frank Edwards, Azzoppardi, Melbourne, 1877.

Brough, William, *Lalla Rookh; or, The Princess, the Peri, & the Troubadour*: A Burlesque and Pantomime in one act, Lacy. London, 1858.

Chatterjee, Sudipto, *The Colonial Staged: Theatre in Colonial Calcutta*, Seagull Books, Calcutta, 2007.

Chatterjee, Sudipto, 'Moor or Less, Othello Under Surveillance, Calcutta, 1848' at sia.stanford.edu/india/Othello%20Paper%20Stanford.doc

Clarence, Richard, *The Stage Cyclopaedia: A Bibliography of Plays*, Burt Franklin, New York, 1909.

Commonwealth Bureau of Census and Statistics, Victorian Office, *Victorian Year Book 1973*, No. 87, 1973.

Dangle, Mr, 'The Rise and Fall of the Calcutta Stage', *The Theatre*, 1 August 1881.

Davis, Richard, *Anna Bishop: The Adventures of an Intrepid Prima Donna*, Currency Press, Sydney 1997.

Denham, Reginald, *Stars in My Hair*, Crown Publishers Inc., New York, 1958.

Dicker, Ian G., *J.C.W.: A Short biography of James Cassius Williamson*, Elizabeth Tudor Press, Rose Bay, NSW, 1974.

Downs, Peter, *The Pollards: A Family and Its Child and Adult Opera Companies in New Zealand and Australia*, Steel Roberts, Wellington, NZ, 2002.

Dressler, Albert, ed. *California's Pioneer Circus Founder Joseph Andrew Rowe*, H. S. Crocker Inc., San Francisco, 1926.

Dutt, Utpal, *Girish Chandra Ghosh*, Sahitya Akademi, Calcutta, 1992.

Foulkes, Richard, 'Sir Ben Greet' *Oxford Dictionary of National Biography*, London, 2004. http://www.oxforddnb.com.ezproxy.lib.monash.edu.au/.

Gänzl, Kurt *Lydia Thompson Queen of Burlesque*, Routledge, New York, 2002.

Gänzl, Kurt, *William B. Gill: From the Goldfield to Broadway*, Rutledge, New York, 2002.

Gilder, Rosamond, *Enter the Actress; The First Women in the Theatre*, George Harrap & Co Ltd., London, 1931.

Gittins, Jean, 'Julia Mat(t)hews', *Australian Dictionary of Biography*, Vol. 5, Melbourne, 1974.

Gittins, Jean, 'Thomas Barry Sullivan', *Australian Dictionary of Biography*, Vol. 6, Melbourne, 1976.
Haan, J. D., 'Thalia and Terpsichore on the Yangtze: A Survey of Foreign Theatre and Music in Shanghai 1850–1865' in *Journal of the Royal Asiatic Society*, Vol. 29, 1988.
Hartnoll, Phyllis, *Oxford Companion to Theatre*, Oxford University Press, Oxford, 1983.
Headrick, Daniel R. *Invisible Weapon: Telecommunications and International Politics, 1851–1945*, OUP, New York, 1991.
Holloway, David, *Playing the Empire*, George G. Harrup, London, 1979.
Howard, Tony, *Women as Hamlet: Performance and Interpretation in Theatre, Film and Fiction*. Cambridge University Press, Cambridge, UK, 2007.
Howe, J. Burdett, *A Cosmopolitan Actor*, Bedford Publishing Company, London, 1888.
Humphreys, H. Morin, *Men of the Time in Australia*, Victorian Series, M'Carron, Bird, Melbourne, 1878.
Ireland, Norton, *Records of the New York Stage*, Bradstreet Press, New York 1867.
Irvin, Eric, *Gentleman George*, University of Queensland Press, St Lucia, 1980.
Kachur, B.A., 'Sir Herbert Beerbohm Tree', *Oxford Dictionary of National Biography Online*, 2004. http://www.oxforddnb.com.ezproxy.lib.monash.edu.au/.
Kelly, Veronica, 'The Banning of Marcus Clarke's *The Happy Land*: Stage, Press and Parliament' in *Australasian Drama Studies*, Vol. 2, No. 1, 1983.
Kelly, Veronica 'Early Australian High Comedy to 1890: Performing the Colonial Bourgeois Self', in *Southerly*, Volume 64, Autumn 2004.
Lawrence, W. J., *The Life of Gustavus Vaughan Brooke*, W. & G. Baird, Belfast, 1892.
Love, Harold, *The Golden Age of Australian Opera*, Currency Press, Sydney, 1981.
Mackay, George, *Annals of Bendigo*, G. Mackay & Co., Bendigo, 1912.
Massey, Montague, *Recollections of Calcutta for over Half a Century*, Thacker Spink & Co, Calcutta, 1918.
Mayer, David, *Harlequin in his Element: The English Pantomime*, 1806–1839, Harvard University Press, Cambridge, Mass., 1969.
Mayhew, Henry, *London Labour and the London Poor*, Vol. III, Griffin, Bohn and Company, London, 1861 [Dover Publications, Inc. New York, 1968].
Mitchell, Tony, *High Art in a Foreign Tongue: Adelaide Ristori's 1875 Australian Tour*, Australasian Drama Studies Association Academic Publications 1, Sydney, 1995.
Mukerjee, S.K. *Story of Indian Theatre*, K.P. Bagchi & Company, Calcutta, 1982.
Orme, Michael, *J.T. Grein*, John Murray, London, 1936.
Parsons, Philip, ed., *Companion to Australian Theatre*, Currency Press, Sydney, 1995.
Pearson, Hesketh, *The Last Actor-Managers*, Methuen, London, 1950.
Peers, Juliet, *More Than Just Gumtrees*, MSWPS, Melbourne, 1993.
Pigots Directory of Sussex 1839–1841.
Said, Edward, *Orientalism*, Routledge Kegan Paul, London 1978; reprint Penguin, 1991.
St Leon, Mark, *Circus in Australia*, The Author, Penshurst, NSW, 2007.
Sands and Kenny; *Sands and McDougall Directories*, 1861–1870.
Sands and McDougall, *Directories of Melbourne*, 1857–1874.
Saxon, Arthur, *Enter Foot and Horse*, Yale University Press, New Haven, 1968.
Schodt, Frederik L., *Professor Risley and the Imperial Japanese Troupe: How an American Acrobat Introduced Circus to Japan and Japan to the West*, Stone Bridge Press, Berkeley, California, 2012.
Shaw, Denis, 'Esther Leach, "The Mrs. Siddons of Bengal"', *Educational Theatre Journal*, Vol. 10, No. 4, December 1958.

BIBLIOGRAPHY

Simpson, Adrienne, *Alice May: Gilbert and Sullivan's First Prima Donna*, Routledge, New York, 2001.
Souvenir of Mrs. G. B. W. Lewis' Professional Jubilee Testimonial Benefit, Theatre Royal October 3rd 1902, Miller Printing Company, Melbourne, 1902.
Speaight, George, *A History of the English Puppet Theatre*, Robert Hale, London, 1990.
Stewart, Nellie, *My Life's Story*, John Sands, Sydney, 1923.
Stuart, Lurline 'Fund-raising in colonial Melbourne: the Shakespeare statue, the Brooke bust and the Garibaldi sword' in *La Trobe Library Journal*, Vol. 8, No. 29, April 1982.
Thorne, Ross, ' Royal Victoria Theatre' in Philip Parsons, ed., *Companion to Australian Theatre*, Currency Press, Sydney, 1995
Toll, Robert C., *Blacking Up: The Minstrel Show in Nineteenth Century America*, Oxford University Press, New York, 1974.
Turner, John (Martin), 'Pablo Fanque, Black Circus Proprietor', in Gretchen Holbrook Gerzina ed., *Black Victorians Black Victoriana*, Rutgers University Press, New Brunswick, 2003.
Turner, J.M., *Victorian Arena*, Vols. 1 and 2, Lingdales Press, Formby, UK, 2000.
Turner, John M, *Historical Hengler's Circus*, Part One, Lingdales Press, Formby, UK, 1989.
Van Der Poorten, Helen, 'Mary Fanny Cathcart', *Australian Dictionary of Biography*, Vol. 3, Melbourne, 1969.
Van Straten, Frank, *Florence Young and the Golden Years of Australian Musical Theatre*, Beleura House and Garden, Mornington, Victoria, 2009.
Varty, Anne, *Children and the Theatre in Victorian Britain: 'All Work, No Play'*, Palgrave Macmillan, UK, 2008.
Vasey, Ruth and Wright, Elizabeth, compliers, *A Calendar of Sydney Theatrical Performances 1870–1879*, Australian Theatres Studies Centre, School of Theatre Studies, University of New South Wales, Sydney, 1986.
Vicinus, Martha, ed., *A Widening Sphere*, Indiana University Press, 1977.
Waterhouse, Richard, *From Minstrel Show to Vaudeville*, New South Wales University Press, Sydney, 1990.
Wearing, J.P., *The London Stage, 1890–1900*, N.J., Scarecrow Press, Metuchen, N.J, 1976.
Wearing, J. P., *The London Stage, 1910–1919*, Scarecrow Press, Metuchen, N.J, 1982.
Wearing, J. P., 'Sir Frank Benson', *Oxford Dictionary of National Biography*, London, 2004. http://www.oxforddnb.com.ezproxy.lib.monash.edu.au/
Williams, Margaret, 'William Anderson', *Australian Dictionary of Biography*, Vol. 7, 1979.
Who Was Who in the Theatre, 1912–1976: a biographical dictionary of actors, actresses, directors, playwrights and producers of the English speaking theatre, compiled from *Who's Who in the Theatre*, volumes 1–15 (1912–1972), Gale Research Co, Detroit, c.1978.
Wild, Sam, *The Original, Complete and Only Authentic Story of 'Old Wild's'... : Being the Reminiscences of its Chief and Last Proprietor, 'Sam Wild'*, ed., 'Trim' [i.e. W. B. Megson], London, 1888, reprinted Society for Theatre Research, London, 1989.
Winseck, D.R. and Pike, R.M. *Communications and Empire*, Duke University, 2007.
Wiseman, Fanny. 'Pleasant Memories', *Illustrated Sporting and Dramatic News*, 1 November 1906, p. 16.
Woo, Celestine, 'Sarah Siddons as Hamlet: three decades, absent breeches, and rife critical confusion', *ANQ*, Volume 20, Number 1, Winter 2007.
Wykes, Alan, *Circus!*, Jupiter Books, London, 1977.

CIRCUS AND STAGE

Newspapers

Advertiser, Adelaide.
Aberdeen Weekly Journal, Aberdeen.
Age, Melbourne.
Albury Border Post, NSW.
Alta California, San Francisco.
Argus, Melbourne.
Australasian, Melbourne.
Australasian Sketcher, Melbourne.
Ballarat Courier, Victoria.
Ballarat Star, Victoria.
Banner of Belfast, Port Fairy, Victoria.
Barrier Miner, South Australia.
Bell's Life in Victoria, Melbourne.
Bendigo Advertiser, Victoria.
Brisbane Courier, Queensland.
Bristol Evening News, UK.
Bristol Mercury, UK.
British Australasian, Melbourne.
Bulletin, Melbourne.
Bulletin, Sydney.
Cape Argus, Cape Town.
China Mail, Hong Kong.
Cornwall Chronicle, Tasmania.
Daily Morning Call, San Francisco.
Daily News and Bengal Hurkaru, Calcutta.
Daily Telegraph, London.
Daily Telegraph, Melbourne.
Dunedin Herald, Dunedin.
Englishman, Calcutta.
Entr'acte and Playbill, Melbourne.
Era, London.
European Mail, London.
Evening Post, Wellington.
Evening Standard, London.
Examiner, Melbourne.
Freeman's Journal, Dublin.
Friend of India, Calcutta.
Geelong Advertiser, Victoria.
Herald, Melbourne.
Hong Kong Daily Press, China.
Hongkong Recorder, China.
Illustrated London News, London.
Indian Daily News, Bengal Hurkaru, Calcutta.
Java Bode, Batavia.
Kyneton Observer, Victoria.
Launceston Examiner, Tasmania.
Leader, Melbourne.
Lorgnette, Melbourne.
Lyttleton Times, Christchurch.

BIBLIOGRAPHY

Maitland Mercury and Hunter River General Advertiser, NSW.
Manchester Times, UK.
Mercury, Hobart.
Morning Chronicle, London.
Mount Alexander Mail. Victoria.
Mount Ararat Advertiser, Victoria.
New York Clipper, New York.
North China Herald, Shanghai.
Observer, Auckland.
Otago Witness, Dunedin.
Ovens and Murray Advertiser, Victoria.
Portland Guardian, Victoria.
Punch, London.
Punch, Melbourne.
South Australian Register, Adelaide.
The Stage, London.
Star, Ballarat.
Straits Times, Singapore.
Sun, Melbourne.
Sydney Mail, NSW.
Sydney Morning Herald, Sydney.
Table Talk, Melbourne.
Tatler, Melbourne.
The Tasmanian, Launceston.
The Theatre, London.
Timaru Herald, NZ.
The Times, London.
Times of India, Bombay.
Today, Melbourne.
Truth, Melbourne.
The Victorian, Melbourne.
Warrnambool Examiner and Western District Advertiser, Victoria.
Weekly Times, Melbourne.
West Australian, Perth.

Unpublished works

Gordon-Clarke, Janette, 'The progress of the Stars: Actresses and their repertories in Australia from the 1850s to the 1890s', Ph.D. Thesis, Department of English, Monash University, 2000.
Holt, Clarence, 'Twice Around the World, or Recollections of an Old Actor', National Library of Australia MS2244.
Lewis Scrapbook, 'Newspaper Criticisms of Mrs GBW Lewis (Miss Rose Edouin) dating from Tuesday 26th July 1892 – her re-appearance in London'.
Spring, John, 'Computerised Listing of Melbourne Public Performances, 1850–1869', Monash University, 1981.

INDEX

Bold type indicates an illustration.

Aarons, Joseph, 128, 130, **131**, **150**, 159, 160, 164, 165
Abbott's Opera House (Auckland), 180
A'Beckett, Gilbert, 110, 165
Aboriginal equestrians, **cover**, 37, 39, **40**
Aboriginal Sammy, 39
Academy of Elocution (Hobart), 194
Academy of Elocution (Melbourne), 205
Academy of Music (Ballarat), 196
Academy of Music (Melbourne), xvi, 127, 128, 130, **131**, 132, 133, 135, 137, 140, **150**, 159, 160, 164, 165, 189, 220
Actor of All Work, The, 28
Actress of All Work, The, 28, 33
Adams, Edwin, 70, 132, 133, 134, 180
Adams, Harry, 37, 41
Addy, Baishnab Charan, 82
Adelphi Theatre (London), 18, 214
Adelphi Theatre (Castlemaine), 38
Adrienne Lecouvreur, 30. 32
L'Aiglon, 208
Aladdin the Wonderful Scamp, 61, 89, 90, 108, 138, 162, 163, 178
Algiers (ship), 24, 25
Ali Baba and the Forty Thieves, 89, 100
Alibaba or, Harlequin Abdalla, 100
Alkanna, Alexander, 37, 40
Allen, John H., 81, 88, 89, 90
Allen, George Benjamin, 115, 118
All for Her, 161
Allison, James, 163
All's Well That Ends Well, 216
Anderson, George, 103, 116
Anderson, John Henry, 23
Anderson, Mrs, 82
Anderson, William, 188
Andrews, Tom, 58, 96, 102
Anstead, Flora, 135, 138, 140
Antony and Cleopatra, 190
Appleton, Frederick Charles, **70**, 90, 94, 196
Ariadne auf Naxos, 215
Arrah-na-Pogue, 79
Ashton, Helen, 139, 140, 167
Ashton's Circus, 40, 49
Asquith, 215
Astley's Amphitheatre (London), **4**
Astley's Amphitheatre (Melbourne), xvi, 7, 8, 12, 14, 15, 26, 30, 46, 50, **68**

Atherton, Alice, 181, 192, 212, 213
Aurora Floyd, 61, 98
Austral Salon, 201
Avoca (ship), 96
Azael the Prodigal, 107, 110

Babes in the Wood, 23
Bachelor's Daughter, The, 29, 32
Bagot, Alec, 16
Bantam V.C., The, 217
Barham, Bill (aka Fanque, Pablo), 12
Barlow, Robert, 9
Barlow, William, 13, 46, 47, 48
Barrett, Wilson, 203
Barry, James, 82
Barry, (Sir) Redmond, 13, 159
Barry, Tom, 11, 41
Bateman, Isabel, 19
Bateman, Kate, 19, 52, 103, 111, 112
Battle of Alma, 3
Battle of Bosworth Field, or, the Death of White Surrey, 43
Beatrice, Miss, 161
Beautiful Haidee, 91
Becket, 193
Beecham, (Sir) Thomas, 215
Belasco, David, 205, 206, 208
Bellhouse & Co., 85
Belphegor the Mountebank, 23, 56
Benison, Agnes, 124
Benjamin, Mr, 14
Benson, Frank, 210, 216
Berg, Adolphe, 8, 12, 13, 14
Berg, Antoinette, 12, 13
Berg, Marie, 12
Berg, Robert, 13
Bernhardt, Sarah, 188, 189
Bijou Theatre Melbourne (aka Academy of Music), xvi, 127, 128, 131, 138, 165–180
Birch, Henry, 8, 9, 14, 43, 46, 48, 49, 60, 61, 81, 87
Birch, Madame, 46, 48
Birch, William (equestrian), 8, 9, 46
Birch, William (panoramist), 49, 79, 202
Bird and Taylor (circus), 15
Bishop, Anna, 26, 83
Bellair, T. S., 95

- 227 -

Benjamin, Mr., 14
Bennett, Charles, 96
Berry, Graham, 110, 142, 165
Blackberries, 213
Blackett, Dr., 183
Black Eyed Susan, 100, 105, 111, 175
Black Sheep, The, 107, 124
Blow for Blow, 177
Blue Beard, 119, 123, **135**, 136, 137, 139, 140, **154**, 162, 163, 178, 179, 180, 213
Bohemian Girl, The, 178
Bombay (ship), 49, 58
Booth, Edwin, 85
Boothman, A, 135
Bosworth Field, or, The Death of White Surrey, 37, 43
Boucicault, Dion (Junior), 186, 198
Boucicault, Dion (Senior), 92, 105, 115, 160, 171, 209
Bourgeois Gentilhomme, Le, 215
Bowring, Adelaide, 161
Box and Cox, 21
Braddon, Mary, 98
Brooke, Gustavus Vaughan, xv, 15, 19, 25, 26, 27, 30, 39, 57, 79, 85, 109
Brooks, Alice, 178
Brooks, Marie, 178
Brother Bill and Me, 107
Brough and Boucicault Comedy Company, 186, 190, 198
Brough Company, 83, 125, 190, 125
Brough Flemming Company, 209
Brough, Florence, xv, 126
Brough, Lionel, 213
Brough, Robert, xv
Brough, William, 57, 91, 94, 99
Brown, Chas, 135
Browne, Pattie, 203
Brown-Potter, Cora, 188
Brune, Minnie Tittle, 207
Brunton, Dorothy, 217
Bryce, Jennie, 196
Bryer, *see also* Edouin and Jones
Bryer, Alice, *see* Atherton, Alice
Bryer, Blanche, 25, 95, 163, 187
Bryer, Charles Edwin (b.1869, son of Charles Edwin Bryer), 95
Bryer, Daisy, 181
Bryer, Edwin Charles, *see* Edouin, Charles
Bryer, Eliza *see* Edouin, Eliza
Bryer, George, 114, 120, 161, 207
Bryer, Herbert Ernest, 25, 33, 95
Bryer, John Edwin, (J. E. Jones), 18, 24, 25, 32, 36, 58, 58, 95, 112, 163, 187
Bryer, John William, 19, 35, 37, 55, 56, 57, 58, 77, 81, 90, 96, 112, 114, 116, 182, 124, 296

Bryer, Julia Lucy, *see* Edouin, Julia
Bryer, Lillie, 209
Bryer, Lizzie (aka Mrs Edouin Bryer), *see* Naylor, Elisabeth
Bryer, Matilda, *see* Earle, Tilly
Bryer, May, *see* Edouin, May
Bryer, Rose, *see* Edouin, Rose
Bryer, Sarah, 17, 18, 24, 25, 32, 50, 81, 84, 102, 104, 106, 163
Bryer, William Edwin, 187, 209, 218, 219
Bryer, William Frederick, *see* Edouin, Willie
Buchanan, McKean, 54
Buckingham, George, 26
Buckingham, L., 98
Buckstone, John Baldwin, 91
Bunch of Keys, A, 213
Burnett, Frances Hodgson, 172
Burton, Henry, (actor), 123, 124
Burton, Henry, (circus), 9, 15, 49, 13
Burtons Circus, 9, 15
Byron, Lord George Gordon, 3, 91, 93
Byron, H. J., 91, 124, 160, 177

Cagli, Augusto, 83
Calabar (ship), 116
Camille, 62
Camille, Floretta, 41
Capital Match, 62
Carandini, Marie, 33, 39
Carandini, Rosina, 33
Carey, William Getston, 114, 116, 120, 123, 124, 125, **144**
Carle, Walter, 135
Carlisle, Richard Risley, *see* Risley, Richard Carlisle
Carrick, Alice, Edith, 118
Carson, Dave, 83, 84, 103
Cartwright, Charles, 202
Caste, 105, 111, 120, 123
Cathcart, Fanny, *see* Heir, Fanny
Catherine (ship), 58
Celeste, Céline, 107, 129, 130
Chakrabarty, S. G., 91, 93
Chain, The, 175
Chapman, Mr and Mrs, 55, 81
Charity Ball, The, 205, 207
China (ship), 106
Chomley, Hussey Malone, 184
Christoff, George, 41, 46, 49
Christopher, George, 41, 46, 49
Cinderella, 110, 217
City of Adelaide (ship), 114
Clarke, Marcus, 110, 165, 169, 179
Clarke, Marian, (née Dunn), **76**, 169, 170, 172
Cleveland, Louisa, 57, **73**, 129, 196

INDEX

Cloches de Cornville, Les, 174, 179
Clouds, 142, 178
Columbus, 107
Colleen Bawn, 90, 103, 105, 108, 122, 159, 175
College Widow, 214
Collins, Wilkie, 115, 155, 135, 173
Come Michaelmas, 214
Coming Clown, The, 213
Compton, Mr., 81
Coogee (ship), 198
Cooke, James (circus proprietor), 11
Cooke, Thomas Taplin (circus proprietor), 11
Cooper, Frederick Fox, 28, 33, 120, 207, 211, 212
Cooper, Rosa, 120, 124
Cooper, Thomas, 165
Coppin, George Selth, xv, xvi, 15, 16, 26, 38, 39, 48, 49, 50, **51**, 85, 96, 97, 159, 160
Cora, L'Article, 48
Corinthian Theatre Calcutta, **117**
Corsican Brothers, The, 108, **143**
Court and Stage, 80
Courtneidge, Robert, 211
Cousins, Jane (Kendall; La Rosiere), 46, 47, 48, 49, 61
Cousins, John Bumpuss, 46, 48, 49
Covent Garden Opera House, 19, 20, 23
Cowper, Captain H., 101
Coyne, Stirling, 27
Crane, Edith, 204, 205
Cremorne Gardens (London), 19, 50
Cremorne Gardens (Melbourne), 15, 38, 40, 49, 50, **51**, 52, **53**, 81
Creswick, J. B, 58, 61, 62
Creswick, William, **137**, 139, 140, 160, 166, 167, 168, 169, 180, 197
Creton, Donald, 101

Daddy-Long-Legs, 217
Dairymaids, The, 214, 217
Daly, Augustin, 92
Daly, Nelly, 135
Daniels, Harry, 135, 159
Darby, William (aka Pablo Fanque), 2, **3**, 12
Darrell, George, 173
Dasi, Binodini, 127
Datta, Michael Madrhusudan, 83
Daughter of Eve, 170, 174
Daughter of the Regiment, 204, 207
Davenport, Jean, 18
Davenport, T. D., 18
David Copperfield, 104
Davis, Fay, 214
Davis, Mrs, 38

Deccan (ship), 97
Deering, Ollie, 81
Deering, Waddy, 81
De Murska, Ilma, **131**, 132, 133
Denham, Reginald, 216
De Sers, Baronne (née White), 114, 115, 116, 118, 120
Devil, The, 214
Dewhurst, Jonathan, 175
Dick Turpin, 16, 37
Did You Ever Send your Wife to Camberwell?, 27
Did You Ever Send Your Wife to Mordialloc?, 27
Dillon, Charles, junior, 140
Dillon, Charles, senior, 23, 56
Douglas, H. A., 81, 178
Douglas (ship), 62
Dovecote, The, 203
Downes, Peter, 174
Dreams, 213
Drew, John, 55
Du Boisgobey, Fortuné, 185
Duchess of Kent Theatre (Ararat), 35, 37
Duggan, Edmund, 188
Duggan, Eugenie, 188
Dunn, Marian, *see* Clarke, Marian
Duret, Marie, 55
Dutt, Utpal, 126

Earl(e) Matilda (Tilly Bryer), 37, 56, 57, 58, 60, 61, 81, 90, 94, 112, 114, 115, 120, 182, 212
East Lynne, 90, 104, 108, 120, 198
Edouin, *see also* Bryer and Jones
Edouin, Charles (Edwin Charles Bryer), 17, 18, 23, 25, 28, 55, 77, 90, 95, 218
Edouin, Daisy, *see* Bryer, Daisy
Edouin, Eliza, 17, 18, 19, 21, 22, 23, 25, 28, 29, 32, 33, 34, 35, **66**, 109, 124
Edouin, Julia (Mrs William Grahame), 17, 18, 23, 24, 25, 28, 29, 32, 33, 36, 50, 54, 55, 57, 58, 62, **66**, 77, 79, 81, 95, 97, 99, 101, 102, 104, 106, 112, 114, **146**, **149**, 170, 188
Edouin, May (Mrs. Fred Edwards), 181, 213, 217
Edouin, Rose (Mrs G. B. W. Lewis)
 children, 79, 80, 86, 87, 91
 images of, **53**, **63**, **66**, **71**, **72**, **73**, **77**, **78**, **121**, **135**, **141**, **148**, **151**, **152**, **153**, **156**, **157**, **200**
 insolvency, 201–202
 marriage, 61, 203
 speeches from stage, 18, 19, 24, 40, 110, 124, 162

CIRCUS AND STAGE

stage career:
   Bombay, 87–102; 114–116; 120–125
   Britain, xv, 19–23; 190–192; 210–217
   Calcutta, 82–91; 95–101; 102–105; 106–113; 119–121
   China, 60–62; 105–106
   Melbourne, xv–xvii, 27–29; 50–58; 79–81; 91–95; 132–181; 195–209
   South Australia, Tasmania and Victoria, 30–39
   Hong Kong, 60–62; 105–106
   select plays and roles:
      Blue Beard (Selim), 120, 136, 179
      Hamlet, 130, 153, 180, 196, 197–199, 201
      Jane Shore, 138, 162–164, 196
      The Jealous Wife (Mrs Oakly), 108, 168, 191
      King Lear (Fool), 167–168, 197
      Lady Macbeth, 108, 162
      Leah the Forsaken, 90, 103, 112, 120
      living marionettes, 20, 25, 28
      Pompadour, 152, 196
      Robinson Crusoe, 140, 141, 142
   teaching, 19, 49, 127, 172, 178, 180, 181, 182, 186, 192, 194, 201, 205, 202, 217, 218, 220
   versatility, 108, 112, 129, 136, 138, 180, 211, 119
   voice, 132, 136, 142, 167, 179, 197, 199, 205
Edouin, Sarah (Mrs Bryer), *see* Bryer, Sarah
Edouin, Willie (William) Frederick, 17, 19, 21, 22, 23, 24, 25, 28, 29, 32, 33, 35, 50, 54, 55, 56, 57, **66, 77**, 79, 96, 99, 119, 136, 140, **147, 154**, 170, 181, 190, 192, 303, 210, 212, 213
Edwards, Fred, 117
Edwards, Henry (Harry), 30, 119
El Hyder, 16
Ellis, Alfred, 151, 193, 198, 200
Ellis, James, 38
English, Elizabeth, 83, 116
English, Mr., 83
Enoch Arden, 134
Ernestine and Georgette, 22
Esmeralda; or, the Sensation Goat, 124
Euripides, 97
Extremes; or, Men of the Day, 134, 136

Faint Heart Never Won Fair Lady, 60
Family Failing, A, 107
Fanque, Pablo, *see* Darby, William, or Barham, Bill
Farnie, H. B., 118, 140, 213
Farquharson, Robert (Smith), 38

Fawcett, George (Rowe), 55, 56
Fenton, Myles, 96
Fielding, Henry, 109
Fille du Regiment, La, 170
Fille du Tambour Major, La, 172
Fitzgerald Circus, 15
Fitzwilliam, Ellen (Mrs Fitzwilliam), 135, 137
Flemming, Herbert, 190, 209
Flexmore, Mr., 135
Florodora, 203, 213
Flower, Sara, 6, 37
Flowers of the Forest, 54, 55, 62
Foley, Kate, 135
Fool of the Family, The, 120
Forbes, Wilson, 135, 178
Forde, J. M., 8
For England, 201
Forest of Bondy, The, 21
Forrest, Edwin, 178
Forty Thieves, 177
Foster, Stephen, 194
Fra Diavolo, 60
Frolics in France, 16, 28, 29, 30, 32, 33, 35, 50, 66, 206, 208, 211
Frou Frou, 62, 100
Frozen North, The, 173
Fun on the Bristol, 178

Gaboriau, Émile, 185
Gamester, The, 58
Gardoni, Jessie, 42
Garner, Arthur, xv, 176
Garrick, David, actor, 168
Garrick, David, scenic artist, 96
Garrick Theatre, 23
Gay Parisienne, The, 202
G. B. W., *see* Lewis, George Benjamin William
George, Carry, 102, 103, 107, 111, 125, 163
Ghosh, Giresh Chandra, 83, 126
Giacometti, Paolo, 138
Gilbert and Sullivan, 115, 168, 171
Gilbert, W. S, 108, 110, 121, 165
Gill, Janet, 61, 62, 90
Gill, S. T., x, 7
Gill, Willie, 58, 61, 62, 83, 90, 92, 94, 95, 96
Gladstane, Mary, xv, 129, 130, 138
Gladstone, William Ewart, 110
Glass, Montague, 217
Goblins of the Gold Coast or Melbournites in California, 26
Golden Horn (ship), 79
Goody Two Shoes, 104, 171
Gordon, George, 186

INDEX

Grahame, Frances May (Lewis), 114, **155**, 170, 188, 192, 194, 198, 199, 202, 203, 204, 205
Grahame, Julia Lucy, *see* Edouin, Julia
Grahame, William Forbes, 104, 114, **146**, 170
Grant Road Theatre Bombay, 102, 115
Graupner, Flora, 161, 169, 170, 173, 220
Great National Theatre (Calcutta), 112, 113, 122
Green Bushes, 90, 91, 106, 108
Greet, Ben, 195, 214
Grein, J. T., 215, 216
Greville, John Rodger, 39, 54, 55, 163
Grey, Jessie, 115, 124, 125, 135, 159, 177
Grey, Ruth, 115, 124, 135
Grist to the Mill, 103
Grundy, Sydney, 125, 220
Gulliver, or, Harlequin King Liliput, 21, 169, 174

Hall, J. L. 103, 160, 177
Hamilton, Octavia, 9
Hamlet, 33, 54, 88, 90, 95, 130, 134, **153**, 168, 196, 197, 198, 199, 201, 220
Handy Andy, 103
Happy Land, The, 110
Hard Cash, 120
Hard Times, 22
Harlequin and Gulliver, 21
Harlequin Blue Beard or, the Heathen Chinee and the Fairy of the Rippling Waters, *see* Blue Beard
Harlequin King Arthur and the Knights of ye Round Table, 89
Harlequin Puss in Boots, 21
Harwood, Henry (nè Biggs), 30, 187
Havilah (ship), 55
Hawtrey, Charles, 206
Hayes, Catherine, 9, 26
Haygarth, E. D., 81, 135, 178
Haymarket Theatre (London), 21, 23, 138, 195, 215
Haymarket Theatre (Melbourne), 16, 55, **68**, 79, 85
Haymarket Theatre (Sandhurst), 35
Hayward, Julia, 175
Heir, Fanny, 30, 54, 56
Heir, Robert, 30
Hengler's Circus, 2, 8
Henry V, 188, 216
Henry VI, 188
Henty, Edward, 81, 187
Herbert(e), Charles, 99, 102
Her Evil Star, 173, 174
Her Majesty's Theatre (Ballarat), 131
Her Majesty's Theatre (Melbourne), 16, 204, 207, 208

Her Majesty's Theatre (Sydney), 203
Hernandez, Alexander, *see* Alkanna, Alexander
Hernandez, James (Mickey Kelly), 37, 41, 42, 43, 45
Hidden Hand, The, 172
Higginbotham, George, 13
Hill, John, 133
His Majesty's Theatre (London), 210, 114
HMS Pinafore, 168, **169**, 170, 171, 172
Hole (Hob)in the Well, The, 16, 28, 29
Holloway, Edmund, 162
Holloway, W. J., 190
Holly Tree Inn, The, 23
Holt, Clarence, 38, 43, 49
Holt, Joseph Bland, xv, 162, 193, 201
Holt, Maud (Tree), 195
Home, 94, 132, 133, 134, 135
Hope of the Family, 55
Howe, John Burdett, 95, 96, 97, 98, 99, 100, 101, **143**, 174, 175, 178, 180
Hoyte, H., 178
Huguenot Captain, The, 107
Hume, Fergus, 185
Humphreys, H. M., 135
Hunchback, The, 201
Hunter, Mr., 81
Husband to Order, A, 58
Hydes, J. P., 135
Hydes, Mrs, 178

I and My Double, 35
Ingomar the Barbarian, 117
In the Soup, 206
Ireland, George Richard, 180
Ireland, Gordon, 152
Ireland, Richard Davies, 13
Irish Emigrant, The, 99
Irving, Sir Henry, 190, 193, 210
Irving Theatre (Seacombe, UK), 212
Island of Jewels, The, 123
Ivanhoe, 115, 117

Jack and the Beanstalk, 89, 176
Jack Sheppard, 21, 55
Jack the Giant Killer: or, Harlequin King Arthur and the Knights of ye Round Table, 54, 89
Janauschek, Francesca, 130
Jane Shore, 138, 142, 162, 163, 164, 178, 180, 196, 197, 198, 220
Janet Pride, 160, 171
Jealous Wife, The, 108, 140, 162, 163, 168, 178, 190, 191
Jefferson, Joseph, 55, 56, **73**, 85

CIRCUS AND STAGE

Jessie Brown, 93
Joan of Arc, 99
Johnson, George Raymond, 187
Jones, Henry Arthur, 125, 202
Jones, John Edwin, *see* Bryer, John Edwin
Julius Caesar, 168
Juvenile HMS Pinafore, 168–172, 174, 179
Juvenile Tambour Major, 172

Kate Wynsley; or, A Woman's Love, 23
Katherine and Petruchio, 140, 168, 175
Kean, Edmund, 98
Kean, Ellen, 129, 130
Keene, Laura, 85
Kelly, Veronica, 110, 165, 173
Kendal, Madge, 97
Kennedy, Mr., 14
Kerry, 119
King John, 57, 61
King Lear, 56, 157, 197
King of the Peacocks, The, 55
Kitts, Edward, 96
Knowles, Conrad, 26
Knowles, Sheridan, 140, 168, 175
Kotzebue, August Friedrich, 19

Lady from Ostend, The, 205
Lady Killer, The, 192
Lady of the Lake, The, 27, 30
Lady of Lyons, The, 27, 90, 118
Lalla Rookh: or the Princess, the Peri, & the Troubadour, 57, 89, 90, 91, 93, 126, 139
Lawrence, Gerald, 214
Lambert, J. C., 30
Lawrence, Robert, 102, 103, 125, 163
Leach, Esther, 82
Leah the Forsaken, 73, 90, 92, 100, 106, 111, 178, 180
Lebedeff, Gerasim Stepanovich, 45
Led Astray, 115, 117
Lee, Emma, 11
Lee, Henry, 20
Lee, Tom, 11
Leonard, George, Herbert, 102, 110
Lewis, Benjamin, 95
Lewis, George Benjamin William
    circus management:
        Astley's Melbourne, 7–10, 12–15;
        Australia, xv, 15, 16, 30, 36–39
        children, employer of: 5, 15, 41;
        China, Hong Kong, India, Dutch East Indies, 1, 41–58
        Cremorne, 15, 20, 38, 48, 49;
        Europe, 2, 3, 5, 8, 9

    personal life:
        builds Georges Terrace, 176, 181, 189
        builds Shanghai Villa, 80, 129, 176
        buys land xv, 1, 81, 189
        death, **155**, 218
        Fanny Perry mystery, 182–186
        images of: **64, 121, 155, 156**
        loses properties in bank crash, 189
        marriage: 5, 61, 203
    theatre management:
        Australia:
            Academy of Music (aka Bijou Theatre) xv, 128–164, 165–180
            employs Marian Clarke, 170
            employs John Burdett Howe, 174–175
            employs William Creswick, 140, 160, 166, 167
            Opera House, 159–164
        India, Hong Kong, Shanghai, 60–80, 81–127
            attacked by actor in Calcutta, 123–124
            employs John Burdett Howe, 96–101employs the Williamsons, 114–120
        New Zealand, 178–180
Lewis, George Encyl, xvi, **78**, 79, 81, 84, 96, 100, 135, 139, 168, **169**, 177, 181, 183, 184, 188, 189, 190, 191, 192, 193, 194, 195, 202, 203, 206, 207, 208, 209, 211, 212, 214, 217, 219
Lewis, Lucy May, 78, 80, 84, 86, 106
Lewis, Rose, *see* Edouin, Rose
Lewis, Susan, (G. B. W.'s mother), 1
Lewis, Tom (real name Tomlinson), 5, 96
Lewis, Victoria May, 86, 87, 114, 123, 124, **158**
Lewis, William (G. B. W.'s father), 1
Lewis, William (Rose and G. B. W.'s baby), 86
Light Blues, The, 217
Like No Other Love, 195, 196
'Lilliputian Tom', 5, 6, 8, 42, 43, 46
Lind, William, 17
Link, Antonietta, 142
Little Mother, The, 108
Little Nell, 119
Little Snow White, 103
Little Tommy Tucker, 105
Living Marionettes, 19, 20, 21, 24
Living Marionette Theatre, 20
Living Statue, The, 138
Liz, 172
Loan of a Lover, 107
Loch, Sir Henry, 192
Locke, Matthew, 99
London Assurance, 56, 90, 100, 105, 160, 174
Lohengrin (burlesque), 52, 174

INDEX

Lohengrin (opera), 142
Lola Montez Spider Dance, The, 55
Lor! Sonnambula, 89
Lost in London, 108
Louis XI, 27
Lovell, G. W., 167
Love's Sacrifice, 178, 187
Lyceum Theatre, Calcutta, 85, 93, 94
Lyceum Theatre, London, 190, 195
Lyceum Theatre, Melbourne, 54
Lyceum Theatre, Shanghai, 60, 62
Lyster, William Saurin, 38, 142, 162
Lytton, Edward Bulwer, 103, 105, 118, 140

Macbeth, 56, 99, 100, 108, 161
McGowan, Mr and Mrs, 30
McMahon, Gregan, 206
Madame Butterfly, 208
Maid and the Magpie, The, 60
Majeroni, Eduardo, 138, 177
Majeroni, Giulia, 138, 177, 182
Mansergh, Peter, 103
Maori (ship), 49
Marble Heart, The, 99, 110, 134, 172
Marie Stuart, 182
Maritana, 178
Marsden, Frank, 142
Marsh Troupe, 19, 46
Marshall, Fred, 177
Marylebone Theatre London, 19, 27, 109, 162
Masks and Faces, 102, 108, 116, 140, 172, 178, 179, 205
Master and Man, 191
Mathews, Charles, 83, 116, 119, 120
Mathews, Julia, 21, 24, 54, 55
Maudsley, Dr., 183
Maugham, William Somerset, 215
May, Alice, 115, 118
May, Caroline, 102, **146**
Mayo, Lord (Viceroy), 97
Mazeppa, 3, 13, 14, 15, 16, 30, **31**
Medea, **97**
Meg's Diversion, 99, 107
Meilhac, Henri, 100
Melba, Dame Nellie
Melford, Mark
Melville, Emelie, 177, 178
Melville, Mr and Mrs, 11, 81
Merchant of Venice, The, 108, 175, 186
Merivale, Herman Charles, 161
Merivale, Philip, 215
Merry Wives of Windsor, The, 216
Message from Mars, A, 206
Middleman, The, 202
Midsummer Night's Dream, A, xvii, 22, **65**, 109

Milner, H. M., 13
Minstrel Shows, 82, 40
Mitra, Dinabandhu, 83
Modern Wives, 192, 213
Molesworth, Robert, 48
Mongo Mongo, **cover**, **40**
Montague Manners Company, 77, 177
Montague Turner Company, 174
Montes/Montez, Lola, 15, 26
Montezuma Theatre, Ballarat, 32, 33
Mooney, Thomas, 8, 14, 16, 90
Moore, Dr., 183
Moore, Maggie (Mrs J. C. Williamson), 114, 116, 117, 118, 127
Mosenthal, Hermann Salomon, 92
Moubray, Thomas, 57
Much Ado about Nothing, 57, 172
Mukerjee, S. K., 126
Murders of the Rue Morgue, 185
Murray, D'Arcy, 14
Musgrove, George, xv, 176, 178, 203, 205, 206, 207
Mutual Hall, Cape Town, 192
My Colonial Cousin, 54
My Son Diana, 104
My Uncle's Intended, 87
My Wife's Daughter, 105, 170
Mystery of a Hansom Cab, The, 185

Naylor, Elizabeth, (aka Mrs Edouin Bryer), 55, 56, 61, 62, **74**, 209
Neild, James Edward, 27, 29, 50, 52, 55, 80, 144, 130, 132, 133, 135, 136, 138, 140, 141, 142, 159, 160, 167, 168, 169, 170, 172, 186, 188, 197, 199, 201
Neilsen-Terry, Phyllis, 215
Nell Gwynne, 110
Nelson, Alfred, 19
Nelson, Carrie (Carry), 174
Nelson, Emma, 73, 74, 75, 87, 102, 111, **146**
Nelson, Sydney, 19, 38, 174
Nephews and Nieces, 138
Nesbitt, Francis, 26
Nethersole, Olga, 192, 204
New Magdalen, The, 62, 115, 118, 124, 135
New Men and Old Acres, 110
New Way to Pay Old Debts, A, 27, 168
Nicholas Nickleby, novel, 12
Nicholas Nickleby, play, 18, 55
Norman, Florence, 96
North and South, 56
Northbrook, Lord (Viceroy), 110
Not Such a Fool As He Looks, 97, 100
Not True, 178
Nunn, Tom, 14

Nye, Jenny, 58, 62, 106
Nymph of the Lurleyburg, The, 54, 55, 105

Octoroon, The, 56, 90, 92, 93, 100, 105, 123, 139
Olympic theatre, Melbourne, 15, 26, 50, **51**, 85, 95
O'Meara, James, 165, 166
O'Neil, Peggy, 117
Opera House (Calcutta), 83, 84, 97, 98, 116
Opera House (Cork, Ireland), 214
Opera House (Melbourne), xvi, 23, 129, 131, 139, 142, 159, 160, 161, 162, 166, 173, 175, 180, 198
Opera House (San Francisco), 213
Orange Girl, The, 107
Orange Tree and the Bumble Bee, The, 139
Othello, 56, 82, 83, 98, 99, 116, 175
Our American Cousin, 54, 55, **73**
Our Girls, 177
Our Loves, 177
Our Traviata, 50
Our Widow, 178

Paddy the Next Best Thing, **157**, 217
Paine, W. L., 196
Palace of Truth, 108
Paladini, Pietro, 142, 159
Pantheon Theatre (Melbourne), 38, 50, **51**, 52, 54, 105, 189
Peachey, Christine (Darrell), 173, 178, 179
Perfect Gentleman, The, 215
Perry, Frances (Fanny), 182, 183, 184, 185, 186
Perry, Martha, 184
Phelps, Samuel, xvii, 22, 23, **64**, 109, 195, 197
Phillips, Hans, 139, 180
Pickwick Papers, 186
Pinero, Arthur Wing, 125, 177, 210, 220
Pizzaro, 58
Placida, the Christian Martyr, 202
Play, 107, 110
Playing With Fire, 105
Plumpton, Alfred, 118
Pluto, 161
Poe, Edgar Allan, 134, 185
Pollards, The, 19, 174, 179
Pomeroy, Louise, 197
Pompadour, La, 195, 198
Pompadour, The, **151**, **152**, 193, 195, 196, 197, 198, 199, **200**, 220
Port Curtis, 38
Porter, Henry, 216
Potash and Perlmutter, 217, 218
Power, Harry, 218

Power, Tyrone, 204, 205
Prince Dorus, 54
Prince of Wales, 118, 119, 122
Prince of Wales Opera House, (Melbourne) xvi, 129, 139, 142, 159
Prince of Wales Theatre, (Melbourne)46, 54
Prince of Wales Theatre (Liverpool), 203
Princess Theatre (Bendigo), 197
Princess Theatre (Dunedin), 178
Princess Theatre (Melbourne), 16, 172, 205, 206, 207
Princess Spring Time, 79
Princess's theatre (Melbourne), xv, xvi, 15, 16, 50, 55, 56, 68, 79, 85, 128, 160, 180, 186, 188
Progress, 159
Pullen, M, 178
Pygmalion and Galatea, 108, 110, 121, 123

Queen Elizabeth, 138, 182
Queen Mary of England, 214
Queens Theatre, Melbourne, 9, 26
Queens Theatre, Sydney, 114, 170, 171
Quinn, Anna Maria, 33
Quinn, Mr., 96

Raphael, Gabriel, 46
Reade, Charles, 79, 120, 205
Redgrave, Michael, 207
Redgrave, Roy, 207
Reed and Barnes, 130
Reed, Joseph, 130, 132, 186
Reeve, Wybert, 161, 174, 177
Reeves, Gemma, x, 191
Reeves, Kate, 135
Richard III, 3, 4, 43, 56, 87, 88, 96
Richelieu, 160
Rickards, Harry, xv, 202, 203
Rip Van Winkle, 97
Risley, Richard Carlisle, 6, 37, 46, 47
Ristori, Adelaide, 130, 138
Rivals, The, 61, 37
Robertson, Edward Shafto, 96, 97
Robertson, T. W., 94, 104, 107, 111, 132, 159
Robert Macaire, 21
Robinson Crusoe, 89, 140, **141**, 142, 164, 213
Robinson, (Sir) Hercules, 47
Robinson, Lady, 42
Rob Roy, 26, 100
Rogers, Emma, 96, 102
Rogers, G. H., 50, 52, **53**
Roland for an Oliver, A, 30
Romeo and Juliet, 107, 107, 108, 201, 207, 214, 215

INDEX

Romeo and Juliet, or, The Cup of Cold Poison, 52, 53, 54, 89
Ronalds, Camile, 218
Rosa Towers Opera Company, 177
Rosnati, Ferante, 133
Rowe, George Fawcett, *see* Fawcett, George
Rowe, Joseph, 5, 6, 7, 9
Rowe, Nicholas, 139
Rowe's Circus, 6, **7**
Royal Academy of Dramatic Art London, 58
Royal Academy of Music, London, 131, 190
Royal Divorce, A, 303
Russell, Florrie, 178
Ryan, Mrs W., 135

Sadhababar Ekadashi, 126
Sadler's Wells Theatre (London), 21, 22, 23, 197
Salway, William, 177, 181, 187
St George and the Dragon, 30
St Lawrence, Mr., 178
St Leon, Mark, 37, 41, 46
St Leon's Circus, 15
Saint Saens, Camile, 215
Samuell, Josephine, 219
San Souci Theatre, Calcutta, 82
Sanders, Dr., 18
Saratoga, 136
Saville, Harry, 135
Saxon, Arthur H., 45
Sayers, Alice, 187
School, 104, 110, 121
School for Scandal, The, 87, 90, 95, 103, 108, **143**, 160, 172, 215
Scott, Clement, 193
Scott-Siddons, Frances Mary, xv, 129
Sea Nymph (ship), 46
Searle, Mr., 38
Secret Service, 203
Serious Family, The, 62, 124, 135
Seven Castles of Christendom, The, 50
Shadows, 171
Shaftesbury Theatre, 210
Shakespeare, xvi, 4, 22, 23, 26, 27, 52, 79, 87, 82, 87, 88, 108, 116, 130, 167, 176, 192, 194, 195, 197, 210, 209, 214, 215, 216, 220 passim
Shakespeare Memorial Theatre, (UK) 210
Shakespearian Lunatic, A, 214
Shamus na Leena, 175
Shanghai, Austin, 45, 46, 48, 84, **144**
Shaughraun, The, 90, 139
Shaw, George Bernard, 125, 210, 214, 215, 220
Sheep's Foot, The, 212
Shepharde, Hattie, 133

Sheridan, John F., 178
Sheridan, Richard Brinsley, 87
Shute, R., 38, 55
Siddons, Sarah, 129, 196, 197
Simpson, Adrienne, 115, 179
Simpson, Palgrave, 124, 161
Sign of the Cross, 203
Silver Lining, The, 98
Sister of Mercy, The, 23
Sister's Penance, A, 172
Smith, Edward Tyrrell, 13
Smith, Farquharson, 38
Smith, Florry, 167
Smith, James, 130, 133, 140, 188
Smith, J. L., 6
Smith, Mrs J. W., 187
Smith, John Thomas, 26
Smith, Louis Lawrence, 186
Snazelle, George, 195
South, William, 55
Spoiled Child, The, 28, 211
Spree in Paris and What Happened, A, 211, 114
Squaw Man, The, 208, 209
Squire of Dames, The, 202
Stacy's School, 96, 114, 139
Stebonheath (ship), 12
Stewart, Nellie, xv, 172, 206, 207
Stirling, Fanny, 216
Stirling, Maggie, 202
Stoneham, Mr., 81, 94
Strand Theatre, 19, 21, 23, 190, 191, 202, 213
Stranger, The, 19, 27
Strebinger, Madame, 37
Struck Oil, 114, 118, 119, 120, 127, **145**
Sullivan, Barry, 55, 56, 58, **75**, 85, 129
Sultana, Mr., 94
Susini, Augusto, 133
Sutton, Vane, 201

Taffy was a Welshman, 22
Tagore, Dwarakanath, 82
Tagore, Rabindranath, 82
Take That Girl Away, 62
Taming of the Shrew, The, 140, 168
Tavares, Morton, 160
Taylor, Mr & Mrs Robert, 96, 102, 103
Taylor, Tom, 54, 92
Te Anou (ship), 178, 180
Tennyson, Alfred, 192
Tentation, La, 115
Terry, Ellen, 193, 204
Terry, Phyllis Neilsen, 215
Thatcher, Charles, 37
Theatre Royal (Adelaide), 94, 163, 174, 177, 198
Theatre Royal (Ballarat), 164

CIRCUS AND STAGE

Theatre Royal (Belfast), 211
Theatre Royal (Brighton, UK), 21, 213
Theatre Royal (Calcutta), xv, 43, 98, 103, 104, 106, 116, 118, 119, 120, 122, 126, 127, 129
Theatre Royal (Croydon, UK), 202
Theatre Royal (Geelong), 30, 54
Theatre Royal (Great Grimsby, UK), 202
Theatre Royal (Hobart), 39
Theatre Royal (Melbourne), 13, 14, 15, 16, 25, 26, 27, 29, 30, 31, 46, 49, 50, 56, 57, 58, **67**, 95, 96, 135, 138, 139, **156**, 160, 170, 174, 176, 186, 191, 202, 219
Theatre Royal (Sydney), 203
Thompson, Lydia, 21, 39, 96, 99, 112, 115, 119, 140, **147**, 212, 213
Thorne, Fred, **135**, 136, 141, 159, 161, 162, 172
Three Musketeers, The, 203
Timon of Athens, 23
Timour the Tartar, 12, 30
Tipoo Sahib, 97
Tom Jones, 109
Tomlinson, Bingham, *see* Lewis, Tom
Touzel, Philip, 96
Toy Cart, The, 217
Tree, (Sir) Herbert Beerbohm, 210, 214, 215
Trilby, 204, 205, 207
Il Trovatore, 178
True as Steel, 115
Truebridge, Leonard, 188, 196, 199
Turned Up, 181, 213
Turner, Henry Gyles, 2
Turner, John Martin, 2
Turner, W. G., 202
Turpin's Ride to York, 3
Two Angry Women of Abingdon, The, 216
Two Roses, The, 138, 160

Uncle, 172
Unequal Match, An, 103
Unprotected Female, An, 35
Up at the Hills, 92, 93

Vauxhall Gardens, London, 8
Vernon, Howard, 209, 209
Very Last Days of Pompeii, The, 103, 105, 109
Victoria Theatre Adelaide, 55
Victoria Theatre, Ballarat, 37, **67**, 162
Victoria Theatre, Sydney, 115, 162

Wait and Hope, 107
Wakefield, Clement, 196
Walch, Garnet, 142, 159, 173, 174
Wallace, W. H., **135**

Wallack's Theatre New York, 96, 112, 113
Walsh, Charles, 33
Walton, Henry E., 135, 139
Walton, Mr, 94
Warner, Charles, 186
Weir, Mary (Mrs J. C. Williamson), 161, 173, 178, 179, 220
Wesley College, 139, 177
Westley, Henry, 124, 128, 187
Which is Which?, 62
Wicked Wife, A, 23
Widow O'Brien, The, 178
Wife: a Tale of Mantua, The, 175
Wild, Jessie, 39, 46
Wild, Marie, 39
Wilde, Oscar, 83, 125, 210, 220
William Tell, 168
Williamson, Garner and Musgrove, 176
Williamson, James Cassius, xv, 114, 116, 117, 118, 119, 120, 122, 127, **145**, 168, 169, 170, 173, 176, 178, 193, 204, 207
Willow Pattern Plate, The, 50
Wills, W. G., 138, 139, 193, 195, 220
Wilson, Cooke & Zoyara's Circus, 16
Wing, Isabella Jane, 25, 79, 163, 182
Wiseman, Alice (Mrs Henry Westley), 128, 187
Wiseman, Emily, 103
Wolfe, J. M., 41, 43
Woman in Red, The, 106
Wonder, The, 172
Wood, Mrs Henry, 104
Woodbridge (ship), 4, 5
Worrell's Circus, 46
Wreck of the Inverness, The, 204
Wyndham, Charles, 193, 204

Yeamans, E. 6, 9
Yeamans, Madame, 6, 49
Youl, Richard, 183
Young, P., 178
Younge, Richard, 30

Zaza, 206, 207
Zelman, Alberto, Junior, 202
Zelman, Alberto, Senior, 87, 133